THE JOHNS HOPKINS UNIVERSITY STUDIES IN
HISTORICAL AND POLITICAL SCIENCE

Under the direction of the Departments of History,
Political Economy, and Political Science

SERIES LXXXV (1967) NUMBER 1

MODERN YEMEN: 1918–1966

MODERN YEMEN

1918–1966

BY

MANFRED W. WENNER

THE JOHNS HOPKINS PRESS

BALTIMORE

Library of Congress Catalog Card Number 67–12420
Printed in the United States of America

FOR MY WIFE AND PARENTS

PREFACE

This study of the history and political development of Yemen in the twentieth century grew out of a desire to establish with some accuracy the more important events in recent Yemen history, as well as the motives behind the internal and foreign policies of that country's leaders.

The information which the author was able to find on Yemen when he first began his studies on the Middle East a number of years ago was skimpy, often contradictory, and even more frequently wrong. As the search for material broadened, it soon became clear that an immense body of literature existed; what was required was extensive sifting before it could be put to use.

Quite obviously, this required assistance. The author was lucky to find a large number of individuals from many professions—Arabs, Europeans of all nationalities, and Americans—who offered their services; without them, the following work could not exist.

Some of these individuals requested that their names not be mentioned; this is a difficult condition, for they provided much of the information contained herein which to my knowledge has not been available elsewhere. I owe them a considerable debt of gratitude—one which I hope someday to be able to repay.

Among those who deserve especial mention, first notice unquestionably goes to Dr. Majid Khadduri, of the Johns Hopkins School of Advanced International Studies. Dr. Khadduri provided valuable advice and important information from his own files, as well as introductions to some of the individuals who played important roles in the events in Yemen of recent years. His assistance is much appreciated.

The outbreak of the revolution in September, 1962, and the protracted war which followed led to the dispatch of a number of correspondents to Yemen. The author is indebted to three of them for providing him with their observations on, and reactions to, leading personalities of both Royalist and Republican factions, as well as important events immediately prior to and after the revolution: Arnold Hottinger of the *Neue Zürcher Zeitung,*

Richard Anderegg of the Swiss National Broadcasting Corporation, and Dana Adams Schmidt of the *New York Times.*

Dr. Salah al-Din al-Munajjid, of Beirut, deserves especial thanks for his invaluable assistance in obtaining a number of the important works in the Arabic language which the author consulted. Ihsan Hijazi, the editor of the *Arab World*; Günther Pawelke; Karl S. Twitchell; Hermann Eilts; Tal'at Ghusayn; George C. Moore; Harold Glidden—all provided helpful assistance and advice.

No author, of course, can hope to acknowledge all the assistance he has received. Librarians in institutions in the Middle East, Europe, and the United States are always essential. Perhaps even more so are the authors of the works consulted—the diplomats, doctors, historians, travelers, and even adventurers and confidence men who wrote their accounts in such a way as to make the author's task a pleasant and informative one — all deserve a note of thanks.

Last, but not least, three individuals merit the author's gratitude: his parents, who made it possible, and his wife, whose assistance in editing cannot be repaid.

EDITORIAL NOTE

Final responsibility for the decisions on which materials to use and how to present them, as well as the opinions expressed herein, naturally lies with the author alone.

The translation and transliteration of Arabic words in the text have been made with the assistance of Hans Wehr, *A Dictionary of Modern Written Arabic* (Ithaca: Cornell University Press, 1960).

The following system of transliteration has been used:

Arabic Character	Latin Equivalent	Arabic Character	Latin Equivalent
ص	ṣ	ء	’
ض	ḍ	ب	b
ط	ṭ	ت	t
ظ	ẓ	ث	th
ع	ʿ	ج	j
غ	gh	ح	ḥ
ف	f	خ	kh
ق	q	د	d
ك	k	ذ	dh
ل	l	ر	r
م	m	ز	z
ن	n	س	s
ه	h	ش	sh
و	w		
ي	y		
a long vowel	¯		

The diacritical marks have been placed on nearly all the Arabic words in the text, that is, names of persons and places and uncommon words such as *dāʿī*, *ḥudūd*, and the like. They have, however, been omitted in many instances where the Arabic word or its adjectival form has become commonly used in English, as, for example, Sunni, Pasha, Zaydi, Islam. In addition, the diacritical marks have been omitted from Anglicized forms of Arabic words such as Imamate, Isma'ilism. To avoid spotting the text with an excess of italics, foreign words have generally been set in italic in the first instance and roman thereafter.

CONTENTS

INTRODUCTION

Until well into the twentieth century, Yemen remained one of the most inaccessible countries in the world. Although under the nominal control of the Ottoman Empire during the last decades of the nineteenth century, Yemen's inhabitants remained largely ignorant of the Industrial Revolution, modern technology, and the political, social, and economic theories and practices of the Western world. While most other Middle Eastern nations were stirring under the impact of the West and its technology and ideologies, Yemenis lived as they had for centuries, cognizant only of their own immediate surroundings, indifferent to all but their closest neighbors.

It was not until the end of World War I that the Sublime Porte renounced all its claims to Yemen, thus leaving it to its own devices in a world of which few Yemenis had even the vaguest conception. The ruler of the country by default was Yaḥyā ibn Muḥammad, the Imām (religious leader) of those Yemenis who were adherents of the Shī'a Zaydi faith. It is with the reign of Imām Yaḥyā (1904–1948), his son and successor Imām Aḥmad (1948–1962), and the short reign of the latter's son, Muḥammad al-Badr, as well as the civil war which followed the outbreak of the revolution in September, 1962, that this volume deals.

Imāms Yaḥyā and Aḥmad were remarkable men. Although unschooled in anything except their conservative Zaydi beliefs, they governed with astonishing effectiveness and unity of purpose a country whose population and terrain had defied numerous previous attempts at administration. Throughout their reigns, they kept Yemen isolated from developments which they felt to be heretical and dangerous. That they were able to postpone the revolutionary changes which have affected nearly all the countries of the Afro-Asian world in the twentieth century is attributable partly to the special talents of these two Imāms and partly to the peculiar circumstances which exist in Yemen even today. The problems of internal disunity and foreign policy with which they attempted to cope, however, ultimately resulted in the revolt of 1962, which forced the present Imām from his position as temporal ruler. It is our purpose to study these circumstances and problems in order to better understand the events which led to the civil war which even now continues to be fought in Yemen.

Along with the suzerainty over Yemen which Imām Yaḥyā received through default in 1918 came problems which he had never encountered during the period of Ottoman control. The country was by no means a unified whole. While his coreligionists, the Zaydis, did recognize the Imām's religious and political authority, there was an equally numerous Sunni group in Yemen to whom his religious authority meant nothing. In addition to the difference in religion, the population was divided between the racially mixed inhabitants of the hot and humid coastal plains and the Arabs of the temperate central highlands and also between the nearly autonomous tribal groups and the city-oriented tradesmen and artisans with commercial interests. Imām Yaḥyā, therefore, at first had to concentrate his efforts on welding this complex population into a nation.

The existence of a diverse population required a central authority able to keep order, maintain a certain standard of justice, and defend the country from outside interference or attack. In order to establish such an authority, Imām Yaḥyā believed it was necessary to create an autocratic government in accordance with the theories of Zaydi Islam, wherein the Imām is nearly omnipotent in both spiritual and temporal affairs. Utilizing the Ottoman system of administration as a starting point, Yaḥyā began his attempt to create a strong central government which he hoped would result in a decrease in the political power of others and would enable him to unify the population around one power center—himself.

Unfortunately for Imām Yaḥyā and his successor, Aḥmad, these divisions ran so deep that much of what was accomplished was only superficial. Although the Imāms managed to present a façade of national unity to the outside world, they did not really eliminate the internal pressures which have existed in Yemen almost since the establishment of the Imamate in the ninth century A.D. The two Imāms, in order to create the political stability which they felt might forge these factions into a single nation, were forced to rely on methods which in more advanced countries are considered reprehensible. The "civil service" was drawn from a small privileged portion of the population. Many important political or military positions of power and responsibility were filled by one of the Imām's brothers or sons or by men with independent bases of political power whose loyalty had been bought or coerced through the keeping of hostages. In these ways, Yaḥyā and Aḥmad attempted to insure fidelity to the Imamate and themselves, but in many cases only increased animosity toward their regime.

In addition to their domestic problems, the Imāms also faced difficulties in the field of foreign relations. Because of his intimate acquaintance with the Ottomans as foreign occupiers and his awareness of the tenuousness of his own position within the newly independent state, Imām Yaḥyā adopted a policy of isolationism for Yemen. This policy, followed perhaps less enthusiastically by Aḥmad, was to have disastrous results; it eventually drove those forces inside the country who wanted contact with the outside world and demanded domestic reforms to resort to violence to achieve their objectives.

Paradoxically, this isolationism was not entirely a personal creation of the Imāms. Both Imāms Yaḥyā and Aḥmad were educated and lived according to the tenets of the Zaydi faith, to which they were deeply and sincerely committed. This conservative branch of Islam, its adherents, and particularly its prominent leaders would not tolerate change and consequently disapproved of intercourse with the modern world. No Imām could admit that evolving circumstances required adjustments in the faith, for Zaydi Islam is regarded as of divine origin and therefore eternal and absolute. The Imāms, in other words, were in many ways prisoners of the orthodoxy of their own religion. If they were not willing to continue to exercise their control in strict accord with its tenets, they ran the risk of being called illegitimate pretenders by an opponent who would satisfy the clamor of the orthodox for greater piety and stricter adherence to Zaydi beliefs.

The primary foreign-policy issue the Imāms faced was their relations with Great Britain. Once Imām Yaḥyā had achieved a semblance of internal security, there remained the important goal of expanding the boundaries of his country to include the areas he felt were part of "natural" and "historical" Yemen. Since 1728 Yemen had exercised no effective jurisdiction over territories not today included in the modern state; nevertheless, the historical tradition of Yemeni sovereignty over the "Aden Protectorates" was not forgotten by the Zaydi Imāms. Both Yaḥyā and Aḥmad believed that Great Britain was in unjustifiable occupation of Yemeni territory and wished to establish itself there permanently.

For Imām Aḥmad, who witnessed a considerable increase in the total claimed by the British as part of their " protected area," the problem became an obsession. In an attempt to strengthen his claim to the areas usurped by the British, Aḥmad sought foreign assistance and was consequently forced to compromise the policy of almost total isolationism which his father had followed. With his vastly increased program of foreign military, technical, and economic assistance from a variety of powers, Aḥmad introduced into Yemen those modernizing forces which in the final analysis were an important cause for the overthrow of the Imamate. The presence of such foreigners not only alienated the traditional and extremely conservative elements which provided much of the support the Imāms received but also introduced revolutionary ideas to those who chafed under the many restrictions which the Imāms had imposed.

Despite oppressive methods for insuring internal peace, the Imāms could not resist the powerful pressures which the twentieth century has brought to bear upon all feudal and theocratic states. With the end of World War II, opposition to the Imāms began to mount. Numerous groups tried to overthrow the government and assassinate the Imāms, with the intention of introducing reforms into the political and economic life of Yemen. Only in 1962, after several unsuccessful coups and the natural death of Imām Aḥmad, did a more modern-minded Imām, who announced openly his intention of promulgating reforms, take the throne. His later partial recantation of progressive ideas, however, helped to convince the reformist forces that revolution was the only solution and signaled the beginning of the most extensive and highly organized revolt attempted in Yemen. This time it was directed against the Imamate as an institution as well as against the individual ruler who happened to be the Imām.

The civil war fought in Yemen since that time has seen the intervention of foreign powers on both sides, justifying Yaḥyā's and Aḥmad's fear of outside interference in Yemeni affairs. Whatever the outcome of the current struggle, the changes it has wrought make a return to the era of Imāms Yaḥyā and Aḥmad most improbable. It is with that little-known era and the reasons for its passing that this volume is concerned.

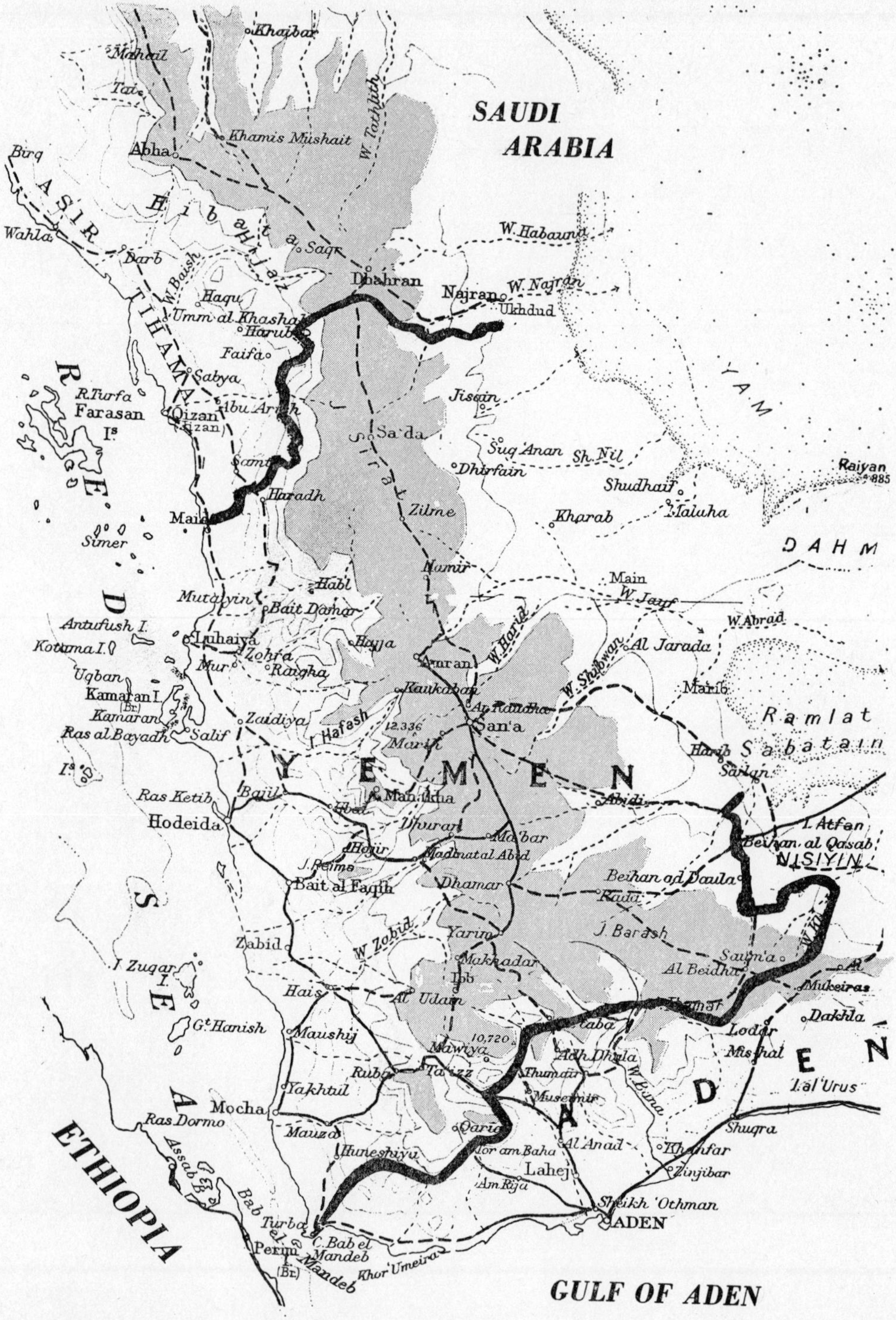

SAUDI ARABIA
Khaibar
Mahail
Abha
Khamis Mushait
W. Tathlith
Birq
ASIR
Wahla
Hibata
Hijaz
Saqr
Darb
W. Baish
Dhahran
W. Habauna
Najran
W. Najran
Ukhdud
Haqu
Umm al Khashab
Harub
TIHAMA
Faifa
Sabya
R. Turfa
Farasan Is
Abu Arish
Qizan
Jisain
Sa'da
Suq Anan
Sh. Nil
Dhirfain
Shudhaif
Raiyan 885
Haradh
Zilme
Kharab
Maluha
Maidi
Simer
DAHM
Habl
Main
W. Jauf
Mutaiyin
Bait Damar
W. Abrad
Antufush I.
Kotama I.
Luhaiya
Hajja
W. Harid
Al Jarada
Zohra
Amran
W. Shibwan
Uqban
Raigha
Kamaran I.
(Br.)
Kamaran
Kaukaban
Marib
Ar Raudha
Zaidiya
Ras al Bayadh
Salif
J. Hafash
12,336
San'a
Ramlat Sabatain
Harib
YEMEN
Ras Ketib
Bajil
Manakha
Abidi
Hodeida
Dhuran
Ma'bar
I. Atfan
Beihan al Qasab
NISIYIN
J. Reima
Madinat al Abid
Bait al Faqih
Dhamar
Beihan ad Daula
Rada
J. Barash
RED SEA
Zabid
Yarim
W. Zabid
Sau'na
I. Zuqar
Al Beidha
Hais
Ibb
Al Udain
Mukeiras
Dakhla
Gt. Hanish
Maushij
10,720
Lodar
Mawiya
Dhala
Mishal
ADEN
Ruba
Ta'izz
Thumair
W. Bana
Yakhtul
Musaimir
I. al 'Urus
Mocha
Ras Dormo
Mauza
Qarie
Al Anad
Shuqra
ETHIOPIA
Assab
Huneshiya
Khanfar
Lahej
Zinjibar
Am Rija
Bab el Mandeb
Turba
Sheikh 'Othman
ADEN
Perim
(Br.)
C. Bab el Mandeb
Khor 'Umeira
GULF OF ADEN

Chapter I

THE LAND AND ITS PEOPLE

The Land

Description

The modern state of Yemen remained until recently one of the least-known countries in the world, despite its strategic location. Its position in the southwestern corner of the Arabian Peninsula astride the Straits of Bāb al-Mandab, where the Red Sea meets the Gulf of Aden, effectively controls the southern outlet of the Suez Canal; but its other geographical features and the deliberately isolationist policy of its rulers combined to keep it aloof from events in the rest of the world until well into the twentieth century.

The frontiers which delimit Yemen were established early in this century by a variety of non-Yemeni governments. The result is not wholly logical either geographically or demographically, and the boundaries have not yet been recognized by Yemen in their entirety. Nevertheless, these borders do contain within them most of that portion of the Arabian Peninsula known to the geographers of the ancient world as "Arabia Felix" and to Muslim Arabs as "al-Yaman al-Saʿīda." [1]

1. Geographical names in Arabic usually describe some characteristic of the area to which the name is applied. Northern Arab writers, seeking to explain the origin of the name "Yemen" many years after that region's incorporation into the Islamic world, created two different theories concerning the word's derivation. This was due to the fact that the Arabic language has two triliteral roots containing the consonants Y-M-N: (1) YaMiN, meaning "right" or "on the right hand"; therefore, Yemen is the country on the right hand. It was argued that from the point of view of a Muslim in Makka, Yemen lay in the south of the peninsula, or on the right hand; (2) YuMaN, meaning "prosperous" or "happy"; it was argued in this instance that Yemen is obviously the climatically most favored portion of the peninsula, for it has sufficient water to grow all manner of fruits and vegetables. Therefore, Yemen is the "prosperous" or "happy land."

Recent paleographical and archaeological studies undertaken in southwestern Arabia, however indicate that the word *Yemen*, like many other place names in this area, is derived from the language of ancient South Arabia—a language whose existence was apparently unknown to later Muslim scholars.

Inscriptions from the region of Mā'rib and other locations indicate that the

Yemen's northern border is with Saudi Arabia, specifically with the province of 'Asīr, the ownership of which was for many years disputed by the two countries. In the south the border touches the Aden Protectorates, a series of small principalities now under British protection which were formerly controlled by the rulers of Yemen and which the Imām's have continued to claim.

To the west lies the Red Sea, while in the east Yemen's borders are completely undemarcated. As the land levels off (from the great central mountain range) toward the east into the Rub' al-Khālī, Yemen's authority gradually wanes, and her frontiers merge with the great desert technically within the confines of Saudi Arabia.

Internally, Yemen is divided into two markedly different geographical regions, a division which plays an important role in the economic, religious, and political life of the country: (1) the coastal strip along the Red Sea, known as the Tihāma, and (2) the mountainous interior highlands.

The Tihāma stretches the entire 450-kilometer length of Yemen's seacoast, from Maydī in the north to Bāb al-Mandab

---

Sabaean kings from the fourth century A.D. on included an area known as YMNT (𐩺𐩣𐩬𐩩) in their kingdom and in their complete titles. The full title of these Sabaean kings was MLK/SB'/WDHRYDN/WḤḌRM(W)T/WYMNT, meaning "King of Saba', Dhū-Raydān, Ḥaḍramawt, and Yamanat." After the expansions of the fifth century A.D., the Sabaean kings added W' 'RB/HMW/TWDM/WTHMT, meaning "and the Arabs (nomads) of the high plateaus and the lowlands." These titles were retained until all of Yemen fell to the Muslim armies in 628 A.D.

Nevertheless, the precise meaning and location of YMNT remain unknown. What is known is that the Sabaean kings did not expand into the southwestern corner of the peninsula until the fourth century and that scholars have established the location and definition of all other Sabaean titles. This would make it reasonable to assume that the area referred to as YMNT, which was added to the realm in the fourth century, is what the Sabaeans meant by the name YaMaNaT. The sole remaining problem which must be explained is the T ending. However, there is sufficient evidence to assume that the T in Ancient South Arabian is the equivalent of the modern Arabic "t marbūta." The fact that there are a number of precedents for the later elimination of the "t marbūta" on certain words and names would seem to make the case for the Ancient South Arabian derivation of the word *Yemen* a near certainty.

It might be added that many modern names in Yemen have been taken over from Ancient South Arabian: Tihāma (cf. THMT above in the title of the Sabaean kings, meaning lowland), Laḥij, Ṣa'da, Dhamār, Najrān, and so on.

See A. Jamme, *Sabaean Inscriptions from Mahram Bilqîs* (*Mârib*) (Baltimore: Johns Hopkins Press, 1962), pp. 373–375.

It should be added that there is as little reason to refer to Yemen in English as "the Yemen" because the Arabic is "al-Yaman" as there is to refer to "the France" because the French is "La France."

in the south. It is a sandy, almost waterless but extremely fertile expanse of desert, covered with sparse vegetation, ranging in width from twenty to fifty kilometers. The high temperatures and humidity make living there extremely uncomfortable for anyone not accustomed to the climate from birth. Behind this coastal plain lies the "upper Tihāma," a region where the sandy desert meets the first low foothills of the mountains. It also varies in width from twenty-five to forty kilometers. Here are stony valleys where the wadis of the mountains empty into the plain.

Farther east the foothills increase in height ridge after ridge, interwoven by narrow valleys, until the highlands of crystalline, volcanic, and limestone rock cliffs are reached. The latter are carved into fantastic gorges by the plentiful rains of the monsoon season. In the area round the capital, Ṣan'ā', the crests of the mountains tower to heights of almost 4,000 meters. On the far side of the central massif, the pattern is repeated, but in a narrower space; the mountains fall off, and the foothills recede into the great desert of the central Arabian Peninsula.

The highlands and their innumerable valleys are extremely fertile, receiving a regular rainfall every year, unlike any other portion of the Arabian Peninsula. This rainfall permits extensive cultivation, and through the centuries the Yemeni plateaus and valleys have been terraced from their rocky summits to the wadi floors below; every drop of water is used and reused before it is finally permitted to reach the valley floor and disappear into the hot sands of the Tihāma.

The climate and fertility of the soil in Yemen permit the cultivation of nearly every vegetable, cereal, and fruit in the world, from bamboo, bananas, citrus fruits, mangoes, pomegranates, and dates to peaches, tomatoes, nuts, grapes, millet, and corn. There are two crops, however, that stand out because of their importance to the economy: coffee and *qāt*.

Yemen's most important and famous cash crop for centuries has been coffee. Although it is thought that the coffee tree was introduced into Yemen from Ethiopia, it is from the former that coffee as a beverage made its way around the world. In so doing, it gave the name of the principal port of export, al-Mukhā, to what is still the most highly prized and expensive of the world's coffees (variously spelled Mocca, Mokka, or Mocha). It is from the sale of this coffee to the United States, Switzerland, Italy, and France that Yemen has earned most of its foreign exchange.

The second most important cash crop is *qāt*, a small shrub also thought to have come originally from Ethiopia, which grows in the same altitude and under the same conditions as coffee.[2] The small young leaves, leafbuds, and tender shoots of the qāt plant are chewed; the juice from them is swallowed and the leaves are thrown away at periodic intervals, after which the chewer drinks water. The feeling derived from this chewing has been described by Yemenis and Europeans alike as being one of mental alertness, wakefulness (bordering on insomnia at night), and a pleasant stimulation of the senses. The effects, in general, appear to be similar to those produced by such other alkaloids as mescalin (peyote), LSD-25, and atropine. The qāt habit is widespread in the cities, but most of the agricultural population and the tribesmen scorn it. In urban centers large qāt parties are held every day, normally beginning at about two o'clock in the afternoon and lasting until early evening. Little business of any kind is transacted at this time, for nearly everyone in the cities can afford the habit.

Qāt chewing is also extremely common in the Protectorates and in Aden itself, where the British authorities once unsuccessfully tried to prohibit it. Fresh bundles of qāt, wrapped in banana leaves or grass to keep them fresh, are rushed to the Protectorates and Aden by truck. Yemeni qāt is also flown daily to Eritrea and Ethiopia, for it is said to be far superior to what is grown there. Habitual users can even distinguish between different varieties from the same general vicinity.

The habit is harmful in several ways. It is credited with debilitating effects on the body after long use; the parties during which it is taken are a waste of time and energy; habitual users will squander any funds they have in order to obtain it; and its cultivation consumes considerable land which could be put to more productive use.

For several reasons individual growers prefer to raise qāt rather than tobacco, grapes, or other produce. It requires less care (but more water) than many more valuable crops. Three harvests in

2. According to a Yemeni tradition, slips of the coffee and *qāt* plants were planted in al-'Udayn (the two twigs) in pre-Islamic times. Neither plant, however, is mentioned in the Qur'ān, ancient traditions, or early Arab poetry.

one year are common. It can be marketed locally, often by the grower himself, thereby assuring him of a far greater and speedier return than that on coffee or grapes. Consequently, many coffee trees (as well as other plants) are being replaced with qāt bushes, and in recent years there has been a considerable decline in the amount of first-class Yemeni coffee available for export. The lack of an organized system of agricultural credit, which might lessen the difference between the return for good coffee and profit for qāt, has long been one of the criticisms which Yemeni reformers have leveled at the government of the Imāms.[3]

The Cities

Even before the birth of Muḥammad, great city-state kingdoms existed in south Arabia. This history and the temperate climate and considerable rainfall of the uplands account for the existence of relatively large and populous cities in Yemen today.

The largest and most important of these is Ṣan'ā'. Located in a fertile valley at an altitude of about 2,500 meters in the central mountains, its history is said to extend back to biblical times. During the nineteenth century, the Zaydi Imāms moved their seat of government there, and as a result it became one of the most important and populous cities of Yemen; estimates of its population range as high as 50,000. It has for centuries been the center of most of the manufacturing and industrial undertakings in Yemen, achieving particular renown for its metalwork and high-quality manganese-steel swords, knives, and daggers. Its size

3. Nearly every Western visitor or traveler to Yemen has had some remarks to make on the qāt habit, and there is, as a result, extensive literature on the subject. Some of the following may be consulted for more information: Charles Moser, "The Flower of Paradise," *The National Geographic Magazine*, XXXII (August, 1917), 173–186; P. W. R. Petrie, "Some Experiences in Southern Arabia," *Journal of Tropical Medicine and Hygiene*, XLII (December, 1939), 257–360; C. E. Sage, "Catha Edulis," *Pharmaceutical Journal*, CLIII (1944), 128 ff.; "Khat" [*sic*], *Geographical Journal*, CXXVI (March, 1960), 52 ff.; Cesare Ansaldi, *Il Yemen nella storia e nella leggenda* (Rome: Sindicato Italiana Arti Grafiche Editore, 1933), pp. 199–202. Probably the most rational opinion on the habit was offered by a recent (1959) visitor, who wrote: "In most articles describing the qāt habit in Yemen a somewhat self-righteous attitude is taken, declaring how much better it would be if the acreage wasted on growing qāt were used for grain or other edibles. This is unquestionably true, but the same accusation could be levelled against any country which permits the cultivation of plants which have no beneficial effect." (Erich Bethmann, *Yemen on the Threshold* [Washington, D.C.: American Friends of the Middle East, 1960], p. 50.)

and location make it the center of trade for the highlands, and its population is generally more knowledgeable and interested in the outside world than the majority of Yemenis. The fact that the Ottoman authorities made it their administrative capital added considerably to its economic importance, size, and population.

Although not nearly so old as Ṣan'ā', Ta'izz also has a long history and has served as the capital for a variety of lesser dynasties. It is the major city of the south and is located in a predominantly Shāfi'ī area. With the accession of Imām Aḥmad in 1948 it became the capital, although this distinction was returned to Ṣan'ā' in 1962 by the revolutionary government. The transfer of government to Ta'izz and the establishment there of foreign embassies, permitted for the first time by Aḥmad, added measurably to the city's stature, size, and population. Its position near Aden has made it an entrepôt for Yemeni trade carried on through that port.

Yemen has numerous ports, but only one is today of real commercial importance: al-Ḥudayda. From the sixteenth century to the twentieth, the Ottoman authorities used it as their chief base and port of entry to Yemen, and both the government and private contractors constructed harbor facilities there from time to time. The most extensive of these modernization projects was undertaken recently by Soviet engineers; as a result, nearly all international trade which Yemen conducts passes directly through al-Ḥudayda.

Al-Luḥayya, Maydī, and al-Mukhā were formerly ports of greater significance; the growth of the port of Aden under the British and al-Ḥudayda under the Ottoman administration, however, eliminated nearly all of their trade, and all three now serve only their immediate hinterland.

Other towns of some interest in Yemen are: Bayt al-Faqīh, once an ancient seat of learning; Dhamār, an unwalled town which was the seat of a Zaydi university and is still the center of the horse-breeding industry (which has considerably declined in recent years); Ibb, one of the most beautiful and architecturally interesting interior cities; Manākha, an almost impregnable fortress town which was a former Ottoman administrative center; Ṣa'da, the ancient seat of the Zaydi Imāms and the burial place of the first one; Ḥajja, another fortress town of the northwest and a Zaydi stronghold; Mā'rib, the present-day town built on the ruins of one of the ancient pre-Islamic cities and the major town in the eastern desert; and Zabīd, a Tihāma town formerly of importance as a Shāfi'ī theological center.

THE PEOPLE

A census has never been taken in Yemen, but according to reliable estimates the total population numbers approximately 3,500,000 to 4,000,000 people. The inhabitants can be divided and classified according to many criteria. For an understanding of the internal forces which exist in Yemen, the most important classifications are made on the basis of historical criteria, religious criteria, and whether they are tribally oriented or urban.

Historical Divisions

The Arabs of the peninsula have been divided into two groups since the beginning of recorded history. Although they are racially related and their languages in pre-Islamic times were of the same family, they formerly differed widely in habits and ways of life. The northern Arabs of the Ḥijāz and Najd were primarily nomads, while the Arabs of the south were settled cultivators or town dwellers ever since the time of the highly civilized ancient south Arabian kingdoms.

In order to explain the differences in language, culture, and even race (for there are still marked differences in the physical characteristics of northern and southern Arabs), Muslim historians and genealogists had recourse to the legend that all Arabs are descended from a common ancestor, but in two different lines. The common ancestor was Sām ibn Nūh (Shem, the son of Noah). The "pure" or southern Arab (Qaḥṭānī) is descended from Qaḥṭān ibn 'Abir, or Hūd, as he is often called in southern Arabia (Joktan ben Eber); the "derived" or northern Arab ('Adnānī) is descended from Ismā'īl (Ishmael) through 'Adnān.[4]

4. Hugh Scott, *In the High Yemen* (London: John Murray, 1942), pp. 204, 209; G. W. Bury, *Arabia Infelix* (London: Macmillan, 1915), pp. 27–28. For the genealogy, see Genesis 10:25. Muslim genealogists often adopted Hebrew traditions and genealogies.

The tomb of Hūd is located in the Ḥaḍramawt (Eastern Aden Protectorate), in the Kathīrī State. The entire area is, as a result, forbidden to Jews, and it is the only portion of the southern Arabian Peninsula which has never had any Jewish colonies. See Harold Ingrams, *Arabia and the Isles* (2nd ed.; London: John Murray, 1952), pp. 199–201; D. van der Meulen and H. von Wissmann, *Hadramaut—Some of Its Mysteries Unveiled* (Leiden: E. J. Brill, 1932), pp. 158–161.

This distinction among Arabs is particularly important among those of south Arabia. Many of today's feuds and differences go back to this pre-Islamic split—a division which some Arabs have carried with them through their many migrations and conquests and which has become one of the causes of political and inter-family hostilities in other Muslim Arab countries.

Within Yemen the Rassī Dynasty, to which Imāms Yaḥyā and Aḥmad belonged, profess to be the inheritors of the Ḥimyarite civilization which ruled Yemen before its conquest by the Muslims; in other words, they claim Qaḥṭānī ancestry. In fact, they are 'Adnānīs, as their other (more reasonable) claim to descent from the Prophet Muḥammad through Ḥasan indicates.[5]

Religious Divisions

The conquest of Yemen by Islam produced the second great division in the population, for religious schisms soon fractured the unity of Islam throughout the Muslim world, dividing it into major sects: Sunni and Shī'a. The best estimates which can be made today indicate that these two sects are almost evenly represented within Yemen, although both the Sunnis and Shī'as claim over half of the inhabitants as adherents of their sect.

Because Yemen early revealed its sympathy for 'Alī, the son-in-law of the Prophet, many of those Muslims who believed that only descendants of 'Alī should succeed to the Caliphate took refuge in its mountain fastnesses. These adherents to the 'Alid claim (the Shī'a) later were themselves divided into several sects. Only two of these Shī'a groups were successful in creating a following and perpetuating themselves into the twentieth century: the Zaydis and the Ismā'īlīs.

The Zaydis

The rise of the Zaydi Imamate in the ninth century A.D. was undoubtedly the most important event that occurred in Yemen after the coming of Islam. The establishment in the Yemeni highlands of the religious and later political overlordship of the Zaydi sect influenced the social structure, the attitudes, and the life of

5. The Quraysh, the northern tribe to which Muḥammad's clan, the Hāshim, belonged, is 'Adnānī. Of course, it is possible that through intermarriage the Rassī Dynasty has legitimate claims to both these distinctions.

The Ismā'īlīs

The other group of Shī'as historically associated with Yemen are the Ismā'īlīs. They, like other Shī'as and unlike the Zaydis, believe in the Mahdī (hidden Imām), who will one day return to save the world. In Ismā'īlī theology, the last recognized Imām was the seventh, Ismā'īl ibn Ja'far al-Sādiq. A number of religious differences have grown up within this particular set of Isma'ilism; those resident in Yemen are of the Sulaymānī division, which in the twentieth century has become limited solely to certain small districts in Yemen and the oasis of Najrān, on the Yemeni-Saudi Arabian border. Since the disappearance of their Imām, this sect has been governed by a *dā'ī* (he who calls, or propagandizes, that is, originally, the director of missionary work).

In Yemen, the Ismā'īlīs are referred to as al-Makārima, as a result of the fact that during the seventeenth century the leadership devolved to the al-Makramī family from which all dā'īs since that time have come. The original seat of these dā'īs was the town of Ṭayyiba, located in the Wādī Ḍahr northwest of Ṣan'ā'. At the present time, however, the few remaining colonies are found in isolated mountain ridges, particularly in the Manākha (Jabal Ḥaraz) region. Their number today probably does not exceed 25,000. The last dā'ī whose fate is known to the West was 'Alī ibn Muḥsin; he acceded in 1912 and died in 1936. His successor, Ḥusayn Aḥmad, was exiled to Makka by King 'Abd al-'Azīz of Saudi Arabia during his occupation of the Najrān Oasis. He was not permitted to return to Najrān, and little further information is available on the fate of the Ismā'īlī community in Najrān or in Yemen since that time.[11]

---

they sometimes intervened in tribal disputes in order to mediate for peace. See R. B. Serjeant, "The Mountain Tribes of the Yemen," *The Geographical Magazine*, XV, No. 2 (June, 1942), 72; W. R. Brown, "The Yemeni Dilemma," *The Middle East Journal*, XVII (Autumn, 1963), 349–367.

11. On the Ismā'īlīs of Yemen, see "Isma'ilism," *Encyclopedia of Islam*, Supplement (1938), pp. 99 ff.; Ettore Rossi, *L'Arabo parlato a San'ā'* (Rome: Istituto per l'Oriente, 1939), p. 140; H. St. J. Philby, *Arabian Highlands* (Ithaca: Cornell University Press, 1952), pp. 356 ff.; Muṣṭafā Murād al-Dabbāgh, *Jazīrat al-'Arab* (Beirut: Dār al-Talī'a Press, 1963), I, 270; Aḥmad Fakhrī, *Al-Yaman* (Cairo: Jāmi'at al-Duwal al-'Arabiyya, 1957), p. 21, which has a map indicating the areas where Ismā'īlīs were still to be found in 1956.

Some writers have reported that the Ismā'īlīs have suffered persecution at the hands of the Zaydi Imāms during the past fifty years. It is known that Imām Muḥammad ibn Yaḥyā (d. 1904) in 1902 managed to capture many of their

the people there and has continued to do so into the twentieth century.[6]

The Zaydis derive the name of their sect from Zayd, one of the two grandsons of Ḥusayn. As is the case with other Shī'as, the Zaydis recognize as their spiritual leaders (Imāms) only descendants of the Prophet Muḥammad through his daughter Fāṭima and his son-in-law and cousin 'Alī and their two sons Ḥasan and Ḥusayn. The Zaydis differ from other Shī'as, however, in their recognition of Zayd as the fifth Imām rather than his brother Muḥammad al-Bāqir.[7]

The first of the Zaydi Imāms to establish himself in Yemen, al-Hādī ilā al-Ḥaqq Yaḥyā, however, was not descended from this branch of the Prophet's family. He and nearly all of his successors are of the House of Rassī—descendants of Ḥasan through his two sons. This illustrates another point on which Zaydis differ from the majority of Shī'as. According to the Zaydis, 'Alī's succession to the Imamate was due to his particular merits. As a consequence, the Zaydis have made the Imamate selective and have never accepted inherited familial rule as its only criterion. A candidate for the Zaydi Imamate must fulfill certain conditions required by Zaydi law and tradition. Within Yemen, the only condition which effectively eliminates the majority of the population is that the candidate must be a descendant of Fāṭima and 'Alī. An important corollary of this reasoning, and one which has profoundly influenced Yemeni history, is that a candidate for the Imamate must stand forth publicly and claim recognition.[8]

6. For a detailed description of the rise of the Zaydi Imamate, see C. van Arendonk, *Les Débuts de l'Imamat Zaidite au Yemen* (Leiden: E. J. Brill, 1960).

7. The first Imām was 'Alī; the second, 'Alī's son Ḥasan; the third, 'Alī's son Ḥusayn; the fourth, Ḥusayn's son 'Alī Zayn al-'Ābidīn. The divergence of the Zaydis from other Shī'as after the fifth Imām has resulted in their characterization as "the Fivers" among other Muslims.

8. There are fourteen commonly recognized prerequisites for the Imamate. The candidate must be: (1) male; (2) free born; (3) a taxpayer; (4) sound in mind; (5) sound in all the senses; (6) sound in the ends, that is, perfect hands and feet (this is designed to eliminate criminals who have suffered the Quranic punishment required by the Sharī'a); (7) just; (8) pious; (9) generous; (10) endowed with administrative ability; (11) 'Alawī, that is, a descendant of 'Alī; (12) Fāṭimī (this is designed to eliminate members of Ismā'īlī sects from candidacy); (13) brave (more specifically, this means the ability to resort to the sword if necessary for offense or defense and is designed to eliminate children and "concealed" Mahdīs from candidacy; it is a specific statement to the effect that the Zaydis must have a living Imām); (14) a Mujtahid, that is, one learned

The position and powers of the Imām in Zaydi religious theory are unlike those of any other ruler in either Shī'a or Sunni Islam. Upon his accession, an Imām is considered to be imbued with the "guiding light of God"; his decisions on matters of faith, morals, law, and even the personal lives of the community of believers, of which he is both spiritual and temporal head, are infallible. Nevertheless, the Imām's power is limited by the Qur'ān, the Sunna (tradition), and Islamic law according to the Zaydi theoreticians. He is not technically required to consider even a unanimous decision of the council of religious elders of the country (the 'Ulamā') as binding, but in practice both Imām Yaḥyā's and Aḥmad's freedom of action were partially restricted by the conservatism of this body.

Upon assuming office, Zaydi Imāms have always adopted other names, usually descriptive phrases indicative of their piety and/or learning. Imām Yaḥyā, for example, styled himself "al-Mutawakkil 'alā Allāh" (the relier on God). Among their various titles are "Amīr al-Mu'minīn" (commander of the faithful) and "Khalīfa" (successor to the Prophet); both of these titles emphasize the Zaydi Imāms' right to be the head of the true Islamic community. As a result of the thesis that other Muslims have deviated from the true path, there is a strong tendency among Zaydis toward fanaticism in their treatment of other Muslims.[9]

---

in Muslim law and theology and able to interpret the Qur'ān and therefore make new laws when required.

A number of religious authorities, however, have claimed additional conditions which must be fulfilled. Among the most commonly listed is excellent horsemanship. The frequent listing of this attribute and the stress on bravery have, perhaps, placed an unfortunate amount of emphasis on unrestrained might or power as the major determinative. It is to this factor that many trace the frequency of civil wars which have plagued Yemen for centuries.

Zaydi theory permits the existence of multiple Imāms if one Imām is unable to fulfill all the conditions. Consequently, there have been Imāms for war and Imāms for theology and law at the same time. There have also been frequent "anti-Imāms"; if an anti-Imām is able to oust his predecessor or rival, he is recognized as the legal Imām. See Ameen Rihani, *Arabian Peak and Desert* (London: Constable, 1930), pp. 108–110; R. Strothmann, "Zaidiya," *Encyclopedia of Islam*, IV (1936), 1196–1198.

9. The Zaydis, however, as is the case with other Muslims, recognize the existence of "peoples of the book," that is, Jews, Christians, and others who deserve special status within the community of Islam. The Imāms, like the Ottoman Caliphs, treated the Jews (the only non-Muslim community in Yemen) as a millet (nation), subject to its own laws and government.

Within the Zaydi state, which was based on the right of the descendants of Muḥammad to rule, all Sayyids were a privileged class. It is no exaggeration to say that Yemen under the Zaydi Imāms was administered largely in the interest of this elite, variously estimated to number between 5,000 and 50,000. Their claim to descent from the Prophet was enough to assure them special privileges and status.

The Imām, theoretically elected by his fellow Sayyids, was forced to take the interests and desires of the community of Sayyids into consideration. In order to content this large "interest group," the Imāms dispensed patronage in the form of government positions. As a result, many of the affairs of the state were in the hands of Sayyids; they administered justice, assessed taxes, and supervised tax collection as well as all the myriad functions of even a relatively primitive government. The Sayyids, who were not an independently wealthy landed or commercial aristocracy, were forced to obtain their wealth from other sources. Their control of the administration of justice and taxation naturally provided them with innumerable opportunities for the extortion of funds from the farmers and commercial classes of the cities. The income of the government itself was not large, however, and very few Sayyids were able to amass real fortunes in the Western sense.

The Imāms were largely separated from the population by this intervening oligarchy of Sayyids, against whom there was much popular resentment. In his dealings with the government, the average Yemeni never encountered the Imām or even his personal aides, who were usually commoners (non-Sayyids) raised to important positions as advisers and assistants to the Imām. They dealt with this Sayyid oligarchy, and consequently the generally tyrannical nature of the Imām's regime was largely associated in the popular mind with the Sayyids. It was they whom the average Yemeni had to bribe and mollify if he wanted decisions made or affairs settled. The Imāms themselves, therefore, were able to command a good deal of public respect, loyalty, and even love from a large portion of the population.[10]

10. Despite much opposition to the Sayyids, especially among the commercial class, individual Sayyids were held in esteem in particular tribal districts, where one of their ancestors might be the local saint (*walī*) and another family member the *mansab* (curator of the tomb). By right of their birth and disinterestedness,

The Shāfiʿīs

Orthodox, or Sunni, Islam is represented in Yemen by the Shāfiʿī school of law, whose adherents outnumber other Sunnis in the southwestern corner of the peninsula. Shāfiʿīs predominate in the Tihāma, the foothills, and the southern regions of the country in general, whereas the Zaydis live almost exclusively in the highlands of the center and north as well as most of the eastern desert regions. Certain towns in the lowlands of Yemen, particularly Zabīd, have been famous in the past as the site of universities of Shāfiʿī theology and still retain their spiritual importance for Shāfiʿīs of the south.[12]

The Shāfiʿīs, as adherents of Sunni Islam, recognize no legal or religious right of the Zaydi Imām to interpret or create law. They acknowledge (with varying degrees of sincerity or passivity) his position as temporal ruler of the state, but they do not accept him as their religious leader. This difference in attitude has naturally led to considerable disagreement on the Imām's powers, and the conflict between Sunni and Shīʿa Muslims has been a frequent accompaniment to the various civil disturbances affecting the course of Yemeni history, particularly in the twentieth century.

Nevertheless, the average person in Yemen understands very little, if anything, of the doctrinal differences between Shāfiʿīs and Zaydis, which deal largely with minute points of law. The greatest distinctions between them are found in their oral traditions, histories, epics, and tales concerning themselves and others, which each sect has as a part of its culture. Outward signs of the division between the two sects concern matters relating to prayer and other devotional duties. Because prayer is one of the five

---

sacred writings, containing the names of their Imāms and other holy personages written in a secret code. There is no information on what became of these records. It is possible that the Zaydi Imāms, who alternately feared and reviled the Ismāʿīlīs because of their former power in Yemen, may have used the opportunity presented by the capture of these documents to increase pressure on the Ismāʿīlī community. It seems likely in the light of Zaydi theory that the Imāms would oppose their continued autonomy. For actions taken against them immediately after independence, see ʿAbdullāh ibn ʿAbd al-Karīm al-Jarāfī, *Al-Muqtaṭaf min Tārikh al-Yaman* (Cairo: Dār Ihyāʾ al-Kutub al-ʿArabiyya, 1951), p. 233.

12. During the Middle Ages, the Shāfiʿī Tihāma was independent of the Zaydi highlands, and its capital was Zabīd. Although today it is a small town, it retains much of its importance for Shāfiʿīs, who will sometimes travel great distances in order to have their legal disputes settled there.

" pillars " of Islam, these differences affect one of the most important features of each Muslim's life and have led to considerable rancor at times.[13]

It is, however, possible to exaggerate the differences between Shāfi'īs and Zaydis. It must not be assumed that the division between them runs so deep that it does not permit interfaith cooperation on many political problems, for Shāfi'īs have often acted in the interests of the Imām and the Zaydi state in times of revolution and public disorder. And it is not uncommon for Shāfi'īs and Zaydis to intermarry and use each other's mosques.

Despite their Shī'a origins and their refusal to recognize any spiritual leader not descended from Muḥammad, Zaydis are, in general outlook and philosophy, closer to Sunni Islam than any of the other Shī'a sects. They are often called, particularly by Sunnis of south Arabia, *al-madhhab al-khāmis* (the fifth school) of Islamic law.[14]

The Jews

For centuries the Jews formed the largest non-Muslim minority in Yemen, numbering around 60,000 to 75,000. The Zaydis have always been tolerant toward the Jews, of whom very few lived in the predominantly Shāfi'ī districts. European scholars studying the distribution of Jews in Yemen discovered that Jewish settlements in the northern and central parts closely paralleled Zaydi

13. These differences make it immediately apparent whether one is in a Zaydi or Shāfi'ī settlement and also whether the person praying is a Zaydi or a Shāfi'ī: (1) Zaydi muezzins, in their call to prayer, add the line, " ḥayy 'alā khayr al-'amāl " (come to the best of works); (2) Zaydis say their prayers without ever moving their hands, which are kept rigidly at the sides of their bodies, and at the close of prayers they do not say " amen." Sunnis (Shāfi'īs) begin praying with their hands at their sides, but they then raise them to their heads and place them in front of their bodies with the hands crossed right over left. See Rossi, *L'Arabo parlato a San'ā'*, p. 140; William Robertson [P. W. R. Petrie], " San'a', Past and Present," *Moslem World*, XXXIII, No. 1 (January, 1943), 53.

Some writers have also noted that Zaydis will shift their times of prayer (especially to accommodate their qāt parties, which last into early evening), while other have remarked that Zaydis apparently pray only three times a day instead of the customary five. See, for example: François Balsan, *Inquiétant Yemen* (Paris and Geneva: La Palatine, 1961), p. 58.

14. Among the points of dogma in other Shī'a sects which the Zaydis either ignore or actively discourage are saint worship, mysticism, temporary marriage, and the great celebrations associated with the tenth of Muḥarram (the death of Ḥusayn). See Robertson, " San'a', Past and Present," p. 53; Strothmann, " Zaidiya," p. 1197.

settlements in the same areas.[15] Under the Imāms the Jews were considered a millet and were taxed the non-Muslim tribute (*jizya*), for the collection of which the chief rabbi of the Jewish community was made responsible. While it is likely that the Imāms adopted this system from the Ottomans, Muslim legal theory concerning the status of *dhimmīs* (protected peoples) specifically organizes taxation on this basis.

Although the Jews were subject to a number of special laws concerning housing, clothing, and transportation, they were permitted to manufacture alcohol and follow any occupation they chose (with the exception of the military, from which all protected peoples are exempt). They became the craftsmen of Yemen, and in time fine metalwork, jewelry, certain kinds of embroidery, window tracery, and other crafts devolved almost entirely into their hands.

Despite reports to the contrary, the Imāms were usually scrupulously fair to the Jews and were apparently genuinely sorry to see the majority of them leave for the newly created state of Israel during the years 1950–1951.[16] The many Jewish villages, as well as the large Jewish quarter in Ṣan'ā', are today almost wholly deserted, and the total number of Jews probably does not exceed 1,300.[17]

15. H. von Wissmann and C. Rathjens, *Südarabien Reise*, Vol. III: *Landeskundliche Ergebnisse* (Hamburg: Friederichsen, De Gruyter, 1934), pp. 133–136.

16. Imām Yaḥyā, for example, entrusted all his purchases of European arms during the interwar period to a Jewish friend, Iṣḥāq Subayrī. Upon hearing of the desire of the Jews to establish a "national home" in Palestine, the Imām, in order to avoid complete dependence on his own advisers and/or on the Jewish community in Yemen, invited a prominent Palestinian rabbi to come to Yemen and explain to him personally the arguments and proposals which the Jews had. See Ladislas Farago, *Arabian Antic* (New York: Sheridan House, 1938), p. 183; Hans Helfritz, *Land without Shade* (New York: National Travel Club, 1936), pp. 215, 223.

When Imām Aḥmad realized that in the course of time nearly all the Jews would be leaving Yemen, they were told to teach their trades to the Arabs. Although this training cannot have been exhaustive, the country does not seem to have suffered very much as a result of the Jewish exodus. See B. W. Seager, "The Yemen," *Journal of the Royal Central Asian Society*, XLII, Pts. 3–4 (July–October, 1955), 229.

For taxation and population distribution, see Nello Lambardi, "Divisioni amministrative del Yemen; con notizie econòmiche e demografiche," *Oriente Moderno*, XXVII, Nos. 7–9 (July–September, 1947), 143–162.

The literature on the Jews of Yemen, their origins, culture, and departure, is too extensive to be discussed here.

17. J. S. Simmons *et al.*, *Global Epidemiology* (Philadelphia: J. B. Lippincott, 1954), Vol. III: *The Near and Middle East*, p. 318.

Tribal-Urban Divisions

More important, perhaps, for an understanding of the modern history of Yemen is the division in the population between those who are tribally oriented and the commercially inclined independent town dwellers. As has already been pointed out, the vast majority of the population of Yemen are settled, either as cultivators or as merchants or artisans within the towns and cities. The traditional tribesman, the nomad who ekes out a meager existence in his lifelong trek from water hole to water hole in search of grazing lands for his flocks, represents only a small minority of the population, confined to the arid, relatively barren eastern areas and some regions of the north.

Nearly all the tribes of Yemen long ago settled themselves into the innumerable valleys which cleave the great Yemeni plateau. They have established small villages, and following the traditions of their ancestors, they keep large flocks of animals which necessitate some seasonal migration. At the same time, they are involved in at least a minimum of agricultural activity on land which they usually own. They produce most of their own food and fodder for their animals, as well as some products which they exchange at weekly markets.

Although the majority of the tribes are semisettled cultivators, their traditions of independence and fierce dislike of the permanent town dweller engaged in commerce or manufacture have diminished little over the years. They cherish an attitude of contempt for the comfort and effeminacy of city life and the inability of city people to settle their arguments and feuds themselves. In other words, they denigrate urban residents' dependence on a government which has undertaken to protect their lives and property and to apply certain standards of justice. They also criticize the townsman's inability or unwillingness to carry arms—the certain sign of a tribesman in Yemen.

Shāfiʿī tribes constitute about one-fifth of the total number of tribes in Yemen. They are located primarily in the Tihāma foothills, while the remaining four-fifths, the Zaydi tribes, are located in the central and northern mountains. The fact that the population is almost evenly divided along religious lines means that more Shāfiʿīs than Zaydis are engaged in commerce, manufacturing, and trade and resident in cities and towns. This means that the religious differences among the population are, in many cases, strengthened by this tribal-urban division.

Tribal people consider themselves to be the elite of Yemen because of their ancestry. They are nearly all Qaḥṭānī, and most can trace their genealogies to the great pre-Islamic civilizations and confederations.[18] In many ways they do form a privileged class, primarily because they constitute over half the population and hold the preponderance of power in the state. All Yemeni tribes are very conservative; any attempt to introduce administrative, religious, or other innovations is extremely difficult. They have their own unwritten laws and usages, called *'urf*, which are passed down from generation to generation, and their own courts for settling water, boundary, and other kinds of disputes which arise between them, including, in many instances, criminal cases.

Each tribe is, in reality, a small nation, with its own territory, grazing ground, wells, market towns, allegiances, friends, enemies, history, and the like. All its members give fealty to their own leader or shaykh, who, in the case of a Zaydi tribe, in turn owes allegiance to his spiritual leader, the Imām. Most tribes have their own system of shifting alliances, which they utilize when they believe that a wrong has been done them. Unless the central government is capable of prohibiting it, intertribal warfare is used to settle even the most petty grievances.

Until the twentieth century most of the tribal districts, because of their geographical isolation, had never come under any type of foreign rule.[19] Under the Ottoman Empire, for example, only

18. Traces of the ancient pre-Islamic kingdoms persist in the names of many tribes, although these tribes may be of much diminished stature today. Most are no longer located in the areas from which they first derived their names: the Banū Ma'an (Ma'īn), Banū Ḥimyar, Banū Ma'āfir (Maphar), Quṭaybi (Qaṭaba), for example, all are now located east and southeast of the areas covered by the great pre-Islamic kingdoms. T. E. Lawrence is undoubtedly correct in attributing this movement to population pressure in the interior, with stronger clans pushing weaker ones into the desert, where they became nomads in order to keep alive. See T. E. Lawrence, *The Seven Pillars of Wisdom* (New York: Doubleday, 1935), pp. 35–37.

19. "Foreign rule" to the Zaydi tribes of central and northern Yemen means anyone who is not Qaḥṭānī and not from among the immediate tribal group and its extensive system of alliances and associations, whether for purposes of war and defense or commerce and trade. This idea is so strictly held by some tribes that, after nearly a thousand years, the Sayyids and even the Hāshimite Imāms are still considered interlopers and foreigners to the Yemeni plateaus. See Brown, "The Yemeni Dilemma," p. 364.

four of the many tribes belonging to the two largest confederations in northern Yemen, the Ḥāshid and the Bakīl, were under the Porte's suzerainty: the Bāl-Ḥarīth (or Banī Ḥarīth), the Khawlān, the 'Iyāl Sarīh, and the tribes of Bilād Bustān.[20] Because of this long history of tribal independence, it might be assumed that any attempt to establish a superior authority, even though it be of Yemeni origin, would not be welcome.

20. *Encyclopedia of Islam*, II (1927), 285.

Chapter II

THE ROAD TO INDEPENDENCE

The twentieth century opened inauspiciously for Yemen. By virtue of its being Muslim and because of its strategic position on the Red Sea, the Ottoman government was determined to maintain its hold on the country. In accordance with this policy, and as a result of previous rebellions, the Porte had appointed a particularly harsh and oppressive governor, Wālī 'Abdullāh Pasha. In the south, in territory once ruled by the Imāms, Great Britain considered its possession of Aden and the Protectorates of primary importance to the cohesion of its vast colonial empire.[1] Yemen involuntarily became the arena in which the two great empires met and finally compromised on their " spheres of influence " in southern Arabia.

The interests of both the British and the Ottomans in the southwestern portion of the peninsula extended many years into the past. The ambitions of the Ottoman Empire were first directed toward Yemen as a result of the Porte's desire to control the Red Sea route to India and because it considered control of Yemen a logical extension of its administration of the Ḥijāz and the eastern Arabian Peninsula. During the apogee of Ottoman might, the rule of Sulaymān the Magnificent, his fleet captured Aden in 1538. It is unknown exactly when, but shortly thereafter a Pasha was installed in Ṣan'ā' as Governor of Yemen. The Ottomans maintained their rule for almost a century, until 1630. In that year

1. British policy in Aden was conditioned by the port's strategic location on the trade route to India. As a result, both Aden and the Protectorates were administered by the Bombay Presidency—later the Government of India Office in Delhi—until 1937, when it became a Crown Colony administered directly by the Colonial Office in London.

Even into the 1960s, Aden ranked third in the Commonwealth (behind London and Liverpool) in total shipping handled. However, the merger of Aden into the South Arabia Federation (March, 1963), and the violence and political uncertainty occasioned by the promise of independence for the Federation by 1968 had begun, in 1966, to affect adversely Aden's military and commercial significance.

they evacuated the country, partially because of a series of Arab uprisings and partially because the Red Sea route had declined in importance as the use of the route around the Cape of Good Hope increased, making the expenditure of large sums on the rebellions of the distant Wilayat seem extravagant. The territories formerly administered by the Ottoman authorities were simply abandoned to the Zaydi Imāms, who were to remain undisturbed for nearly two centuries thereafter, except for occasional visits by European travelers.

In 1728, however, a number of minor rulers under the dominion of the Zaydi Imām declared their independence. By far the most important of these was the chief of the 'Abdalī tribe, whose capital is the town and oasis of Laḥij, located in the foothills of the Yemeni mountains south of Ta'izz. He took the title of Sultan, retained ever since by his successors. When, 101 years later in 1829, agents of the East India Company, acting as representatives for the Bombay government, appeared off the shores of Aden in search of a likely spot for a coaling station, they made contact with the Sultan of Laḥij as the overlord of Aden. Ten years later a skirmish took place between the British forces and those of the Sultan, and the former captured the city and port of Aden on January 11, 1839. To the British, their spoils logically included a portion of the hinterland, not only because this area was claimed by the Sultan whom they had defeated but also because they wished to establish some geographical security for their new possession. It is this hinterland which later came to be known as the Aden Protectorate.[2]

YEMEN UNDER THE OTTOMANS

The Ottoman authorities reappeared during the 1840s, when they sent an army deep into the Arabian Peninsula to quell a

2. Great Britain, it should be added, was also concerned with Muḥammad 'Alī's increasing influence in the Arabian Peninsula. Egypt's ruler had sent his armies into the Najd in order to crush the Wahhabi movement in an effort to ingratiate himself with the Sultan, as well as increase his own power and prestige. It seems reasonable to assume that Great Britain was sufficiently concerned with the possibility of long-term Egyptian control of the peninsula that her leaders felt it prudent to establish a prior claim to at least a portion of it.

For greater detail on this early background, see H. L. Hoskins, "Background of the British Position in Arabia," *The Middle East Journal*, I, No. 2 (April. 1947), 137–147.

Wahhabi uprising in the Najd. This expeditionary force occupied al-Ḥudayda and portions of the Tihāma in 1849 as part of the Porte's plans to bring the whole peninsula under its control once more. No serious attempt was made to occupy the hinterland until 1872, when an Ottoman army swept inland and occupied Ṣanʿāʾ with the assistance of the local population, whose patience had been exhausted by fratricidal wars undertaken by competing contenders for the Imamate.[3] The Porte used the cause of one of the contenders as a pretext for its re-entry into the capital and thus gave the first *de facto* recognition to an Imām as overlord of the Zaydi-dominated highlands.[4] That same year the first of the new Ottoman Pashas of Yemen was installed. This second occupation of Yemen was to last until 1918, when the Empire went down to defeat in World War I and as a result renounced all its possessions in the Arabian Peninsula.

The Ottoman Turks, during their second occupation of Yemen, had to contend with a series of violent rebellions against their authority from various Imāms who considered themselves to be autonomous, if not independent. The most important of the revolts were centered in the Zaydi highlands; the accession of a new Imām was the signal for renewed fighting against the Pashas in 1891 and again in 1904.[5]

The Imām of the Zaydis at the opening of the twentieth century was Muḥammad ibn Yaḥyā, styled "al-Manṣūr Billāh" (the victorious one with [the help of] God). During his reign he did nothing to alter the endemic state of revolt which existed among the Zaydi population, although he was sometimes amenable to concessions and negotiations with the enlightened Ottoman Wālī, Aḥmad Fayḍī Pasha. Upon his death in June, 1904, his son Yaḥyā ibn Muḥammad received the *bayʿa* (oath of allegience)

3. The fact that the Ottomans decided to occupy Yemen was, in no small measure, due to the opening of the Suez Canal in 1869 and the re-emergence of the Red Sea as an important maritime route.

4. During all the periods of Ottoman hegemony over Yemen, the Imāms and their followers never managed to convert the whole of Yemen to their Zaydi religious views, nor did they usually exercise political control over the whole country. Instead, the Zaydi Imāms were confined to their historic seats in the north—usually Shahāra or Ṣaʿda—while the other Islamic sects administered their own religious and political affairs.

5. For a description of the rebellion of 1891, at the time of the accession of Imām Muḥammad ibn Yaḥyā, see B. Harris, *A Journey through the Yemen* (Edinburgh: William Blackwood, 1893).

and became the new Imām, styling himself "al-Mutawakkil 'alā Allāh" (the relier on God).

Imām Yaḥyā was destined to rule Yemen for the next forty-four years, during which he became the temporal ruler of the independent state of Yemen as well as the spiritual ruler of the Zaydis. Although it was said that he never saw the sea in his lifetime and never visited a foreign country, he demonstrated a remarkable political perspicacity and shrewdness in his dealings with other powers; his dedication and zeal for the cause of his faith and Yemen's independence cannot be doubted.

The new Imām, who had never concealed his dislike for the Ottoman Turks as occupiers, immediately upon his accession called for a revolt against them. In so doing, Yaḥyā exhibited not only his general resentment of the Ottoman occupation but also his specific disapproval of the demarcation of Yemen's southern frontiers. In May, 1904, the month before his accession, the Anglo-Turkish Boundary Commission finished its work of drawing a border between the Wilayat of Yemen and the Aden Protectorates. The Imām, who considered himself the legitimate ruler of Aden as well as Yemen, vigorously contested this boundary's validity.

Anglo-Turkish Frontier Demarcation

The origins of this binational border commission extended back into the eighteen-nineties, some two decades after the second Ottoman occupation of Yemen. A series of incidents involving the tribes which inhabit the Adeni hinterland and the Yemeni lowlands had so endangered the stability of the area that the British requested that a joint commission be established to determine the boundaries. The Porte's administrators were at first unwilling because they cherished the hope of making use of the Zaydi Imām's claims to authority over these tribes in order to assert their own sovereignty over all or part of the Protectorates. After some particularly vicious incidents on the Ḍāli' plateau during 1900 and 1901, the Porte finally expressed the wish that the frontier between the two empires be demarcated. A joint Anglo-Turkish Boundary Commission was created and met for the first time in January, 1902, in al-Ḍāli'.

The work of defining the boundary was extremely difficult.

Although the two teams were accompanied by armed columns for protection, raids and harassment by the native tribes proved to be a considerable problem. The innumerable tribal territorial disputes which had to be resolved and the difficult, mountainous terrain made progress extremely slow. In May, 1904, the Commission finished delimiting a frontier from Turba on the south Arabian coast (near Bāb al-Mandab) to a point slightly north-northeast of the Yemeni town of Qa'ṭaba and then withdrew. The remainder of the boundary between the British and Ottoman spheres of influence was thereafter drawn on a map; the line from Qa'ṭaba was extended at a 45° angle into the Rub' al-Khālī; it was then turned north and drawn across the entire southern portion of the peninsula until it met the base of the Qaṭar Peninsula on the Persian Gulf. The whole border agreement concerning Yemen and the Protectorates and the line bisecting what is today Saudi Arabia was ratified much later, in March, 1914, by the two parties in the Anglo-Turkish Convention.[6]

The boundary thus created is important, not only because it set the southern frontier of Yemen as it remains to this day but also because it was, and has continued to be, the main bone of contention between the governments of Yemen and Great Britain. Imām Yaḥyā and his successor Aḥmad considered the boundary demarcation by the Anglo-Turkish Commission to be without any legal applicability to them or their country. In the view of Yaḥyā, the establishment of this frontier was the result of a convention signed by two foreign powers during their temporary military occupation of Yemeni soil. They had no sovereign rights in Yemen, which had been neither a member of the Commission nor a party to the Convention.

Imām Yaḥyā's Revolts

The initial success of Imām Yaḥyā's revolt occasioned the recall to Yemen of the Pasha sent to suppress the rebellion of 1891, Aḥmad Fayḍī. With the aid of fresh soldiers, he was able to expel Imām Yaḥyā from Ṣan'ā', forcing him and his supporters to retreat to the plateaus of northern Yemen and to the traditional Zaydi places of refuge—Shahāra and its vicinity. Resolved to

6. For background on this dispute and an account of the difficulties the Commission experienced, see especially Abdullah Mansur [G. Wyman Bury], *The Land of Uz* (London: Macmillan, 1911), Chaps. 3–5; Tom Hickinbotham, *Aden* (London: Constable, 1958), pp. 55–58.

inflict a complete defeat upon the Imām's forces, the Ottoman army entered this difficult territory. It was soon under heavy pressure, due to poor supply lines and efficient guerrilla action by the Imām's forces; its Arab auxiliaries deserted en masse, and a smoldering mutiny grew up within the remaining ranks.

The Ottoman officials prudently adopted a more conciliatory attitude and embarked upon a series of negotiations. After the first talks failed in 1906, a delegation formed by the 'Ulamā' of Makka was sent to Yemen to study the situation. Upon its recommendations, concessions were made to the principal demands of the Imām. The most important concession Yaḥyā wanted was the reinstatement of the Sharī'a (the Islamic code of laws regulating both religious and civil life within Islam) as the legal system for Yemen.[7]

Many other minor demands were unofficially conceded to Yaḥyā during the governorship of Ḥasan Taḥsīn Pasha (1908–1910), and relations between the Ottoman government and the Yemenis improved for the time being. The record of uprisings and attacks on government positions during this period is slight, leading one to the conclusion that a conciliatory phase had opened in Ottoman-Yemeni relations. In fact, however, the revolt of 1904–1905 had been disastrous in its economic aftereffects, for its was famine that was the largest single factor in bringing about the defeat of the Ottoman garrisons. It seems likely that the general economic decay, destruction, and anarchy which had accompanied the revolt left the country temporarily exhausted, while the grievances and hatreds created by it were being nursed for another onslaught.

The next Wālī, Muḥammad 'Ali Pasha, who arrived in 1910 to replace Taḥsīn Pasha, reverted to harsh measures in administering the country. This served as the signal for a new revolt. In 1911 the Imām stormed out of his northern stronghold at the head of a large army of tribesmen and besieged San'ā' for three months. An Ottoman army was dispatched, under Aḥmad 'Izzat Pasha, who fought his way over the mountains toward Ṣan'ā' in order to relieve the city.[8]

7. The Ottomans formerly had insisted on administering the country in accordance with their own civil code, called the Qānūn. See 'Abd al-Wāsi' ibn Yaḥyā al-Wās'ī, *Tārīkh al-Yaman* (Cairo: Al-Maṭba'a al-Salfiyya, 1927), pp. 236–239.

8. For a description of this siege, see A. J. B. Wavell, *A Modern Pilgrim in Mecca and a Siege in Sanaa* (London: Constable, 1912), pp. 180–331.

'Izzat Pasha adopted a conciliatory policy toward the Imām. After he replaced Muḥammad 'Alī and became military governor—for Yemen was now under military law—he aimed at producing a lasting agreement. 'Izzat Pasha was shrewd enough to see that the military exigencies of the situation demanded some kind of negotiated settlement if the Ottoman Empire was to preserve its nominal sovereignty in Yemen, and he and the Imām were able to come to an agreement.[9]

Treaty of Da'ān (دعّان)

The Treaty of Da'ān, named after a small town northwest of 'Amrān, was drawn up in October, 1911, to last a period of ten years. When the treaty was first submitted to the Ottoman Parliament for ratification, however, it was rejected. 'Izzat Pasha thereupon left for Istanbul in order to lobby for its approval, considering it to be of paramount importance for continued Ottoman rule in Yemen. He left as his successor in Yemen a civilian of Syrian origin, Maḥmūd Nadīm Bey, under whose governorship the agreement was faithfully observed by both sides.[10] 'Izzat Pasha's activities in favor of the treaty bore fruit, for on September 22, 1913, an imperial firman ratifying the treaty was publicly read in Ṣan'ā', proclaiming an entente with the Imām, "for the sake of peace between Muslims."[11]

The terms of the treaty granted most of the demands made earlier by Imām Yaḥyā. Article 1 specifically recognized him as spiritual and temporal head of the Zaydi community. Other articles made the Sharī'a the official legal code for the Zaydi districts; granted the Imām the power to appoint all governors and judges there; limited the functions of the Ottoman Wālī to executing decisions reached by the Zaydi courts; gave the Imām an almost completely free hand in matters of taxation and waqf (religious endowment), requiring him to pay only one-tenth of his revenues to the Ottoman government; granted a general amnesty; and exempted from taxation certain districts specified by the Imām (the Arḥab and Khawlān) for a period of ten years,

9. It is worth remembering that the Ottoman Empire was at this time engaged in fighting a war with Italy over other portions of its domains in North Africa.
10. Bury, *Arabia Infelix*, p. 16.
11. *Ibid.*

due to the economic aftereffects of the war.[12] The Imām, from all accounts, appeared pleased with the results.

The Treaty of Da'ān represented the most far-reaching recognition of the role of the Imām of Yemen up to that time, and Yaḥyā had good reason to be pleased. The country was, in effect, split into two administrative divisions, for the Ottoman authorities reserved to themselves the right to appoint officials and collect taxes in the Shāfi'ī portions of the Wilayat; they also used every opportunity to emphasize the differences between Shāfi'īs and Zaydis for their own purposes. Nevertheless, the Imām had established a strong legal precedent for his assumption of power once the Porte abandoned the Wilayat. Benefits to the Imām did not stop there, for he was also granted a yearly subsidy of 2,500 Turkish gold pounds, presumably in order to subsidize some of the more important tribes, to maintain internal security.[13] The terms of the treaty, which were almost all based on Yaḥyā's demands, pointed up those items which were to be of the greatest interest and concern to the Imām in the future: the applicability of the Sharī'a as the sole legal code and his prerogative to appoint all officials of the government.

World War I and Independence

During World War I, Yemen played only a minor role. At the outbreak, the Ottoman government had a force of about 2,000 men and 4,000 Yemeni auxiliaries there.[14] The British, in anticipation of an Ottoman attack, landed troops in Aden in order to strengthen their garrisons. After a series of preliminary skirmishes in which both sides accomplished little, the Ottomans and their Yemeni allies attacked the British garrison at Laḥij, which fell to them on July 5, 1915.[15] Eager to gain control of Aden, the Porte dispatched in early 1916 a force of 3,500 men, accompanied by a small German mission, in order to reinforce the troops at Laḥij. The attempt was foiled by the interruption of Ottoman communications in the Arabian Peninsula brought about by the

12. For the text of this treaty, see al-Wāsi'ī, *Tārīkh al-Yaman*, pp. 136–139.

13. Edouard Brémond, *Yémen et Saoudia* (Paris: Charles-Lavauzelle, 1937), p. 76.

14. *Ibid.*, p. 80.

15. For interesting sidelights on this campaign, see "A Sad Little Sideshow of Desert War," *The Times* (London), July 19, 1965.

beginning of the Ḥijāz Revolt and the work of T. E. Lawrence in the same year. Any further attempts to accomplish the same goal were impossible, for the Red Sea very early in the conflict became a British-controlled "lake," and Yemen remained an isolated province of the Empire without communication lines to Istanbul.[16]

At the outbreak of hostilities, the British government was hard pressed to establish a comprehensive set of alliances among the various states in the south of the Arabian Peninsula. It therefore began a campaign to bring Yemen over to the Allied cause. After a difficult and delicate diplomatic trip, the political officer in Aden, Lt. Col. Harold F. Jacob, obtained a letter from the Imām promising special consideration for Great Britain, but clearly affirming his fidelity to the Ottoman government.[17] In addition to money, arms, and ammunition, the Imām demanded recognition of his sovereignty over the area bounded in the north by Cape Hālī, to and including Ḥaḍramawt on the Arabian Sea, with the exception of the city of Aden and its immediate hinterland (the area covered by the present Crown Colony). This claim included all the territory of the Idrīsī, the Amīr of ʿAsīr, who had been an ally of Britain since 1915, as well as all of the Western Aden Protectorate and a large portion of the Eastern Protectorate. Although the British refused to consider these terms, Colonel Jacob never ceased to remain in touch with Ṣanʿāʾ and continued negotiations with the Imām for a number of years afterward.[18]

The economic consequences of the war for the numerous petty states in the Western Aden Protectorate were disastrous, and by 1918 nearly all the Arab rulers there had deserted the British for the Ottoman-Yemeni side. This precedent and the later occupation of these areas by Yemen were to make the amicable settling of border disputes between Yemen and Great Britain extremely difficult.

At the end of World War I, the Ottoman-Yemeni detachment which had occupied Laḥij was divided into two parts. The Turkish commander, ʿAlī Saʿīd Pasha, and a little over half of his troops surrendered to the English and were repatriated to Turkey. The

16. The Ottoman garrison in Laḥij was able to retain its position there without reinforcements until 1918.

17. Brémond, *Yémen et Saoudia*, p. 81.

18. *Ibid.*, p. 84.

remainder, including a number of officers, took the major portion of the weapons and armaments and decided to enter the service of the Imām. This process was repeated in every Ottoman garrison in Yemen. The post at al-Ḥudayda, for example, included enough military equipment for a full division, and the 500 Ottoman Turkish and Arab troops of the garrison there who entered the Imām's service took this matériel with them. In Ṣan'ā' nearly all the Turkish soldiers and most of their officers, including the former Wālī, Maḥmūd Nadīm Pasha, who had become military governor of Yemen at the outbreak of the war, opted to remain in Yemen. Another prominent personality who decided to stay was Muḥammad Rāghib ibn Rafīq Bey, the Mutaṣarrif of al-Ḥudayda, who later became Imām Yaḥyā's Foreign Minister.[19]

In late 1917 the Imām had moved his entourage to the town of al-Rawḍa, north of Ṣan'ā', perhaps anticipating his early entry into the capital. He was visited there by delegations of tribal leaders and important personalities while the Ottoman Turks were evacuating their positions in the highlands. In November, 1918, the Imām entered Ṣan'ā' triumphantly; shortly thereafter he was officially recognized by the Turkish Wālī as the latter's successor in Yemen.[20] Imām Yaḥyā apparently considered Yemen independent after the withdrawal of the Ottomans and expected others to automatically grant him at least *de facto* recognition. He reasoned that Ottoman rule in Yemen had never been anything other than foreign occupation and therefore never bothered to issue a formal declaration of his independence. Nevertheless, it is possible to argue that Yemen was the first of the former Ottoman territories to become an independent Arab state.

As far as Yaḥyā was concerned, however, this was merely the first step in making Yemen a nation-state; obtaining universal (*de jure*) recognition of its independence and incorporating into it those areas of neighboring states which he considered to be

19. *Ibid.*, pp. 86–87. These were by far the most important of the Ottoman officials who remained to serve the Imām. Maḥmūd Nadīm Bey handled a number of delicate diplomatic negotiations for Yaḥyā until his return to Turkey in 1925. Muḥammad Rāghib ibn Rafīq was, until his death in 1959/1960 (1379 A.H.), intermittently the Foreign Minister for both Imāms Yaḥyā and Aḥmad.

For the text of the Imām's plea to the Ottoman administrators to stay and help him, see Günther Pawelke, *Der Jemen—Das verbotene Land* (Düsseldorf: Econ Verlag, 1959), p. 116.

20. Al-Wāsi'ī, *Tārīkh al-Yaman*, p. 261.

integral parts of Yemen temporarily occupied by foreign powers were still to come. Obstacles to the Imām's goals, however, were numerous and complex. Therefore, the account of succeeding events will be divided into the two major arenas in which he tried to achieve his purposes: internal and external affairs.

PART II: INTERNAL AFFAIRS

Chapter III

INTERNAL GOVERNMENT

For many years before 1918, the territory which Imām Yaḥyā inherited chiefly by default had not been governed as a single, unified whole. It had been divided into minor principalities and incorporated into a large empire by foreign conquerors. Nothing had been done to create a governmental structure specifically for Yemen, taking its problems of terrain and population divisions into consideration.

In facing these problems, Imām Yaḥyā was not without previous experience in the intricacies of governmental administration. Because the Treaty of Daʿān made him responsible for the appointment of provincial administrators and Sharīʿa judges for the Zaydi districts, he had already begun creating an administrative cadre for Yemen. In addition, although the treaty did not spell it out, the Imām was, in effect, responsible for the security of the Zaydi areas—probably the most difficult of the tasks that he faced. Because ultimate responsibility for the whole Wilayat remained with the Ottoman government, however, there was no special police or military organization created for the Zaydi areas alone.

Military Organization

Left almost without military or police organization after the departure of the Ottoman administration in 1918, Imām Yaḥyā was forced to set about creating a military establishment which would maintain internal security, collect taxes, prevent rebellious tribes from interfering with commerce, and protect the frontiers of the new state.

Fully aware that the few thousand auxiliaries the Ottomans had trained during their occupation would not be able to undertake these tasks, Imām Yaḥyā persuaded the Ottoman officers who remained behind to take up service in his army, which they were to help create. As a result, the Yemeni Army continued for many years to have an unusual mixture of Turkish, German,[1] and Arab training methods, commands, and organization; even today it retains many Turkish commands and military titles.

The new army was divided into two primary sections: (1) al-Jaysh al-Difāʿī (the defense army or militia) and (2) al-Jaysh al-Niẓāmī (the regular army). There were, in addition, two minor military groups: al-Jaysh al-Barrani (the volunteer army) and the Sawārīs (cavalry). The volunteer army consisted of "free soldiers," that is, young men, primarily from the northern highlands, who served without pay and were allowed to leave the service whenever they desired. The primary function of the cavalry was service on ceremonial occasions and holidays.

Both of the two main armies were commanded by Syrian officers, specifically brought in by Imām Yaḥyā for that purpose in the nineteen-thirties and given the title *raʾīs arkān al-ḥarb* (chief of staff). These two officers fulfilled their duties until their retirement under Imām Aḥmad soon after his accession to the Imamate. Both were ultimately responsible to the Minister of War (or Defense), who was usually the Imām himself, for he preferred to maintain as much control as possible over matters affecting the military and internal security.

Militia

The Ottoman Turks had used primarily their own soldiers during their occupation of Yemen, with some auxiliaries drawn from other portions of the Empire, and had trained very few Yemenis. Consequently Imām Yaḥyā set out to create a national militia and to train every young man in the country to be a soldier. The normal procedure was for twenty-five per cent of the adult males of a given *liwāʾ* to be called up for a training period of six months; this process was repeated until all the adult men in every liwāʾ were supposed to have been trained. Every man could expect to be recalled about once every three years for retraining on this rotational basis.

The training area for the militia was located outside Ṣanʿāʾ, where the Turks had constructed extensive military facilities

1. The German influences in the Yemeni Army are derived from the training which many Turkish soldiers and officers received from German officers in the early years of the twentieth century.

during their occupation, called by them al-Urdī (military garrison). Training was in the hands of a military expert and a number of assistants, usually brought from Iraq or Syria.

Estimates by observers during the nineteen-forties and fifties placed the number of men undergoing training at any one time at about 15,000 to 20,000. Registers were kept of the men who had been trained as a reserve list for the regular army if the latter should fall below strength. It was, however, possible for a man who was called into the militia to hire a substitute if he did not wish to serve. This happened frequently, for members of the poorer classes were often willing to undertake a number of terms of service in order to obtain the food and clothing which accompanied the training. In general, therefore, it cannot be said that Imām Yaḥyā's goal to have every Yemeni trained for the defense army was a success.

Regular Army

The regular army in theory consisted of full-time professional soldiers. Its members were largely volunteers, and the period of service required was life. Anyone who wished to retire was permitted to do so; the only condition was that he find and pay someone else to take his place. In many cases, sons replaced fathers, and an army career became traditional in some families. If a particular district failed to provide the number of volunteers thought proper by the Imāms, as was sometimes the case with some of the Shāfi'ī areas and the tribal districts of the north and northeast, conscription was enforced. The strength of this army was also estimated at between 15,000 and 20,000 men at about the same time that the above estimate for the militia was made.

The regular army, like the militia, was poorly paid, and many of its soldiers had to furnish their own uniforms. In addition to the small sum of cash which each soldier received, he was given a ration of food each day, and on festivals, national holidays, feast days, or his own birthday, he was customarily given a sheep, some clothing, or other gifts from the Imām; the clothing, however, did not constitute a uniform.

The regular army was used for a variety of other duties in addition to the defense of the frontiers. Probably the most common was the protection and accompaniment of foreigners who visited Yemen; nearly all travelers were given a small contingent of soldiers during their stay. Each *'Āmil* (governor) in every district also had a small company of troops (called a *katība*) directly under his command; these soldiers, however, were often stationed in Ṣan'ā' in order to prevent their unauthorized use. As the control which Ṣan'ā' could exert on the rest of the country increased, 'Āmils were frequently granted permission by the Imām to use their katības for a variety of police duties, such as the apprehension of highwaymen.

The most important of these police duties was that of tax collection. When called out for tax duty, a katība was dispatched to the delinquent village or area, and simply quartered itself there. During their stay, the troops took their rations from the citizens. It may be assumed that more than food was appropriated by the soldiery, and consequently it is not hard to understand why tax delinquency in Yemen was not very common.

Like the militia, the professional army was trained by foreign military experts, usually Syrians or Iraqis. At first, officer candidates were taught in a small military school established in Ṣan'ā'. After Yaḥyā signed a treaty of friendship and mutual assistance with Iraq, many were sent to the Military College in Baghdad for further training. The first group of young cadets left Yemen in 1934; after their return, most of them became involved in attempts to overthrow the governments of Imāms Yaḥyā and Aḥmad. Because these officers' opposition to the Imām became evident almost as soon as they returned home, Imām Yaḥyā soon changed his policy in this matter, and cadets destined for officer positions within the army were either trained locally by imported military missions or sent to other countries, primarily Egypt.[2] Both Imāms

2. The following men were in the first group to go to the Baghdad Military College for training:

Muḥyī al-Dīn al-'Ansī (leader of the group): Executed in 1948 for participating in the al-Wazīr coup.

Aḥmad al-Thalāyā: Executed for participating in the 1955 attempted coup against Aḥmad.

Muḥammad al-'Alfī: Committed suicide after participating in the 1961 attempted assassination of Aḥmad.

'Abdullāh al-Sallāl: Chief of State after September, 1962, *coup d'état* against Imām Muḥammad al-Badr.

Ḥamūd al-Ja'ifī: Minister of Defense, September, 1962.

Ḥasan al-'Amrī: Minister of Transport, September, 1962.

Other members were Aḥmad Ṭāhir, Muḥammad 'Amr, Aḥmad al-'Ansī, Aḥmad Iṣḥāq, Muḥammad Ḥamr, Muḥammad al-Zaydī, and Aḥmad al-Marrī. See Amīn Sa'īd, *Al-Yaman* (Cairo: Dar Iḥyā' al-Kutub al-'Arabiyya, 1959), p. 49; Aḥmad

came to believe that it was wiser to bring foreign military advisers into Yemen, where presumably they could be more easily controlled and their influence on Yemenis limited. This experiment also was to prove disastrous, for later events revealed the participation of these military advisers, as well as their students, in antigovernment plots.

Effectiveness of Armed Forces

The military establishment which Yaḥyā created cannot be compared to the armies of more advanced states. Although the troops used in the campaigns against tribal rebellions during the nineteen-twenties and thirties gave a good account of themselves, their weapons and techniques were quite different from those of a modern army. Even today the mountainous Yemeni terrain and the tribesmen, who are the country's most effective fighters, determine the nature of the military tactics in Yemen.

Consequently, any kind of organized armed force has limited effectiveness there, and both Imāms Yaḥya and Aḥmad were aware of this fact. They, therefore, never seriously tried to make the army a political tool, whose only loyalty was to the Imāms, for they knew that the tribesmen who made up the bulk of the army already had other affiliations and loyalties. If these loyalties did not a priori include fidelity to the Imām, it would be difficult to make devotion to him supersede older and more traditional allegiances. Consequently, after initially subduing the tribes' rebelliousness, the Imāms concentrated much of their effort on manipulating tribal alliances in order to obtain the loyalty of shaykhs capable of fielding well-armed fighters who, although untrained in modern techniques, were the equal of any regular army soldier when it came to armed combat in the Yemeni highlands.

The emphasis placed on the army and the monies spent on its training and equipment varied in proportion to the difficulties the Imāms had in maintaining their authority in the tribal areas. During the late nineteen-fifties, when increased opposition arose among the Zaydi tribes of the north, Imām Aḥmad placed greater

---

Sharaf al-Dīn, *Al-Yaman 'ibr al-Tārīkh* (Cairo: Maṭba'at al-Sinna al-Muḥammadiyya, 1963), pp. 248, 329.

For more information on foreign-trained officers and their participation in revolts, see below, Chap. V.

emphasis on having a trained military force which received its orders only from him. Consequently, after his alienation of many tribes in 1959 and 1960, more foreign arms and military experts were imported to increase the strength and fighting effectiveness of the regular army.

More recent events have proved that the importance placed on tribal warriors by Yaḥyā and Aḥmad was justified. In the civil war of 1962–1967, it was demonstrated that the tribal adult male population make effective guerrilla fighters, capable of holding their own on their home territory against a modern mechanized army. The desertion of large numbers of soldiers from the ranks of the organized armies to their native areas in order to participate on the side which their tribe supported revealed the wisdom of the Imāms' policy of placing great emphasis on the tribes and commonly depending on them for support.

CIVILIAN ADMINISTRATION

Once Yemen became independent, Imām Yaḥyā was wise enough to see that he alone could not govern the entire country. The added administrative chores formerly carried out by the Ottoman administrators, plus the addition of the predominantly Shāfi'ī districts, necessitated additional personnel with administrative experience. Imām Yaḥyā had the foresight to persuade a number of Ottoman officials who represented the Porte in Yemen to remain and assist him in governing the country.

Nevertheless, Imām Yaḥyā seemed unable or unwilling to delegate much authority to assistants. He had been the only person responsible to the Porte for the Zaydi districts prior to 1918 and had become accustomed to personally attending to nearly all governmental work during his period of autonomy. Perhaps the Imām never considered making any changes in this established pattern.

Therefore, the system of government which developed as the temporal power of the Imāms expanded became increasingly autocratic. The Imāms were responsible for every item of government business: finances, the army, education, health, transportation, and justice. They delegated little, if any, independent decision-making power to officials within a regular hierarchy, with staffs and specific functions to fulfill. There were, instead, only advisers and secretaries appointed by the Imām. From time to time they were called upon to provide the Imāms with specialized information on specific subjects; for the most part, however, their duties consisted simply of presenting petitions from citizens to the ruler and then seeing that his decisions were passed on to minor officials, who implemented them. These secretaries were either trusted relatives or, more frequently, commoners (non-Sayyids) of exceptional ability who had no claim to the Imamate.[3]

The average Yemeni expected and wanted the Imām to deal with the myriad affairs of government personally. In the tradition of their ancestors, the Imāms were available daily to the most humble of their subjects, who at that time presented their requests and personal problems to him. The remainder of the day, and usually much of the night, were devoted to the dispatch of similar petitions which had been delivered to the palace, in addition to more important affairs of state. The Imāms took their tasks seriously, and observers of Imāms Yaḥyā and Aḥmad at work marveled at the efficiency and speed with which these administrative matters were personally handled.[4]

This concern of the Imāms for detail, however, was one of their weaknesses as well as one of their strengths, for it resulted in an unwillingness to delegate authority to any subordinates, prevented the creation of a trained cadre of administrators, and opened Yaḥyā and Aḥmad to the charge that theirs was an absolute and tyrannical rule.

It should be remembered that there were good reasons for their hesitancy in delegating authority; the traditions of an all-powerful Imām placed a considerable strain on the rulers, but could not be ignored. They knew there was only a limited number of people on whom they could rely—usually commoners. The Zaydi tradition that any Sayyid who can accumulate and wield the requisite power can become Imām, even if one already exists, naturally made the Imāms guard what power they had jealously. If they showed themselves incapable of exercising all the duties of office

3. For example, the al-'Amrī family provided advisers and officials to each of the Imāms, and all were very talented and loyal commoners.

4. See Scott, *In the High Yemen*, pp. 174–174; Claudie Fayein, *Une française médecin au Yemen* (Paris: René Julliard, 1955), pp. 46–47; Rihani, *Arabian Peak and Desert*, pp. 104–107, 128–130, 221 ff.; Eva Hoeck, *Als Ärztin unter Beduinen* (Einsiedeln, Switzerland: Benziger Verlag, 1958), pp. 38–39.

that were expected of them, it was a foregone conclusion that someone who felt himself better qualified would see the office and be certain of at least the tacit support of the conservative religious hierarchy.

Provincial Divisions

For some time after independence, the Ottoman internal administrative structure for Yemen remained unchanged and largely in the hands of officials who elected to stay on their jobs under the new government.[5] Soon, however, certain designations of its subdivisions were altered in order to conform with Yemeni administrative terminology.[6] Later, as the Porte's officials retired and returned to Turkey, died, or were replaced, the vestiges of the former system were slowly erased.

According to Yemeni custom, the governor of a province is an Amīr, which title was substituted for that of *mutaṣarrif*. Unlike most other Muslim countries (where Amīr means a prince of the royal blood), in Yemen a provincial governor held this title as a result of his position as Amīr al-Jaysh (Commander-in-Chief of the Army). It meant specifically that he was chief of the troops located within his particular province. This was, and still is, abbreviated simply to Amīr, while the full title of Amīr al-Jaysh is reserved for the Minister of War.

Similarly, according to Yemeni usage, the title of 'Āmil is reserved for the governor of a *qaḍā*, the subdivision of a liwā'. However, there is some confusion in later reorganizations as a

5. The Wilayat of Yemen was divided as follows: (1) the sanjaq of San'ā', including the *qaḍās* of Ḥarāz, Kawkabān, Ānis, Ḥajja, Khamār, Yarīm, Riḍā', and 'Amrān; (2) the sanjaq of al-Ḥudayda, including the qaḍās of Zabīd, al-Luḥayya, Zaydiyya, Jabal Rīma, Ḥajūr, Bayt al-Faqīh, and Bājil; (3) the sanjaq of Ta'izz, including the qaḍās of Ibb, 'Udayn, Qa'ṭaba, Ḥijariyya, al-Mukhā, Qamā'ira, Dhū Sufāl, and Mawiyya. Attached to the Wilayat were a number of independent districts, more an indication of the inability of the Ottoman authorities to govern them directly than of any particular sophistication in administrative subdividing. In the north, these were Abū 'Arīsh, Qaḥṭān, Wadā'a, and Bilād Yām; in the east, Bilād Kitāf, Jabal Baraṭ, al-Jawf (including Bilād Arḥab and Nihm), Mā'rib, Khawlān, Ḥarīb, Bayḥān, Bilād Yāfi'ī, the Oasis of Khabb, and the Faḍlī region. See "Yemen," *Encyclopedia of Islam*, IV (1934), 1155. For the administrative structure of Yemen before 1913, see, among others, Vincenzo Rossi, *Le quistioni del Medio Oriente* (Rome: Casa Editrice Italiana, 1906), pp. 14–16.

6. The first apparent change was the renaming of the sanjaqs, now called *liwā's* (provinces); the sanjaq of Ṣan'ā' because the northern liwā'; the sanjaq of Ta'izz, the southern liwā'; and the sanjaq of al-Ḥudayda, the Tihāma liwā'.

result of the additional application of the title 'Āmil to the governor of a *nāḥiya*, the subdivision of a qaḍā.

Further confusion is created by the ambivalent use of the word *Qāḍī* in Yemen. While in other Muslim Arab countries Qāḍī is used to designate one learned in Islamic law, its primary denotation in Yemen is as an honorific title given to a commoner who has been elevated to a responsible position in the government, such as an 'Āmil or even Amīr. Thus, it is not unusual to find persons with the title Qāḍī acting as 'Āmils of a qaḍā, but having no particular knowledge of law and fulfilling a purely political position.

In 1944 the main administrative divisions of the country were recast. This reorganization was apparently undertaken with the express purposes of apportioning certain districts to a particular son of Imām Yaḥyā and strengthening the control of the central government over all portions of the country. Yemen was divided into four liwā's, as follows:

1. The liwā' of Ta'izz, governed by the Crown Prince, Sayf al-Islam Aḥmad, Imām Yaḥyā's eldest son.[7] This liwā' included all of the former southern liwā' and a few portions of the old northern liwā'. Aḥmad was living in Ta'izz at this time and governed the southern portions directly, with little reference to Ṣan'ā' or his father. His brother Sayf al-Islam Muṭahhar acted as deputy governor for the northern portions and usually lived at Qafla.

2. The liwā' of Ṣan'ā', governed directly by Imām Yaḥyā and Sayf al-Islam 'Abdullāh. Although 'Abdullāh was in theory the governor of another province (given below), he resided almost permanently in Ṣan'ā' with his father. The liwā' of Ṣan'ā' was by far the largest of the new liwā's and was designed to contain all those rebellious districts which had proved hard to govern.

3. The liwā' of al-Ḥudayda, actually governed by Qāḍī 'Alī al-'Amrī (the brother of Yaḥyā's "prime minister" and adviser, Qāḍī 'Abdullāh al-'Amrī), acting as Sayf al-Islam 'Abdullāh's deputy.

4. The liwā' of Ibb, governed by Sayf al-Islam Ḥasan. This liwā' consisted of portions of the old central amirate of Dhamār,

7. All the sons of an Imām are given the title "Sayf al-Islam" according to Zaydi custom.

many parts of which had been transferred administratively to the liwā' of Ṣan'ā'.

Incorporated into this new administrative scheme were the following subdivisions:

1. Liwā'—governed by an Amīr (also, a *nā'ib al-liwā'*, a deputy governor).

2. Qaḍā—governed by an 'Āmil (usually a Sayyid).

3. Nāḥiya—governed by an 'Āmil.[8]

4. *'Izla*—governed by an 'aqīl, shaykh, and sometimes by a *ḥākim.*[9]

Apparently soon after the 1944 reorganization (the date is uncertain), Yaḥyā felt that additional improvements could be made. Accordingly, the country was redivided, this time into six liwā's: Ta'izz, Ṣan'ā', al-Ḥudayda, Ibb, and the new liwā's of Ṣa'da in the northeast and Ḥajja in the northwest. The most likely explanation for the new system is afforded by the fact that, as Yaḥyā's health deteriorated during the middle nineteen-forties, he decided to delegate some of the responsibilities of governing the immense liwā' of Ṣan'ā' to other members of his family.

The accession of Imām Aḥmad in 1948 brought few changes to the administrative structure. The main change was the addition of another liwā', the seventh. Created in 1949 and called the liwā' of Bayḍā', it included a number of the more unruly areas around Ḥarīb in the southeast. A part was also taken from the former liwā' of Ṣan'ā', which probably had been for too long the catchall for rebellious eastern districts.[10]

This last arrangement apparently comes closest to a rational division of Yemen for the present time, and it was taken over whole by the Republican government formed after the September 26, 1962, revolt against Imām Muḥammad al-Badr.[11]

8. In most cases, the 'āmils of nāḥiyas were Zaydi Sayyids, or commoners who had received the title of Qāḍī. Even in the Shāfi'ī districts of the south and southwest, some of these officials were Zaydi Sayyids; the number of Shāfi'ī 'āmils was always very low, a continual source of friction between the two sects.

9. There were a variety of other subdivisions employed by different officials in their own provinces. For more detailed information, see Lambardi, "Divisioni amministrative del Yemen," pp. 143–162.

10. Fakhrī, *Al-Yaman*, pp. 19–20.

11. 'Adnān Tarīsī, *Al-Yaman wa Ḥaḍārat al-'Arab* (Beirut: Dār Maktabat al-Ḥayāt, 1963), pp. 203–209.

Local Officials

Traditionally, each tribe and village in tribal areas elected its own chief, whether his title was shaykh or ʿaqīl; in practice, of course, tribal leadership in most cases was hereditary. Under the Ottoman authorities, the people were permitted to retain this privilege, and villages and tribes were allowed a considerable amount of local autonomy.[12] During the nineteen-thirties and forties, however, Imām Yaḥyā undertook to change this system. Under his rule, these officials of small towns and villages came to be nominated by the Amīr of the liwāʾ and confirmed by the Imām.

Because the right to appoint officials and judges had been granted to Imām Yaḥyā by the Treaty of Daʿān, it was not a complete novelty to have Imām-appointed administrators in Zaydi districts. For Imām Yaḥyā, the terms of the treaty also provided a logical basis for the extension of his appointive powers over additional administrators and governors throughout the new state.

The tribes objected violently to this new policy, and for nearly twenty years Imām Yaḥyā worked to impose his interpretation of his powers of appointment on them. The Imām did finally succeed in asserting his right to select the tribal shaykhs, who were also administrators of tribal law. Consequently, through this power he was able to play a role in selecting not only the political leader of the community but also the judicial head. In the final analysis, it must be seen as a victory for him that many tribes, although grudgingly and never wholeheartedly, accepted his appointment of many of their leaders and decision makers.

Purposes and Motivations

The motivations behind such changes were varied. A major part of every reorganization was due to the Imām's policy of attempting to weaken the cohesion of the tribes in order to prevent their uniting or presenting a common front against the central government. At the same time, however, Yaḥyā also tried to do away with the ancient tribal divisions and interfamily and kin-group feuds; the purpose in this case was to create a greater amount of internal stability and peace, to permit an expansion of domestic trade.

12. Basil W. Seager, "The Yemen," *Journal of the Royal Central Asian Society*, XLII, p. 225.

Another goal of the reorganizations was to concentrate more power in the hands of the reigning Ḥamīd al-Dīn clan. Many key government positions had been held traditionally by members of other prominent Sayyid families, a situation which Yaḥyā wished to alter in order to reduce the power of other contenders for the Imamate. During the nineteen-thirties many prominent personalities were removed from positions of responsibility and replaced with members of Imām Yaḥyā's immediate family. As other officials died, their posts were either abolished or, in a few cases, given to other families whom Yaḥyā trusted—usually families from his own clan.

By making appointments on all levels of government, including the smallest village, Imām Yaḥyā hoped to strengthen the controls which the central government in Ṣan'ā' could exert over them and thereby incorporate them into the larger government apparatus and reduce their independence. To a degree, he was successful, for as local officials came to be involved in the assessment and collection of taxes for the central government from their areas, their positions became very desirable sinecures. The amount of influence which could be brought to bear within the court at Ṣan'ā' (or Ta'izz under Imām Aḥmad) and the amount of " commission " paid to the Amīr of the liwā' and other government officials became the deciding factors in the distribution of these positions.

One other reason for the Imām's desire to control the appointments of local shaykhs was his long-sought goal of establishing the Sharī'a as the only legal code in Yemen, for the appointees in their role as arbiters of local law were in a position to alter considerably the legal systems in their own areas.

YEMEN'S LEGAL CODE

The Sharī'a (the path) is the " canonical law for all Islam." There are, however, many different interpretations of its meaning among Muslims; the Sunnis, for example, have four different schools of legal thought. In Yemen, the Quranic commentators and the 'Ulamā' of the Zaydi community have their own view of the life of Muḥammad, the origins and attributes of the Qu'rān, God, and the proper means for arriving at legal judgments.

In general, one may characterize the Zaydi interpretation of the Sharī'a as considerably more strict than that practiced in most other Muslim countries. The traditional punishments for crimes, for example—decapitation for capital crimes and mutilation for some lesser offenses—are still applied in accordance with Zaydi theory, which holds that it is impossible to alter, modify, or ignore any of the terms of a legal system which is of divine origin.

As the Imām of the Zaydi community of believers, it was incumbent upon Yaḥyā to live and rule according to the tenets of the Zaydi faith. There is no reason to doubt that Imām Yaḥyā was sincere in his attempt to do so. Consequently, soon after independence was achieved, Imām Yaḥyā set out on a campaign to make the Sharīʿa the only code of law in all districts of the new state.

Although the Porte had recognized the Imām's right to administer the Sharīʿa exclusively in his own Zaydi districts, this did not mean that the Islamic legal code was, in practice, the only one applied there. In fact, the Imām faced more problems in enforcing his will on the tribes, many of whom were Zaydis, than he did in applying the Sharīʿa to the city dwellers. Because of the long tradition of tribal independence, as well as the endemic state of anarchy which prevailed in Yemen after the fall of the pre-Islamic kingdoms, a system of common law had arisen. From the tenth to the twentieth centuries there had been only nominal obeisance given by the tribes of Yemen to Islam.[13] Consequently, the system of law which grew up in these tribal areas had little connection with, or respect for, the Sharīʿa.

Types of Legal Code

In Yemen at the beginning of the twentieth century, people and their lives were regulated according to one or more of the following systems of law: (1) the Sharīʿa, which was commonly used in those areas where the Imām had temporal power and

13. The great tenth-century Yemeni historian al-Ḥamdānī called the Yemeni tribes "heathens," although they call themselves Muslims, because they have no knowledge of the "holy law" (the Sharīʿa), and there is no one to teach it to them, and because they ignore all Muslim duties; quoted in Pawelke, *Der Jemen*, pp. 88–89.

Twentieth-century travelers have similarly reported many pagan beliefs among Yemeni tribesmen and their ignorance of Islamic practices and beliefs. See Rosita Forbes, "A Visit to the Idrisi Territory in Asir and Yemen," *Geographical Journal*, LXII, No. 4 (October, 1923), 276; C. S. Coon, *Measuring Ethiopia and Flight into Arabia* (Boston: Little, Brown, 1935), pp. 234–235.

could enforce judgments made under Islamic law; (2) 'urf, or common law,[14] which was primarily used by the tribes living outside the settled areas; and (3) the *manqad* system, administered by a castelike itinerant group of "justices of the peace," found in the extreme eastern sections of Yemen and the Ḥaḍramawt, applied in conjunction with 'urf.

Tribal Law

Tribal law is intended to maintain order by applying sanctions to those who have, either intentionally or accidentally, caused damage to others; Islamic law, being later and more advanced (although based on tribal law), attempts to deal also with morals, something completely outside the scope of tribal law, even though the latter contains rules for nearly every aspect of life.

'Urf is a system only in the sense that it is a collection of unwritten laws, usages, and traditions, passed down orally from generation to generation, embodying the decisions of tribal chiefs and wise men. It represents a stage of law just one step beyond intertribal anarchy, by which the tribes regulate, without undue bloodshed, disputes over water rights and grazing grounds as well as personal quarrels, debts, and other disagreements which may arise.

The headman, or elder, usually called an 'aqīl, and often shaykh, acts as "judge"; no special training is necessary for this office. The concept of punishment for crime is unknown in 'urf, for everything operates on the principle of revenge and reparation for deeds. Another important principle is that of collective responsibility by a tribe or clan, for it is the clan or family kin group which is the unit to be protected, not the individual. From this concept it is a short step to the blood feud, one of the characteristics of the 'urf system and one which has caused untold hardship in both human and economic terms in those areas where it is common.

Under common law there is a very strong emphasis on the right of a clan to settle arguments and redress wrongs. As a result, the tribesmen have great contempt for men who permit someone else to set their laws and right their wrongs; the concept of

14. 'Urf can be translated as custom, usage, tradition, or habit. In Yemen, tribal law is also often called *ḥukm al-qabīla* (precisely, tribal law), or *ḥukm al-badū* (Badu law).

committing a crime against a " state," that is, an outside legal and/or moral force, is completely foreign to them.[15]

The Manqad System

Under the manqad system, the chief manqad (judge) is elected and known as *manqad al-manāqid* (judge of judges); [16] he chooses others from outside his family and clan to assist him in making decisions, and his choice is not limited in any respect. These assistants all receive the title " manqad," and either separately or together they perform the functions of a final court of appeal. Their judgments are given according to the widest possible code, which they themselves describe as being based on " al-Sharī'a, al-'Āda, wa al-Ḥaqq " (the Sharī'a, custom [tribal law], and the truth).

No tribesman, having once put his case to a manqad, may withdraw it or refuse to abide by the decision handed down without forfeiting his tribal honor and being considered guilty of a great shame—in this portion of the world, a strong enough punishment to force compliance. The manqads dress as poor men and go about unarmed. They are treated by chiefs and tribesmen alike with great respect. Nevertheless, due to the increase in breaches of custom by the rapid rush of developments in recent years, their power has declined; today they appear to be a dying caste, limited almost wholly in their influence to the Ramlat Sab'atayn in the extreme Eastern regions of Yemen and the deserts north of the Wādī Ḥaḍramawt.[17]

15. For additional information on the legal systems and traditions which govern life and relations within and between the Yemeni tribes, see:

Carl Rathjens, " Tâghût gegen scherî'a," *Jahrbuch des Linden-Museums* (Stuttgart), Neue Folge I (1951), pp. 172–187.

Ettore Rossi, " Il diritto consuetudinario delle tribù arabe del Yemen," *Rivista degli Studi Orientali*, XXIII (1948), 1–36.

Eduard Glaser, " Die Kastengliederung im Jemen," *Das Ausland*, LVIII (March 16, 1885), 201–205.

16. Manqad is derived from the root N-Q-D, meaning " to pick out, or investigate." Nevertheless, it is believed that this system of independent legal arbitrators can be traced back to the legal systems of the ancient pre-Islamic kingdoms, possibly that of Ma'īn.

17. A. Hamilton (The Master of Belhaven), *The Kingdom of Melchior* (London: John Murray, 1949), p. 154. On the basis of reports by Yemeni historians and Western writers and travelers in the areas named during recent years, it seems safe to assume that the influence of the manqads in areas directly controlled by the Imāms had died out by the time the eastern districts were being subjugated.

Attempt to Establish the Sharīʿa System

If the Sharīʿa was to become the sole system of the law in Yemen, it would mean the elimination of both ʿurf and the manqad system. As a first step toward eradicating them, Imām Yaḥyā sought to control them through appointing their administrators. Since both ʿurf and the manqad system were administered in each tribal community by men with little or no special religious training or inclination, it was necessary for the Imām to gain control of the appointment of secular leaders, which he was able to do in a considerable degree. In the process, he hoped to be able to select men of religious training and loyalty to him who would be willing to replace, if only gradually, their traditional law with concepts and decisions based on the Sharīʿa.

In this desire, however, he was less successful. The final result of Imām Yaḥyā's campaigns was a compromise; by the middle nineteen-thirties he was compelled to give official recognition to the continued existence of ʿurf, as evidenced by his policy of appointing two judges for each administrative district: one for Sharīʿa cases and one for ʿurf cases. In modern terminology, then, Yemen in effect had two legal systems: a civil and secular law, administered by the ʿāmil (governor) of the district, and the (canonical) Sharīʿa law, administered by the ḥākim (judge).[18]

Most of those shaykhs whom the Imām did appoint continued to rule by common law; undoubtedly most feared the reaction among their fellow tribesmen should they cease to do so. The simple fact that a tribal leader derived much of his authority from the acquiescence of the tribe to his leadership, and not derivatively from the Imām, meant that if a shaykh wished to retain his position, his first loyalty and basic concern would be for the wishes of his followers. Consequently, it was rare indeed that tribal leaders did as the Imām wished unless the tribesmen them-

18. The highest court of appeal for cases from both systems was the Imām, although he could also be the court of first instance. Appeal from the shaykh in the tribal areas went to the ʿāmil in ʿurf cases, then to the amīr of the province, and finally to the Imām. In Sharīʿa cases, appeal went to a higher ḥākim (with the approval of the local ʿāmil) and finally to the Raʾīs al-Istiʾnāf, the high court of appeal, located in Ṣanʿāʾ. From this court's chief judge it was possible to go to the Imām, but this occurred infrequently.

For the above information on the legal system and the court organization, the author is indebted to one of his most helpful friends among those who formerly acted in an advisory capacity to the Imāms, but who wishes to remain anonymous for the present.

selves also approved. Even those inroads which the Imām did make in the political life of the tribes were achieved only after many long and bloody rebellions had been successfully put down.

THE ESTABLISHMENT OF INTERNAL SECURITY

The method by which Imām Yaḥyā attained his limited control over the tribes' political life was long and complex. One important element was, of course, the appointment of shaykhs and other officials who were loyal to the Imām. This was possible, in many instances, only through extensive use of his new army and the military prowess of his son and successor, Aḥmad. In addition, Imām Yaḥyā's own intimate knowledge of intertribal relationships, feuds, and loyalties, the result of his long association with them during Ottoman rule, was another factor which enabled him finally to establish internal security.

The primary reason for the Imām's difficulty in asserting his authority was the fact that most Yemeni tribes had known centuries of independence, due largely to the inability of any government to administer effectively the difficult terrain in which they lived. The Ottomans, during their occupation, had attempted to maintain some order among these tribes and, as a result, were forced to contend with innumerable tribal outbreaks—many of them led by the Imāms themselves, who relied on their closest allies among the Zaydi tribes of the mountainous interior for their forces.

The Ottoman authorities made an effort to limit the desire of certain tribes to undertake pillaging expeditions against neighboring tribes and villages, whether for economic reasons, revenge, or sport, by adopting the time-honored method of bribery. Certain tribes were paid a monthly stipend, and although such payment was an implicit admission that the Porte could not directly control them, it amply demonstrated that gold could purchase not only the pacification of some tribes but, indeed, in many cases their loyalty. By far the most important of these stipends, after that given to the Zaydi Imām himself, was paid to two of the most powerful tribal confederations in northern Yemen, the Ḥāshid and the Bakīl. Thirteen hundred Turkish pounds per month, until the end of World War I, was necessary to purchase peace between tribal enemies of these two groups and their neighbors.[19]

19. Rihani, *Arabian Peak and Desert*, p. 114.

Campaigns in the North

The relaxation of authority and the cutting off of the Porte's subsidies immediately after the Ottoman evacuation brought about a rash of tribal outbreaks against the new government and also unleashed intertribal hostilities which had been building up. One of the first of these occurred after the elimination of the Ḥāshid-Bakīl subsidy; it was a protracted conflict, which no doubt had its origins in the period when the subsidy was paid, between tribes of the Ḥāshid and the 'Iyāl Sarīh of the latter.[20]

Imām Yaḥyā had already begun to create an army and to appoint tribal shaykhs, and it was not long before the first opposition to these efforts were also felt. In 1922–1923 (1341 A.H.), certain tribes in the regions north of Ṣan'ā' objected to enforced conscription into the regular army. Subdued after a short campaign, they temporarily accepted the decisions of the new government.[21]

Perhaps the severity with which this outbreak was put down tempered the rebelliousness of some other tribes, for it was not until two years later that the next disturbances occurred. In 1924–1925 (1343 A.H.) some of the powerful and turbulent tribes of al-Jawf, the great plain in the northeast of Yemen, rose in revolt. The Imām considered the outbreak of sufficient seriousness to send a large portion of the new army, under the leadership of one of the most prominent men in Yemen, al-Sayyid 'Abdullāh ibn Aḥmad al-Wazīr. 'Abdullāh was successful in putting down the revolt, and on the trek back to Ṣan'ā' was forced to crush another minor outbreak among the tribes to the north of that city.[22]

Yemeni accounts report the fact that al-Sayyid 'Abdullāh appointed a "judge and teachers of religion" for the area after defeating the tribes, undoubtedly in connection with Yaḥyā's campaign to replace 'urf in these districts with the Sharī'a.

20. *Ibid.*, p. 83. Although some writers have referred to the Ḥāshid and Bakīl confederations as the "two wings of the Imamate," indicating their unswerving loyalty to the Imāms, there is nothing to indicate this in Yemeni descriptions of the reigns of Yaḥyā and Aḥmad; throughout the twentieth century, there is sporadic fighting between different subsections of these two, as well as outright opposition to the policies of the Imāms.

21. Al-Wāsi'ī, *Tarīkh al-Yaman*, p. 265; Ḥusayn ibn Aḥmad al-'Arshī, *Bulūgh al-Marām*, ed. Père A.-M. de St. Elie (Cairo: C. E. Albertiri, 1939), pp. 93–94.

22. Al-Wāsi'ī, *Tārīkh al-Yaman*, p. 273; al-'Arshī, *Bulūgh al-Marām*, p. 94; al-Jarāfī, *Al-Muqtaṭaf*, p. 233; Sharaf al-Dīn, *al-Yaman*, p. 403.

Campaigns in the Tihāma

Following his successful campaign in al-Jawf, al-Sayyid ʿAbdullāh was ordered into the Tiḥāma in order to assist Sayf al-Islam Aḥmad, at the head of another force there. The purpose of the two-pronged attack was to wrest the coastal regions from the Idrīsī; [23] this was accomplished in a short campaign, after which Imām Yaḥyā set about establishing his authority by appointing judges, administrators, and teachers for the newly acquired territory.[24] Most, if not all, of these new government officials were Zaydis. It may be assumed that the Imām did this to insure the loyalty of at least the government personnel in the Tihāma, for the Shāfiʿī population of Yemen had co-operated fairly well with the Ottoman administration and cared little for the prospect of Zaydi rule.

The first revolt against this Zaydi rule in the Tihāma was not long in coming. In the following year, 1926–1927 (1345 A.H.), during the ʿĪd al-Aḍḥa (Feast of Immolation), part of the population attacked and killed some troops of the Imām. Sayf al-Islam Aḥmad's army once again went into the area and quickly put down the revolt.[25] The peace which followed lasted a little over one year, for a new rebellion broke out in 1928–1929 (1347 A.H.) which proved to be one of the most serious challenges to the Imām's authority since independence.

The Shāfiʿī tribe of al-Zarānīq, in the Bayt al-Faqīh–Zabīd–al-Ḥudayda area, decided again to assert its independence.[26] Although Zarānīq fighting strength probably does not exceed 10,000 men, they are among the strongest and most numerous tribes in the Tihāma [27] and have been a source of trouble to all who have tried to govern them. Under the Porte's administration, they were strong enough to assassinate one of the *qāʾimmaqāms* without

23. The Idrīsī was the ruler of the principality of ʿAsīr, and had been established in the entire Tihāma after World War I by his former British allies.

24. Al-Wāsiʿī, *Tārīkh al-Yaman*, p. 274; al-ʿArshī, *Bulūgh al-Marām*, p. 94.

25. Al-Wāsiʿī, *Tārīkh al-Yaman*, p. 277; al-ʿArshī, *Bulūgh al-Marām*, p. 96.

26. Reports of rebellions on the part of the Zarānīq against any form of administrative control over them extend back into the nineteenth century and the first arrival of the Ottoman Empire's troops.

27. More recent writers have given the figure as 90,000, the number to be found in almost all contemporary Arab sources. See, for example, al-ʿArshi, *Bulugh al-Marām*, p. 190; Dabbāgh, *Jazīrat al-ʿArab*, I, 253.

Older writers, with firsthand experience in Yemen, give the 10,000 figures, which the author considers a closer approximation. See Bury, *Arabia Infelix*, p. 24; Amīn al-Rayḥānī, *Mulūk al-ʿArab* (Beirut: Dār al-Rayḥānī Press, 1960), p. 276.

suffering any retaliatory punishment and to levy road tolls on Ottoman infantry which desired to pass through al-Zarāniq territory.[28] While many travelers have described their "fractious independence," at least one has called them a "friendly, hospitable people," who have no fanatical xenophobic tendencies and love their poverty-stricken and unhealthy land (referring to the unpleasant climate of the Tihāma), who defend their freedom with fierce tenacity, and who, as a result, are often harassed by the Imām's soldiers with confiscations and destructive raids.[29]

The desire of the Zarāniq for freedom from outside interference led them to undertake one of the most pathetic gestures the opponents of Zaydi rule in Yemen have ever tried. In 1925, immediately after the occupation of the Tihāma by the troops of the Imām, Shaykh Aḥmad al-Fuqaynī of the Zarāniq sent a telegram to the League of Nations asking that an independent Shāfiʿī-Zarāniq state be established in the Tihāma with al-Ḥudayda as the capital.[30]

Apparently despairing of receiving foreign recognition of their independence, the Zarāniq declared war on the Imām in late 1928. They began their rebellion by attacking a number of police posts and cutting the roads and communications throughout their territory. Imām Yaḥyā again called upon his son, Sayf al-Islam Aḥmad, to quell the revolt. Primarily because of the victory which he achieved in this campaign against the most unruly tribe in Yemen, the fame of Aḥmad as a warrior became a national legend in his own lifetime, around which lengthy poems were composed.[31]

28. Bury, *Arabia Infelix*, pp. 23–24.

29. Hans Helfritz, *Glückliches Arabien* (Zürich and Stuttgart: Fretz und Wasmuth, 1956), p. 179.

30. Yemeni sources attribute the origins of this uprising to foreign incitement and encouragement. This seems unlikely, however, because these same sources cannot agree on whether the Zarāniq received British or Italian assistance; the disagreement developing between these two powers over the status of the Red Sea at this time makes it unlikely that there was Anglo-Italian collusion in the matter. In addition, Yemeni sources have produced no evidence for their claim—the accusation seems to suffice. Nevertheless, it should be added that the former chief of the French military mission in Saudi Arabia also accuses the English of complicity in the revolt. In his case, a general willingness to attribute all the evils of the peninsula to British policy tends to weaken his statement. See al-ʿArshī, *Bulūgh al-Marām*, p. 190; Fakhrī, *Al-Yaman*, p. 169; Sharaf al-Dīn, *Al-Yaman*, p. 314; Brémond, *Yémen et Saoudia*, p. 103.

31. E. Rossi, *L'arabo parlato a Sanʿa* devotes many pages to a long poem composed at the time concerning Aḥmad's military exploits as an exercise for students learning Ṣanʿānī Arabic.

Aḥmad, as was his custom, gathered together his own army, drawn mainly from the Ḥāshid confederation and other northern mountain tribes. In addition, he forced some Tihāma tribes, neighbors of the Zarānīq, to assist him. Because of the fact that the Zarānīq had prepared themselves for a prolonged war and fortified a number of positions dominating the overland routes to their territory, Aḥmad was finally forced to attack them from the sea. He succeeded in capturing their primary port, Ghulayfiqa, and seized their collection of sailing craft. Once he had secured the coast, he fought his way inland and eventually managed to divide and surround his opposition. After almost a year of fighting, Aḥmad was able to march into the Zarānīq capital of Bayt al-Faqīh in October, 1929, and " establish peace and security " in this portion of Yemen.[32]

Fighting in the East

Imām Yaḥyā's campaign against the Zarānīq had scarcely ended when the eastern regions of al-Jawf and al-Mashriq rose in rebellion. By 1929–1930 (1348 A.H.) two brothers, 'Alī and Ḥamad ibn Nāṣir al-Qarda'ī, acting as governors, were in control of the entire region from Bilād al-Jūbah in the north to Ḥarīb-Bayḥān in the south. Imām Yaḥyā sent troops under the leadership of al-Sharīf 'Abdullāh al-Ḍumayn al-Hamzī, the Amīr al-Jaysh at the time, and al-Sayyid 'Abdullāh al-Wazīr to quell the uprising. 'Abdullāh al-Wazīr managed to capture and arrest 'Alī and send him to prison in Ṣan'ā', from which, however, he later escaped to plague to Imām.[33]

In the view of Yaḥyā, the conditions prevailing in his eastern districts were far too insecure to be ignored, and he felt it necessary to undertake a series of campaigns in order to establish his hegemony over these areas once and for all. He began with the dispatch of a large portion of the regular army, again commanded by 'Abdullāh al-Ḍumayn and 'Abdullāh al-Wazīr, to the Bilād Khawlān area, the Ṣirwaḥ area, and Mā'rib in 1931–1932 (1350 A.H.). Until this time, the area around Mā'rib had remained an

32. Al-Jarāfī, *Al-Muqtaṭaf*, p. 240; al-'Arshī, *Bulūgh al-Marām*, pp. 190–191; Fakhrī, *Al-Yaman*, p. 169; E. Rossi, *L'arabo parlato a San'a*, p. 115.

33. Al-Jarāfī, *Al-Muqtaṭaf*, p. 240; H. St. Philby, *Sheba's Daughters* (London: Methuen, 1939), pp. 300–301; Helfritz, *Glückliches Arabien*, p. 80; A. Hamilton, *The Kingdom of Melchior*, pp. 63, 66, and 133–157 *passim*, describes some of the other adventures of the Qarda'ī brothers both in and out of the Imām's service.

automonomous province under its own Sharīf since 1640.[34] Government troops, under the "able and energetic" 'Abdullāh al-Wazīr, after fighting a series of fierce battles with the 'Abīda tribesmen, finally managed to occupy Mā'rib and depose the last prince of the line, Muḥammad ibn 'Abd al-Raḥmān.[35]

In 1932–1933 (1351 A.H.), Sayf al-Islam Aḥmad was ordered by Imām Yaḥyā to pacify three northeastern regions over which the government had yet to exercise effective control: (1) the Sufyān region of the Duhma tribes; (2) the Jabal al-Aswad region of al-Jawf; and (3) Jabal Baraṭ, where the Dhū Ḥusayn and Dhū Muḥammad, two powerful and warlike tribes, had kept the whole area lawless and unproductive for a number of years. The Crown Prince himself, at the head of a large force, pacified the first two, and his brother Sayf al-Islam Ḥasan, the third.[36]

Oasis of Najrān

With the armed forces of Aḥmad and Ḥasan engaged in calming areas adjacent to the oasis of Najrān, Imām Yaḥyā apparently felt that he had an excellent opportunity for occupying that oasis.[37] The major tribe of the area, the Yām, came to the assistance of one of the Yemeni tribes just defeated by Aḥmad which was attempting to reverse its defeat, and both Aḥmad and Ḥasan marched their armies into Najrān. In ordering this action, Imām Yaḥyā hoped not only to punish the allies of the recalcitrant Yemeni tribe but also to annex the oasis to his domains.

While Sayf al-Islam Aḥmad was still in the city of Ṣa'da, a

34. In 1640, Sharīf Ḥusayn of al-Zāhir in al-Jawf, who had helped to expel the Turks in that year, took the title of Amīr and started his own kingdom in the area of Mā'rib. He was able to extend his dominions from Raghwān to Bayḥān, but his sons were unable to maintain the little domain in its original size. It soon amounted to scarcely more than a principality of Mā'rib and the immediately adjacent areas. See Adolf Grohmann, "Mā'rib," *Encyclopedia of Islam*, III (1936), 293.

35. Al-Jarāfī, *Al-Muqtaṭaf*, p. 240; Philby, *Sheba's Daughters*, p. 396.

36. Al-Jarāfī, *Al-Muqtaṭaf*, pp. 241–242.

37. Najrān is a large and fertile region lying in the northeastern border area between Saudi Arabia and Yemen. Nominally under Ottoman suzerainty during their administration (as part of the independent district of Bilād Yām), and claimed by both Imām Yaḥyā and King 'Abd al-'Azīz ibn Sa'ūd of Saudi Arabia, its precise ownership had yet to be established. Because of the almost certain disputes which would arise if either of the two claimants attempted to exercise his authority, it had remained until the nineteen-thirties a buffer region between these two monarchs.

deputation of notables under the leadership of Shaykh Ḥasan ibn Zayd called on him from Najrān, advising him of their loyalty and offering hostages in witness of their allegiance to him.[38] Whether this group made its appearance out of fear of reprisals or genuine allegiance to the Zaydi Imām is not known. For Imām Yaḥyā, however, it effectively justified his claim to administer and control the Yām tribe because of its relationship with certain other tribes residing primarily in Yemen, notably the Ḥamdān and the Ḥāshid.[39] Yaḥyā's attempt to annex the Najrān Oasis ended in failure, for 'Abd al-'Azīz ibn Sa'ūd was unwilling to lose this territory, and his forces easily defeated those of the Imām.

Acceptance of Yaḥyā's Control

This war signaled the end of Imām Yaḥyā's attempted expansion toward the north, as well as the end of almost uninterrupted war against many tribes in opposition to the new government and its policies. In 1938–1939 (1357 A.H.), after receiving the bay'a as Crown Prince, Aḥmad was able to undertake an extensive tour of the country without experiencing difficulty or opposition. This trip demonstrated the extent of internal peace which had been established as a result of the many campaigns Aḥmad and other leaders had waged for Imām Yaḥyā and his policies.

In 1940–1941 (1359 A.H.), after a minor rebellion,[40] a further indication of the growing public acceptance of central government

38. *Ibid.*, pp. 243–244.

39. The tribal claim was based on the fact that the Yām are a *batn* (subdivision) of the Ḥamdān. See 'Umar Riḍā Kaḥḥāla, *Mu'jam Qabā'il al-'Arab* (Damascus: al-Hāshimiyya Press, 1949), II, 1259); al-Jarāfī, *Al-Muqtaṭaf*, p. 19; al-Dabbāgh, *Jazīrat al-'Arab*, I, 235.

However, Yaḥyā obviously felt also that the military situation was favorable. Just prior to the events outlined above, he was quoted as saying, "Fortunately I have a large standing army in San'ā' assembled for the purpose of defeating Ibn Sa'ūd." Quoted by Coon, *Measuring Ethiopia*, p. 228.

40. In this year, 1359, Imām Yaḥyā had to send his army Commander-in-Chief, al-Shārif 'Abdullāh al-Ḍumayn, to quell a minor revolt in the Bayḍā' region. A Hijāzī self-exile, al-Sayyid Muḥammad al-Drabbāgh, who had tried for a number of years to find support in the peninsula for his campaign to oust King 'Abd al-'Azīz from power and bring about a return of the Hāshimite dynasty, had managed to organize a small force of Yāfi'ī tribesmen from the Western Aden Protectorate. With them he had invaded several small villages in al-Bayḍā'. The invasion-uprising was quelled in short order, and al-Sayyid al-Dabbāgh was sent back to Aden under arrest. See Farago, *Arabian Antic*, pp. 84–85; al-Jarāfī, *Al-Muqtaṭaf*, p. 254; Sharaf al-Dīn, *Al-Yaman*, p. 314.

control was demonstrated by the visit of a large delegation of prominent personalities from the Tihāma to Imām Yaḥyā in Ṣan'ā'. The delegation was specifically created for the purpose of providing a " confirmation of the brotherly ties " between the two parts of Yemen, the Tihāma and the highlands; it is quite unlikely that such a public display could have been organized only a few years earlier.[41]

Hostages

It would be a mistake to assume that tribal unrest or all opposition to Imām Yaḥyā's policies ceased to exist, but the number and ferocity of such outbreaks diminished considerably as Yaḥyā consolidated his hold over the state in the nineteen-thirties. As his armies and tribal warriors extended his control over regions formerly left to their own devices, in order to retain this newly won control, Imām Yaḥyā came to rely more and more on an age-old tradition in Yemen: the taking of hostages.

Over the centuries, Zaydi Imāms had sought some guarantee of the loyalty of tribes on whose fighting prowess they were dependent for the maintenance of their position and authority. The method which proved most effective was the incarceration of one or more near relatives of the chiefs of important tribes in a number of prison schools maintained directly by the Imāms. Determined to perpetuate internal stability, Imām Yaḥyā, and after him Aḥmad, imitated their predecessors; in the campaigns against the tribes outlined above, the Imām's armies took hostages from the tribal leaders whom they had defeated.

These hostages were normally small boys between the ages of five and fifteen, although in rare cases older hostages were also kept. Generally speaking, only a son, nephew, or cousin of a tribal leader was considered near enough in blood relationship to provide the required guarantee of good behavior. During the reign of Imām Yaḥyā, most of these hostages were held in the citadel in Ṣan'ā', although a few were distributed in the Imām's other palaces and forts around the country, usually in the place farthest from their own homes. Under Imām Aḥmad, the major hostages were kept in the citadel al-Qāhira near Ta'izz.

The treatment which the hostages received was dependent on the current behavior of the particular tribe to which they belonged.

41. Al-Jarāfī, *Al-Muqtaṭaf*, p. 255.

If a tribe had been passive and law-abiding, its hostages were allowed to go home on national holidays and feast days. They were provided with clothes, food, and an above-average education until the age of fifteen. At fifteen, when a Yemeni is considered to reach manhood, they were manacled or chained. In practice, however, this rarely occurred, for they were usually replaced by a younger relative; the elder was permitted to return to his father.[42]

Because certain tribes and regions of the country were always more unruly and less amenable to government control and administration then others, they were usually represented by the largest number of hostages. Visitors to Yemen have made various estimates concerning the total number kept by the Imāms in all the prison schools. One estimate of 4,000 hostages was made as the series of campaigns against the tribes was drawing to a close;[43] a more recent estimate (1955) placed the figure at approximately 2,000.[44] If one takes into consideration the improvement in internal security after the early nineteen-thirties, the reduction in numbers would seem appropriate.[45]

Although it has been argued that " no feature of the [*sic*] Imām Yaḥyā's system, not even his notorious parsimony, was more unpopular in the country than [the] taking and keeping of hostages," [46] its effectiveness for achieving internal security cannot be denied. An accurate summation of the importance of this

42. Although nearly all travelers have written on the subject of the hostages, most have failed to see the context in which the system developed and its historical background. For the observations of two relatively objective European travelers, see Pawelke, *Der Jemen*, pp. 74–75; Helfritz, *Glückliches Arabien*, p. 138.

43. Helfritz, *Glückliches Arabien*, p. 138.

44. Seager, " The Yemen," p. 218.

45. The figure of 2,000 for 1955 may even be high, due to the fact that additional hostages were taken as a result of an attempted coup in the early part of that year.

The only reasonably reliable figures on the number of hostages taken after a particularly difficult campaign against some notoriously unruly tribes are given by al-Jarāfī, *Al-Muqtaṭaf*, pp. 243–244. After the 1932–1933 campaign against the tribes of the Jabal Baraṭ region, Aḥmad and Ḥasan took 300 hostages. This figure stands out in al-Jarāfī's account because of its size. It seems safe to assume that this was an abnormally high amount, if we consider that the author writes from a pro-Imām point of view and the fact that this campaign was particularly long and fierce. There is, consequently, no reason to consider it an average figure, applicable to all the tribes which had been defeated or required to send hostages to the Imām.

46. Philby, *Sheba's Daughters*, p. 45.

practice for both Imāms Yaḥyā and Aḥmad was made by a German observer:

> Die Stellung von Geiseln durch alle verantwortlichen Persönlichkeiten ist im Laufe von Jahrhunderten so zur Regel geworden, dass man das Geiselsystem als einen der Pfeiler bezeichnen kann, auf dem die Macht des Imams, ja, Ruhe, Ordnung und Sicherheit im Staate beruhen.[47]

THE EFFECTS OF INTERNAL SECURITY

By far the most important achievement of Yaḥyā's reign was the establishment of internal peace and security in Yemen—a very considerable accomplishment considering the endemic anarchy which existed before and during the Ottoman occupation. The majority of the population, including most of the tribes, accepted and even welcomed the enforced peace, for it provided them with a respite from continual fighting and freedom from sudden and senseless death.[48]

A comparison of Yemen under Imām Yaḥyā and the state of affairs which existed in the Ḥaḍramawt in the nineteen-thirties provides a relevant contrast. In the words of the British official who was the chief architect of the truce which later was to bring stability to the Ḥaḍramawt, the difference between the standard of public security in the two areas was striking:

> The contrast was vividly brought home by the constant sight of men and women working in the fields [of Yemen] without a thought of being raided by their neighbors. I had lived at close quarters with the Protectorate for so long that I was more accustomed to see cultivation confined to the immediate neighborhood of fortified homesteads in which refuge could be taken as soon as the first shot cracked. I had ridden for hours over land still marked by ancient irrigation bunds and seen fertile oases turned to desert which report said had been cultivated in the long long ago. In the Yemen the humblest traveller could move alone from place to place

47. Pawelke, *Der Jemen*, p. 75.

48. Seager, "The Yemen," p. 218, on the basis of his experiences even claims that the tribes were "well aware that their behaviour warrants such a system" (the keeping of hostages for the maintenance of peace and security).

> without fear; in the Protectorate it was necessary to take at least . . . a companion who acted as a kind of living visa, a guarantee that one was under the protection of the tribe through whose territory one passed. Caravans from the Yemen interior on their way to al-Yemen's Eye [Aden] moved safely on the traderoutes as long as they were in the Imām's territory; once they had crossed into the British Protectorate they were often subject to plunder by marauding tribes.[49]

The importance of this achievement of peace inside Yemen is evident, and it must be credited to the single-minded determination of Imām Yaḥyā. There is little doubt that life in Yemen before the establishment of internal security was " solitary, poor, nasty, brutish and short." One need only study the architecture to imagine the conditions prevailing in the countryside before the establishment of law and order. Nearly all the older towns and villages are surrounded by thick stone walls; the houses of individual farmers are imposing bastions of rock, constructed on almost completely unapproachable rock ledges.

There is no doubt, on the other hand, that the methods used to obtain this standard of public security were tyrannical and even reprehensible by Western standards. As was perhaps to be expected, no such system could last long without arousing opposition; the reaction to it had already begun under Yaḥyā, and it was to grow steadily under his successors.

49. Harold Ingrams, *The Yemen* (London: John Murray, 1963), p. 32.

Chapter IV

OPPOSITION TO IMĀM YAḤYĀ

Imām Yaḥyā was determined to keep his country as free as possible from all foreign entanglements, alliances, and influence, for he believed that foreigners would jeopardize Yemeni independence, if they were permitted too great freedom inside the country, as well as undermine the traditional religious way of life of the Yemenis, which he was determined to preserve.[1]

This policy of isolationism earned him considerable respect from the educated classes and leaders of other Arab states, most of whom spent part of the interwar period under European colonial occupation. Most educated Yemenis also agreed with his policy of keeping the Western powers out of their country. They did not, however, approve of his internal policies which were based on the suppression of local autonomy, the concentration of all political and economic power in the Imām's own hands or those of near relatives and a few trusted retainers, and the prohibition of all modern conveniences.

During the nineteen-thirties and forties, many Yemenis who had been exposed to the foreign ideas and techniques which Yaḥyā feared began to agitate for reforms within the country. They were joined in their opposition by other groups who had specific grudges or complaints against the Imām's policies: the Shāfiʿīs and extremely conservative Zaydi religious circles.

Progressive Opponents

As World War II drew to a close and other Arab countries also achieved their independence, increasing numbers of young Yemenis wanted to see their country become a part of the larger Arab world. Although Imām Yaḥyā eventually gave permission for his country to join the Arab League and the United Nations,

1. For further information on Yaḥyā's policy of isolationism, see below, Chap. VII.

these events had no effect on Yemen's political life, and the reformers became convinced that violent revolution was the only way to remove the person who appeared to all opposition groups as *the* obstacle to their goals.

Foreign-Educated Yemenis

Imām Yaḥyā's policy of isolationism, which had succeeded in keeping Yemen free of foreign interference, had to be modified by Yaḥyā himself in order to achieve certain other goals. Aware of new developments in arms and other military equipment, and anxious to obtain the benefits of these advances for his own purposes—that it, waging a more effective campaign against the British in the Protectorates and the Saudis in the north, as well as against his own rebellious tribes—Yaḥyā resolved to obtain these new weapons.

In order to get such equipment, it was necessary to deal with various European powers. Because of the arms' complexity and foreign origin, it was obvious that the unsophisticated Yemeni soldier would need instruction in their use, maintenance, and repair, for which trained personnel were needed. Imām Yaḥyā was able to buy weapons from Europe with little difficulty; he was not, however, willing to allow Europeans to train his troops, for he feared the consequences to Yemen's independence. In order to find the needed teachers, Yaḥyā turned to what he considered to be his most reliable ally: another Arab state.

In 1931 Imām Yaḥyā signed his first treaty with another Arab state: Iraq. The latter thereby became the first Arab country to recognize the Imām not only in his religious role but also in his temporal role as King of Yemen. As a result of Iraq's recognition of his position, and because it also was independent (after 1932) and possessed of greater military power and better training facilities, Iraq seemed the logical place for the Imām to send Yemeni cadets he wanted trained in the use of modern equipment and military technology.

The students who were sent to Baghdad on this first mission were hand-picked by the Imām on the basis of their presumed political reliability; they were all commoners with no political influence and no claim to the Imamate. This precaution, however, was taken in vain. While studying modern military techniques in

Iraq, it was inevitable that the young Yemenis would also become acquainted with more progressive ideas on many subjects than they had encountered at home: politics, economics, social justice, and the proper functions of a government. They made the acquaintance of other technological developments, modern inventions, and public services performed by governments in more advanced societies. On the basis of future developments, one can only conclude that the "cultural shock" these young Yemenis suffered was considerable.

The course of studies in Baghdad lasted two years, and it was not long before the first students returned home and received appointments to positions in the ranks of the army or the personal service of the Imām. Less than two years after their return, at least one of the graduates was sentenced to prison for "spreading modern ideas." [2]

Apparently this officer's disaffection was not an isolated occurrence, for soon after his trial the Imām ordered that the dispatching of young Yemenis for military or technical training abroad be stopped, at least temporarily. Yaḥyā had originally permitted these students to study away from home on the assumption that it would be wiser to have trained Yemenis in important positions in his military establishment than imported foreigners. He soon changed his mind, however, as a result of the subversive activities undertaken by these students upon their return, and decided that imported foreigners were easier to control and keep within prescribed limits of activity than such foreign-educated Yemenis.

Some of those young officers who had been sent abroad managed to retain their positions in the regular army. Most, however, were transferred to the personal service of the Imām, for there he could keep a watchful eye on their activities. But because he no longer trusted them, they were given no duties or functions to perform. Many spent their time in idleness; others began to engage in serious plots to modify the system of government. Their first objective was to remove Imām Yaḥyā from the Imamate, for they considered him too old, too infirm,[3] and too traditional

2. Sharaf al-Dīn, *Al-Yaman*, p. 248.

3. Imām Yaḥyā, described by various travelers throughout the nineteen-twenties and thirties as "vigorous and energetic" (see, for example, Scott, *In the High Yemen*, p. 172), apparently began to age rapidly during the nineteen-forties, his

and despaired of his ever introducing the reforms they wished to see.

The Imām's plan to prevent the spread of subversive ideas among his officers by bringing in foreign teachers was also doomed to failure. Through personal association with their students, individual members of the Iraqi military missions soon convinced many of them of the need for introducing changes into their country's political and economic structure. Consequently, during the early nineteen-forties the number of army officers disaffected with Yaḥmā's regime increased considerably, even though most of them had never left Yemen.

Although they were in the majority, military personnel were not the only Yemenis to leave their homes for education abroad during Yaḥmā's reign. Most of the nonmilitary students were financed by their own families and went to Cairo, drawn there by al-Azhar University's outstanding reputation for Islamic theological studies; their education in Yemen, the traditional Islamic one, scarcely prepared them for any other course of study. Considerably impressed by the great gulf separating Yemen from Egypt in nearly all fields of human endeavor, many resolved to return to Yemen in order to initiate some of the benefits of modernization there. Others went home to take a miscellany of meaningless positions in the service of either the Imām or one of his sons and soon became disillusioned with the royal family's lack of desire to make any changes in the existing state of affairs.

Shāfiʿī Commercial Interests

Imām Yaḥyā's basic distrust of all foreign influences required that he prohibit all but the most unavoidable contacts with other states and their citizenry. One of these essential contacts was commerce, for even Yemen was dependent for some products on other countries. The foreign trade of Yemen had long been a near

health becoming an acute problem. Although earlier visitors had speculated that the Imām probably did suffer from arthritis and rheumatism and perhaps gout, as evidenced by his frequent trips to the famous hot springs of Yemen to ease his pains (al-Jarāfī, *Al-Muqtaṭaf*, p. 225), it was not until 1945 that a medical diagnosis was made by a competent physician. This was Dr. Alfred M. Palmer, Lieutenant-Commander, U.S.N.R., who on March 29, 1945, diagnosed the Imām's condition as "chronic poly-articular rheumatoid arthritis with cardio-renal disease." At the time, Dr. Palmer estimated that the Imām had no more than five years to live. (Department of State Despatch No. 52 [Aden], 23 April 1945.)

monopoly of the Shāfiʿī portion of the population, primarily because of their location in the coastal regions and in the south, near the port of Aden, the economic center of the area. Imām Yaḥyā, however, was not willing to permit trade with foreigners to remain in the hands of the Shāfiʿīs, and direct measures were taken to restrict their economic influence. Most foreign trade was thereafter handled by appointed agents of the Imām. The Shāfiʿīs naturally resented the stringent measures which Yaḥyā took.

It should be remembered that in the early years of his reign Yaḥyā did nothing to appease the Shāfiʿīs or make them feel that they were equal partners in the new state. The fact that the Shāfiʿīs had been favored during the period of Ottoman control had not been forgotten by the Imām.[4] Almost immediately after independence, many prominent Shāfiʿīs were arrested and their wealth and property confiscated, while Zaydi governors and officials were appointed for numerous Shāfiʿī districts. Neither of these actions had helped to create a feeling of unity between the two religious groups.

The stringent governmental controls which Yaḥyā inaugurated on foreign trade, to the detriment of the livelihood and economic power of many Shāfiʿīs, naturally increased their bitterness. Nevertheless, it was impossible to eliminate completely all the commercial activities of the Shāfiʿī merchants. They continued to have contact with the outside world—a fact which only served to make the oppressive regime of Yaḥyā, by contrast, all the more detestable to them. Many naturally resolved to undertake some action to change the political and economic conditions under which they chafed. Most were drawn to the opposition groups outlined below and helped to finance their activities.

Aden as a Focus for Progressive Opposition

Because of the primitive facilities of Yemeni ports such as al-Mukhā, al-Luḥayya, and even al-Ḥudayda, much of Yemen's trade had long been carried on through the port of Aden. As a result, many Yemeni importers had established offices there, drawn

4. The fact that both Ottomans and Shāfiʿīs were adherents of Sunni Islam was undoubtedly one of the major causes for this. The Ottomans, needing some allies in the troublesome Wilayat, had emphasized and sharpened the differences for their own purposes.

by Aden's commercial possibilities as well as its relative political freedom.[5] In addition, poorer Yemenis often emigrated to Aden for varying periods of time in order to earn a living in the many enterprises which had employment opportunities for unskilled and semiskilled labor.

It was, perhaps, inevitable that the many Yemenis who visited Aden in search of employment, and the merchants who went there to avoid the excessive taxation and governmental regulation of their businesses, would begin to protest against their home government. Because of the efficient system of internal intelligence which the Imām had established in Yemen to ferret out opposition to his rule, and the lack of legitimate channels for the expression of views contrary to those of the government, it was impossible for such protests to be made publicly in Yemen. Therefore, the proximity of Aden, combined with its all-important political freedom, made it a natural focal point for progressive opposition to Imām Yaḥyā among a collection of Yemeni self-exiles.

It was in Aden, in the late nineteen-thirties, that the first public voice of protest against the oppressive features of the regime of Imām Yaḥyā was heard[6]—that of the poet Ibrāhīm al-Ḥadrāni. Al-Ḥadrānī claimed to have spent many years in Yemeni prisons before fleeing the country and going into exile in Aden. His poems against the rule of Yaḥyā seem to have been rather popular, and for some time he was considered the leader of Yemen's political refugees.[7] This was a relatively small group in the late nineteen-

5. Other wealthy Yemeni merchants had also established themselves in important trade and entrepôt centers in this area; for example, Djibouti in French Somaliland, Massawa in Eritrea, and Suakin in the Sudan. None of these is, however, as important as Aden, especially for trade with the Yemeni interior.

Sizable colonies of Yemenis had also established themselves in other countries; for example, Marseilles in France and Cardiff (Wales) in Great Britain. Most of these *émigrés* were Shāfi'īs, but although their remittances contributed greatly to the foreign-exchange earnings of Yemen, their energies and interests were increasingly absorbed by the issues and problems of their more immediate environment.

6. Although it has been claimed that there were earlier expressions of opposition to the Imamate, including, for example, the rebellion of the Zarānīq, all the available evidence indicates that it was not until the nineteen-thirties that such opposition became primarily political in nature. On alleged earlier opposition, see Muḥammad Sadīq 'Aql and Hiyām Abū 'Āfiyyah, *Adwā' 'ala Thawrat al-Yaman* (Cairo: Kutub Qawmiyya, 1963), pp. 131–132.

7. Farago, *Arabian Antic*, pp. 78–81. Cf. *Al-Usbū' al-'Arabi* (Beirut), IV, No. 24 (July 15, 1963), 48; Abdul Wahab el-Sciami, "Aspetti della moderna letteratura Yemenita," *Levante*, I, No. 2 (October–December, 1953), 42–44.

thirties; but it was swelled considerably, as the years passed, by influxes of laborers and young foreign-trained Yemenis who got into political trouble at home or left voluntarily, frustrated by the Imām's policies.

Two students who returned to enter the personal service of Crown Prince Aḥmad during the nineteen-forties soon became disillusioned with the outlook and actions of the latter and went to Aden in 1944. These two personalities, who occupied an important position in all exile political movements until the revolution of September, 1962, were (1) Aḥmad Muḥammad Nuʿmān, whose family are the hereditary shaykhs of Dubhān (near Ḥijariyya), who, although Shāfiʿīs, had always wielded a large amount of political influence in southern Yemen; and (2) Muḥammad Maḥmūd al-Zubayrī, a Zaydi from Ṣanʿāʾ, whose family had produced many prominent judges and lawyers and who himself was an accomplished poet and author.

Like these two personalities, other influential Yemenis who went into exile in the middle nineteen-forties added considerable prestige to the fledgling association of reformers and modernists existing in Aden. As their numbers and organization grew, it attracted greater interest among other politically sophisticated groups in Aden. The newspaper *Fatāt al-Jazīra* (The Youth of the Arabian Peninsula) then took up the cause of the exiles and began to publish articles on the state of affairs in Yemen. Although the exiles claimed to publish serious and constructive criticism dealing only with the rule of Imām Yaḥyā, his economic policies, internal political policies, and the like, it may be assumed that a large portion of these articles were scurrilous in content. In any event, the fact of their publication soon attracted the Imām's attention, and he promptly protested to the British authorities, who were able to make the newspaper tone down its attacks on him for the time being.

CONSERVATIVE OPPONENTS

Opposition to Imām Yaḥyā was by no means limited to progressive reformers who wished to see changes in Yemen. On the contrary, conservative religious circles also had reason to feel discontent with the Imām's rule; this discontent was largely based on a specific change which Yaḥyā himself wanted to introduce into Yemen's political life. Formerly, when an Imām died, it was considered at least technically a prerogative of the entire Sayyid class to help determine the identity of his successor. Although the Imamate was now in the hands of the Ḥamīd al-Dīn "house" for the second consecutive generation, it was not common practice that the eldest son follow his father as Imām. Consequently, nearly the entire Sayyid community was considerably dismayed when in 1927 Imām Yaḥyā announced that his son Sayf al-Islam Aḥmad should be Waliyy al-ʿAhd (Crown Prince).

Yaḥyā's motivation was not exclusively family pride, although this undoubtedly was partially the reason. He sincerely believed that in order to secure the stability of the country and eliminate the fratricidal wars which commonly followed the death of an Imām, it would be wise to establish continuity through hereditary succession. In his capacity as secular ruler, Imām Yaḥyā felt that it was especially essential that there be a crown prince prepared to assume his responsibilities on his death.

Because Islamic tradition contains no rule of primogeniture and Zaydi tradition specifically discourages it, Yaḥyā was careful to consult some prominent Zaydis before attempting to state his wish publicly. The most important and influential such leader he consulted was al-Sayyid Muḥammad ibn ʿAqīl, whose agreement he obtained in advance. Nevertheless, this by no means stilled the obvious objections of other Sayyids with strong claims to the Imamate.[8]

As might also be expected, the attempt to shatter such an ancient Zaydi tradition was considered equivalent to altering the principles of the faith itself—a move so radical in nature that it was guaranteed to alienate the important Zaydi ʿUlamāʾ—the association of learned scholars, teachers, and academic theologians whose function it is to protect the faith, particularly against the authority of the state.

Grievances of the al-Wazīr Family

Later, in 1935, there were rumors that Imām Yaḥyā was going to abdicate, and, of course, feverish discussion concerning his suc-

8. Ingrams, *The Yemen*, p. 67. Because the prerequisites for the Imamate eliminate most of the population from eligibility, certain prominent families have provided the majority of the Imāms. Of course, they did not wish to see this office become the monopoly of one family. Among these important Sayyid clans are the al-Wazīr, the Sharaf al-Dīn, and the Zabāra, as well as the Ḥamīd al-Dīn to which Yaḥyā belonged.

cessor took place even though the nomination of Aḥmad had been announced eight years previously.[9] There was also considerable maneuvering among other prominent personalities who considered themselves eligible candidates. One of the names widely mentioned was that of al-Sayyid ʿAbdullāh ibn Aḥmad al-Wazīr, who had achieved renown as an army leader and skilled negotiator.

There proved to be nothing to the rumor, and shortly thereafter Imām Yaḥyā began an extensive revision of his administration which effectively eliminated all those men who had been mentioned as contenders for the Imamate other than his son. Quite possibly the whole incident had been merely a ruse on the Imām's part in order to determine where the chief opposition to his policies lay, although it is equally possible that he simply made good use of an unexpected opportunity.

The first to be dismissed was al-Sayyid ʿAlī al-Wazīr, the Amīr of Taʿizz, the eldest member of the al-Wazīr clan, who was well known for his penchant for internal political maneuvering.[10] Next to lose his position was al-Sayyid ʿAbdullāh al-Wazīr, his younger brother, who held the post of Amīr of al-Ḥudayda, one of the richest in Yemen. Because of his military skill, learning, and political power, however, he continued to be mentioned as a possible candidate for the Imamate.[11] When another member of the al-Wazīr family, al-Sayyid ʿAbd al-Qaddūs, died in 1944 while Amīr of Dhamār, the most important family in Yemen other than the Imām's own had been politically neutralized. As might be expected, the al-Wazīrs were embittered at this turn of events.

Acceptance of Aḥmad as Crown Prince

The Imām, in other words, had reason to believe that his naming of Aḥmad as his successor had not been accepted by all Sayyids. Consequently, in 1937–1938 he embarked on a campaign to have his son receive the bayʿa (oath of allegiance) from all the major contenders for the Imamate; among these candidates were some of Aḥmad's brothers and a number of other leading political figures of the country.

9. *Oriente Moderno*, XV, No. 9 (September, 1935), 470; *Near East and India*, XLV (September 12, 1935), 322; Brémond, *Yémen et Saoudia*, p. 123.

10. Scott, *In the High Yemen*, p. 89.

11. Although ʿAlī was the eldest of the al-Wazīrs, he was not eligible for the Imamate because of the fact that he had only one eye. Cf. the prerequisites for the Imamate, above, Chap. I, n. 8.

Yaḥyā began his campaign with al-Sayyid 'Alī ibn Ḥamūd Sharaf al-Dīn, the leading member of the Sharaf al-Dīn family and a likely candidate for the Imamate.[12] In return for 'Alī's bay'a and his assistance in obtaining the consent of Aḥmad's other rivals, he was to receive the governorship of the profitable al-Ḥudayda province.

After approximately a year of political maneuvering and bargaining, al-Sayyid 'Alī was able to report to Yaḥyā that he had succeeded in obtaining the acceptance of Aḥmad by the two most important members of the al-Wazīr clan, 'Alī and 'Abdullāh, as well as Ḥusayn, Aḥmad's younger brother. The Wazīrs, it was to be discovered later, only pretended to accept the Imām's wishes while continuing their own intrigues for succession. Apparently satisfied for the time being, Yaḥyā announced the bay'a for Aḥmad in 1938–1939 (1356 A.H.).[13]

Alliance of Opponents

It seems certain that in the early nineteen-forties first contacts were made between the disaffected al-Wazīr family and the increasingly vociferous group of Yemenis domiciled in Aden. The removal of the Wazīrs from positions of influence was completed in the same year (1944) that the two prominent reformers al-Zubayrī and Nu'mān left Yemen for self-exile in Aden.

Free Yemeni Party

By this time the group in Aden had organized itself into a political movement, the Free Yemeni Party (al-Aḥrār al-Yamaniyūn), and had begun to publish propaganda on the situation in Yemen. After the period of relative quiet which had been inspired by the Imām's request to the British for action, another active campaign of propaganda was begun shortly after World War II ended.

Then, on April 11, 1946, Crown Prince Aḥmad paid a visit to Aden. He immediately became involved in a dialogue with the exiled political movement, and in an interview with the newspaper *Fatāt al-Jazīra* it was reported that he said:

12. The last Imām to have been a member of the Sharaf al-Dīn was Muḥsin ibn Aḥmad, who appears to have had little temporal power and acted only as religious Imām during the anarchic period prior to the second Ottoman occupation in 1872.

13. Sa'īd, *Al-Yaman*, p. 144; Ingrams, *The Yemen*, p. 71.

> the Yamani government would be ready to enter into direct relations with the rest of the Arab world, to exchange diplomatic missions with other Muslim states, to exploit the mines of the country and to establish industries with the help of foreign and Muslim technicians. The Government was also ready to spread education in accordance with the policy of the Arab League.[14]

Aḥmad's statement took the Free Yemenis almost completely by surprise; some of them apparently took Aḥmad at his word and hailed him as the " Saviour of Yemen." Most, however, were not so credulous and proceeded to list their demands: (1) the Imām must establish a constitutional assembly of jurists, high officials, and prominent personalities for the purpose of writing a constitution; (2) the Imām must form legitimate ministries with capable men and technicians who knew their jobs; and (3) the Imām must no longer permit his sons to take part in the affairs of the state or administration. They were to receive pensions and remain completely inactive.[15] It was obvious to all concerned that these three conditions could not possibly be met, for they would destroy the basis of the Zaydi state.

For over a month, the battle of words continued to rage in the press of Aden, with Aḥmad and the representatives of the Imām indecisive and losing many of the arguments. Encouraged, the Free Yemenis broadened their attack. Under the leadership of al-Zubayrī and Nu'mān, they established their own newspapers; one was founded in Aden, with the name *Ṣawt al-Yaman* (Voice of Yemen), and one in Cairo (to which their activities soon spread because of the importance of Cairo as a center of Arab political and cultural affairs), called *al-Ṣadāqa* (Friendship).[16]

Contributions were solicited from Yemeni exiles; a number of wealthy Shāfi'ī merchants among the Yemeni communities in Eritrea, French Somaliland, and Aden contributed large sums toward the purchase of a printing press to publish *Ṣawt al-Yaman*,

14. As quoted in J. Heyworth-Dunne, *Al-Yemen* (Cairo: Renaissance Bookshop, 1952), p. 38.

Yemen had joined the Arab League, after long hesitation, in November, 1945. See Sa'īd, *Al-Yaman*, pp. 123–124.

15. Heyworth-Dunne, *Al-Yemen*, pp. 38–39.

16. Al-Jarāfī, *Al-Maqtaṭaf*, p. 257.

as well as the many pamphlets, booklets, and even books which soon came pouring from it.[17]

To the surprise of nearly everyone, on November 21, 1946, the Imām's ninth son, Sayf al-Islam Ibrāhīm, came to Aden in order to join the Free Yemeni movement. As might be expected, his name (soon changed to Sayf al-Ḥaqq, meaning "sword of truth") and position added considerably to the prestige of the movement and helped to undermine the arguments of the Imām and his aides.[18]

Conspirators inside Yemen

The conspiracy which was to culminate in the assassination of Imām Yaḥyā was now beginning to take shape. Contact had been established between those inside Yemen, who only wished to see Yaḥyā's reign ended and their own candidate placed in the Imamate, and those outside Yemen who had more concrete and ambitious plans for the country but considered the dispatch of Imām Yaḥyā as the indispensable first step toward the achievement of their goals. The unifying element between these groups was the character and personality of the person against whom the revolution was directed. Once the primary aim had been achieved, however, there was nothing which could keep the disparate revolutionaries together, for their disagreement on postrevolution developments was to prove insurmountable.

The collection of conspirators within Yemen included six major personalities and groups:

1. The al-Wazīr family, which managed to pre-empt the leadership planned for the new government, as the result of a tacit agreement that (*a*) the Imamate as an institution would not be abolished[19] and (*b*) it would not be allowed to devolve to one of Yaḥyā's sons.

17. For example, *al-Yaman al-manhūba al-mankūba* (Yemen, the unfortunate and plundered), *al-Yaman ẓāhiruhā wa bātinuhā* (Yemen, externally and internally), and so on. All these books were published without any author, publisher, place, or date being given and with no indication of their origin except for the words *Ḥizb al-Aḥrār al-Yamanī* (Free Yemeni Party) on the last page. (Those listed here were catalogued by the American University of Beirut library in 1946.)

18. For further information on the background of Sayf al-Islam Ibrāhīm, see Majid Khadduri, "Coup and Counter-coup in the Yaman, 1948," *International Affairs*, XXVIII, No. 1 (January, 1952), 61.

19. It is worth noting that the revolutionaries never seriously considered

2. A collection of some of Imām Yaḥyā's personal advisers and secretaries, the most important of whom was al-Sayyid Ḥusayn al-Kibsī. Many of them, like al-Sayyid Ḥusayn, who had been Yaḥyā's personal representative to a number of foreign conferences, had served abroad and decided that any change in the conditions prevailing in Yemen could only be for the better.

3. A portion of the officer corps of the Yemeni Army, primarily those officers who had either been sent abroad for training or been trained in Yemen by foreign military experts, such as Jamāl Jamīl. Jamīl had first come to Yemen as a member of one of the Iraqi military missions sent to train the Yemeni Army by Bakr Ṣidqī.[20] During his long association with the Yemeni Army, in which he was an artillery instructor, Jamīl had made the acquaintance of the Imām and had risen to the rank of colonel. By 1948, he had become Director of Public Security for the district of Ṣan'ā'.

During his association with the army, Colonel Jamīl had made the acquaintance of those Yemeni officers who had been schooled at the Baghdad Military College. Colonel Jamīl's own revolutionary sympathies undoubtedly reinforced the revolutionary ideas of many of these officers; it may be assumed, too, that many of his own students within Yemen absorbed similar ideas from him.[21]

4. Al-Faḍīl al-Warṭilānī, an Algerian nationalist who had

---

abolishing the Imamate. The leaders recognized the historical precedent and necessity of having an Imām of the Zaydis; they may also have assumed that since the Zaydi faith requires an Imām, had they abolished the Imamate, all Zaydi support for the coup would have vanished. (At the very least, this would have been true for those conservative religious circles whose tacit support they had already received.) Perhaps even cities like Ṣan'ā', solidly Zaydi, who supported al-Wazīr and the revolution, would have been more hesitant in their acceptance of such a radical step, a chance the revolutionaries obviously did not want to take.

20. Jamāl Jamīl was one of the conspirators in the death of Ja'far al-'Askarī (perhaps even the assassin himself) and the Bakr Ṣidqī coup of 1936 in Iraq. After the death of Ṣidqī, he joined the military mission to Yemen headed by Ismā'īl Safwat. At the end of his period of service, he prevailed on the Imām to retain him as a military adviser and instructor in the army. See Sa'īd, *Al-Yaman*, p. 137; Sharaf al-Dīn, *Al-Yaman*, p. 326; al-Jarāfī, *Al-Muqtaṭaf*, p. 259.

21. Although one of the Iraqi teachers of the first Yemeni student group in Baghdad has said that at least one of his students ('Abdullāh al-Sallāl) already had revolutionary sympathies, it is safe to assume that many of the clandestine revolutionary officers learned their tactics under Colonel Jamīl and his associates while they were in Yemen. See Colonel 'Abd al-Qādir al-'Azzawī's opinion quoted in *Al-Usbū' al-'Arabī* (Beirut), October 8, 1962.

sought refuge in Cairo as a result of his political activities in North Africa and there joined the Ikhwān al-Muslimūn (the Muslim Brotherhood), wherein he had risen to a position of some prominence. Financed by a group of Arab merchants, al-Wartilānī arrived in Ṣan'ā' in order to establish a new trading company, intending to purchase and import automobiles and machinery into Yemen. His financial success undoubtedly earned him a prominent place in Ṣan'ānī society; at the same time, his reputation as an influential speaker on Islam and dedicated opponent of European interference in Arab affairs established him in the confidence of the Imām. It was not long, however, before al-Wartilānī opted to join the growing opposition movement. In this he was motivated by his desire to achieve greater wealth under a government with more enlightened attitudes toward foreign trade and by a desire to see a more progressive form of Islam, as understood by the Muslim Brotherhood, introduced into Yemen.

Because of his economic interests and contacts in Aden and the confidence which he inspired in the Imām, al-Wartilānī was able to go on many trips to Aden without arousing the suspicions of Yaḥyā. As a result, he was soon the liaison between the exile groups in Aden and those opposition forces which remained inside Yemen.[22]

5. Shaykh 'Alī Nāṣir al-Qarda'ī and a collection of dissident tribesmen from the Banī Ḥarith and Banī Ḥishaysh tribes of the Ḥarīb-Bayḥān region. Engaged by Jamāl Jamīl for "police duties," their primary job during the *coup d'état* was the quick assassination of as many members of the royal family as they could find.

The Qarda'ī shaykhs had a long history of personal antagonism toward Imām Yaḥyā. The most important of their conflicts with him concerned the status of the Qarda'ī area, from which the shaykhs were removed as governors during the subjugation of the Ḥarīb-Bayḥān region. The Imām later used them to try to bring the Shabwa district under Yemeni control, an action opposed by the British, who completely humiliated the Qarda'ī, thus embittering them toward the Imām.

There is little doubt that their participation in the conspiracy was motivated solely by personal revenge; the relatively small

22. Sa'īd, *Al-Yaman*, p. 137; al-Jarāfī, *Al-Muqtaṭaf*, p. 259; Khadduri, "Coup and Counter-coup," p. 62.

number of tribesmen (fifteen) who assisted them cannot seriously be considered an indication that the eastern tribes wanted to show their displeasure with the campaigns of the nineteen-twenties and thirties carried out against them.

6. Although the 'Ulamā' of Yemen, the economic and political elite of Ṣan'ā', and other influential religious elders cannot legitimately be considered conspirators in the revolution, the undercurrent of opposition to the perpetuation of the Imamate in the Ḥamīd al-Dīn house was strong among them. This opposition was based on Imām Yaḥyā's attempt to break Zaydi tradition by dictating his successor and by the gradual diminishing of the influence of these groups, as more and more of the political power of the country gravitated into the hands of Yaḥyā and his relatives. This usurpation of power was of considerable importance, for the resultant curtailment of the traditional elite's political influence also affected its economic power. In addition, the increasing monopolization of trade and commerce by Yaḥyā had detrimentally affected the economic life of the larger cities. There is no doubt that the onerous taxes which Yaḥyā had imposed on business not only led to the elite's disaffection with the old regime but also was responsible for the public sympathy which the new government received from a significant portion of the population.[23]

Nevertheless, the 'Ulamā' and the elites did not participate openly in the conspiracy against Yaḥyā. While they did support 'Abdullāh al-Wazīr for the Imamate upon Yaḥyā's demise, they were perfectly willing to let Yaḥyā continue as Imām until that time came. By the beginning of 1948, it was obvious to all that the Imām had only a short time to live; he was seventy-nine years old and suffered from a variety of diseases which made it almost impossible for him to move about.[24]

23. For a description of some of the most onerous and, in Western economic terms, illogical of the taxes imposed, see Rihani, *Arabian Peak and Desert*, pp. 125–126, 164; Serjeant, "The Mountain Tribes of the Yemen," p. 69; Brown, "The Yemeni Dilemma," p. 356, n. 8. (Although this latter article applies specifically to Aḥmad's reign, there was little difference between the policies followed by Yaḥyā and Aḥmad with regard to taxation.)

24. According to the Christian calendar, Imām Yaḥyā was born in June, 1869; his death in February, 1948, would make him nearly seventy-nine years old. According to the Muslim calendar, he was born in Rabī' I 1286; his death in Rabī' II 1367 would make him eighty-one years old. This difference has been the cause of many contradictory reports concerning the ages of Yemeni rulers and personalities as reported in the Western press.

THE REVOLUTION OF 1948

Precisely because it was common knowledge that the Imām was in failing health, the revolutionaries in Aden decided that it was both necessary and opportune to strike without delay. Were they to wait until his death, they would probably have to fight against Aḥmad, who would succeed to the Imamate without much difficulty and present a more vigorous opposition to their aims than that presented by Yaḥyā. They therefore decided to seize the initiative and remove Yaḥyā from the scene before Aḥmad or other members of the royal family had any opportunity to consolidate their power.

Abortive Attempt

Consequently, in the early part of January, 1948, they sent an assassin to the palace in Ṣan'ā' to kill Imām Yaḥyā. Although the assassin was not apprehended, he was prevented from carrying out his task by the faithfulness of the Imām's palace retainers. His successful escape from the palace, nevertheless, was interpreted by the conspirators as the prearranged signal signifying that the deed was done. Before the confusion could be straightened out, the news that Imām Yaḥyā was dead had been telegraphed to Aden, where it was promptly picked up by news agencies and published in the world press.[25] The opposition Yemeni newspapers in Aden published the additional information that 'Abdullāh al-Wazīr had been proclaimed the new Imām and included a list of the members of the new government.[26]

The Imām took immediate action. He summoned al-Wazīr and questioned him about the reports—all of which al-Wazīr denied, apparently to the satisfaction of Yaḥyā, for he was released and permitted to return to his residence. The Imām told the government paper, *al-Imān* (The Faith), to publish a refutation of these reports; the newspaper at the same time published the fact that he had ordered his son Aḥmad, then the Amīr of Ta'izz, to come to Ṣan'ā'.[27] As a result, the revolutionaries and conspirators in Ṣan'ā' and Aden knew they had to act immediately; Aḥmad's great fame as a political-military leader was fully justified. Were he to

25. *New York Times*, January 16 and 17, 1948. Similar articles are reported in *Oriente Moderno*, XXVIII, Nos. 1–3 (January–March, 1948), 36.
26. Sharaf al-Dīn, *Al-Yaman*, p. 326.
27. *Ibid.*, p. 327.

arrive in Ṣan'ā' before the revolution could take place, the chances of its success were considerably less.

Assassination and Attack on the Royal Family

Therefore another attempt was agreed upon; it was to take place on February 17, and this time it was successfully carried out. While Imām Yaḥyā was returning from a visit to his estates at Ḥizayz south of Ṣan'ā', with Qāḍī 'Abdullāh al-'Amrī and one of his grandsons, al-Ḥusayn ibn Ḥasan, the assassins machine-gunned the car carrying them.[28]

Aware of the power which Aḥmad, the Crown Prince, could wield, the revolutionaries had prepared to stage a similar ambush for him on the outskirts of Ta'izz, knowing that he would be informed there of events in Ṣan'ā' and would probably leave Ta'izz via the road to al-Ḥudayda. Aḥmad, surrounded by soldiers, and himself clad as a soldier for the sake of camouflage, was able to avoid assassination. The group which had been sent to do the job was completely outnumbered by Aḥmad's retinue and consequently never even attempted to carry out its task.[29]

Aḥmad, together with his soldiers and the large supply of gold he had prudently packed, made his way north through Hays, Bājil, al-Ḥudayda, and other Tihāma towns to the area around Ḥajja, one of the traditional strongholds of the Ḥamīd al-Dīn house. The population and tribes of this area had been, and were to be time and time again, a dependable source of support for the members of Yaḥyā's family. Once there, Aḥmad began to gather and organize the numerous tribal leaders who were awaiting him, as well as the portions of the regular army who declared themselves for him.[30]

Meanwhile, in Ṣan'ā' other members of the royal family had been informed that Yaḥyā had left the city in order to meet Aḥmad, whose baggage had already begun to arrive. In order to await the arriving party, they collected at the Dār al-Sa'āda Palace. There they were met by Jamāl Jamīl and his special force, which

28. Al-Jarāfī, *Al-Muqtaṭaf*, p. 258; Sharaf al-Dīn, *Al-Yaman*, pp. 327–328; and Sa'īd, *Al-Yaman*, pp. 137–138.

29. The leader of this group was Shaykh Ḥasan ibn Ṣāliḥ al-Shā'if, one of the leaders of the Jabal Baraṭ tribes. See Sharāf al-Dīn, *Al-Yaman*, p. 328; Hoeck, *Als Ärztin unter Beduinen*, p. 32.

30. Al-Jarāfī, *Al-Muqtaṭaf*, p. 261.

quickly shot Sayf al-Islam al-Ḥusayn and Sayf al-Islam Muḥsin. Sayf al-Islam Yaḥyā threw himself to the floor and surrendered, and his life was spared.[31]

Organization of Revolutionary Government

In Aden, the Free Yemeni Party was also informed of these events. According to the prearranged plan, certain members of the Party were to go to various cities throughout the country in order to take up administrative duties there. Although Sayf al-Ḥaqq Ibrāhīm, the Prime Minister of the new regime, was flown directly to Ṣan'ā' by a special plane,[32] the other members of the Party had to make their way into the country by land transportation, notoriously slow in Yemen. This meant that while most of the Party members were entering the country, Aḥmad and his allies had sufficient opportunity to gain further support and consolidate their strength.[33]

Although the Party made no special provisions for getting its representatives into Yemen, it did take the possible role of several provincial cities seriously and sent prominent members of the Party to them. For example, Qāḍī Muḥammad Maḥmūd al-Zubayrī and Aḥmad al-Barāq were sent to the provincial capital of Ta'izz, while Shaykh Aḥmad Muḥammad Nu'mān was dispatched to Dhamār.[34] The fact that the Party's representatives did not reach

31. *Ibid.*, p. 260; Sa'īd, *Al-Yaman*, p. 138.
32. Sharaf al-Dīn, *Al-Yaman*, p. 327.
33. It is worth pointing out that one of Yaḥyā's arguments against the construction of more modern transportation facilities within Yemen was that they would only enable foreigners to invade his country that much more quickly. Ironically, although the argument had been effectively countered by military theoreticians on the grounds that a modern inland transportation network would enable a government to move its troops faster in order to defend its borders, it was, nevertheless, one of the major factors in preventing the Party from sending its men to their preassigned positions with sufficient speed.

With no clear indication of the success of either side or the way the news of the war was being received in other cities, the governors and leaders of different areas adopted a do-nothing policy in order to wait and see which side they should join. If someone representing the revolutionaries had been in these provincial cities, it is likely that the outcome would have been different. On-the-spot pressure, persuasion, and simple propaganda might have put a number of officials into the revolutionary camp, a factor which could have affected the final outcome of the war. For example, Hoeck, *Als Ärztin unter Beduinen*, p. 34, reports that the first members of the Party did not arrive in Ta'izz until more than two days after the beginning of the revolt; reaching Ta'izz is still relatively easy compared with the terrain separating it from other areas farther inland. See also al-Jarāfī, *Al-Muqtaṭaf*, p. 261.
34. Al-Jarāfī, *Al-Muqtaṭaf*, p. 261.

their posts in the provinces until several days after the revolt began, and in some cases not at all, prevented them from gaining control of the situation in any place other than the capital city.

The new central government in Ṣan'ā' began to take shape almost immediately. The 'Ulamā' of Ṣan'ā', together with some other prominent personalities and dignitaries, formally installed 'Abdullāh al-Wazīr as the successor to Yaḥyā on February 18. 'Abdullāh at first took the Imamic title of "al-Dā'ī" (The Appealer), but later had this changed to "al-Hādī" (The Guide), undoubtedly because of the Ismā'īlī associations of the first title.[35]

The new Imām called upon another relative, 'Alī ibn 'Abdullāh al-Wazīr, to form a cabinet, apparently acting in concert with Sayf al-Ḥaqq Ibrāhīm at first; the latter, however, seems very soon after to have been completely ignored by his associates, perhaps because of his relationship with the dead Imām. Appointed to this cabinet were: Sayyid Ḥusayn al-Kibsī, Foreign Minister; Ḥusayn ibn 'Alī 'Abd al-Qādir, Minister of Defense; Muḥammad Maḥmūd al-Zubayrī, Minister of Education; and Aḥmad Muḥammad Nu'mān, Minister of Agriculture.[36] Sayf al-Ḥaqq Ibrāhīm was given the relatively minor post of president of the proposed consultative assembly.[37]

Reaction of Other Arab States

Ḥusayn al-Kibsī, almost immediately after the assassination of Yaḥyā, sent a telegram to the other Arab states and to the Arab League, asking for recognition of the new "constitutional, Sharī'a [regulated]" government.[38] In these cables, however, no mention was ever made of the way in which Yaḥyā had died—a fact that

35. *Ibid.*, p. 260.

36. Sa'īd, *Al-Yaman*, p. 138.

37. The motives behind Ibrāhīm's association with the Free Yemenis are unclear. It was reported that his behavior in Yemen had been ambiguous and brought about sharp disagreements with his father, the Imām. The Free Yemenis naturally welcomed his participation because of the prestige it gave to their cause. However, aware of the personal reasons for his original defection, and determined not to permit members of the Imām's family to regain influence, they appointed him to fill a position which had no responsibilities or functions. See Khadduri, "Coup and Counter-coup," pp. 61, 64; Sa'īd, *Al-Yaman*, p. 138.

Ibrāhīm remained at this post during the duration of the revolution. He was imprisoned and was reported to have died of a "heart attack" shortly after Aḥmad came to power.

38. Sa'īd, *Al-Yaman*, p. 139, contains the text of the telegram.

was to play an important role in building up opposition to the new regime. In Cairo, the Political Committee of the Arab League decided that before any action could be taken on this request, a commission should go to Ṣan'ā' in order to report on the situation there. A two-man commission, composed of 'Abd al-Mun'im Muṣṭafā and Dr. Ḥasan Ismā'īl, arrived in Ṣan'ā' on February 22, 1948.[39]

On the basis of the report which was cabled back by this delegation and a request from the new Imām that a full commission come to Yemen, the Political Committee organized another delegation to investigate the situation for all the members of the League. It was composed of Dr. 'Abd al-Wahhab 'Azzām (Egypt), Maẓhar Raslān (Syria), 'Abd al-Jalīl al-Rāwī (Iraq), Midḥat Jum'a (Jordan), Taqī al-Dīn al-Sulḥ (Lebanon), Dr. Ḥasan Tabīb (Egypt), as well as 'Abd al-Raḥmān 'Azzām, of the Arab League. The new Commission left Suez by steamer on February 17, and when the ship arrived in Jidda on March 3, it was met by Shaykh Yūsuf Yāsīn and Sayyid Ḥasan ibn Ibrāhīm, who requested that the entire delegation visit King 'Abd al-'Azīz ibn Sa'ūd in Riyāḍ.[40]

Having heard that Aḥmad had sent a telegram to the League advising it that the country was considerably disturbed and the visit from such a commission was not necessary, the new Imām hurriedly got together a delegation to present his views on the situation to both King 'Abd al-'Azīz and the League Commission. The delegation, composed of Sayyid 'Abdullāh ibn 'Alī al-Wazīr, al-Faḍīl al-Warṭilānī, and Qāḍī Muḥammad Maḥmūd al-Zubayrī, arrived in Jidda on March 8 on its way to Riyāḍ.[41]

The counteroffensive which Aḥmad had mounted was by this time beginning to tell on the revolutionaries; 'Abdullāh al-Wazīr followed up the delegation with a request of both the Saudi King and the Arab League for arms and equipment in order "to repulse the tribes attacking Ṣan'ā' in order to plunder the treasury of the Imām," as well as asking al-Warṭilānī to request the necessary equipment from King 'Abd al-'Azīz personally.[42]

Although the Saudi King was personally acquainted with

39. Sa'īd, *Al-Yaman*, p. 140; al-Jarāfī, *Al-Muqtaṭaf*, p. 264.
40. Al-Jarāfī, *Al-Muqtaṭaf*, p. 264; Sa'īd, *Al-Yaman*, p. 141.
41. Al-Jarāfī, *Al-Muqtaṭaf*, p. 264; Sa'īd, *Al-Yaman*, p. 143.
42. Quoted in Sa'īd, *Al-Yaman*, p. 143.

'Abdullāh al-Wazīr (through their previous contacts),[43] the question uppermost in his mind was the dangerous precedent such political assassination might create; as a monarch he could hardly afford to sympathize openly with al-Wazīr. It has even been suggested, with some justification, that King 'Abd al-'Azīz invited the Commission to Riyāḍ in order to give Aḥmad as much time as possible before they arrived in Yemen.[44]

The Commission found itself divided upon what stand it should take; the representatives of Egypt, Jordan, and Saudi Arabia were opposed to al-Wazīr; those of Syria and Lebanon at least originally were sympathetic. The Commission was, however, spared the embarrassment of having to come to a decision, for the news soon arrived of the overthrow of the government of 'Abdullāh al-Wazīr and Aḥmad's accession to the Imamate.

Aḥmad's Campaign

For all practical purposes, when Aḥmad arrived in Ḥajja the fate of 'Abdullāh al-Wazīr's coup was sealed. Having been welcomed by the population of the Ḥajja district, where during his period as governor he had been lavish in his largesse in order to prepare for contingencies such as the one he now faced, Aḥmad lost no time in making preparations for the campaign which was to overthrow the revolutionary government within the month.

'Abdullāh al-Wazīr, as soon as he heard of Aḥmad's arrival at Ḥajja, made preparations for the defense of the approaches to the city of Ṣan'ā', the obvious goal of Aḥmad's forces. One of these approaches leads through the Kawkabān district, to which 'Abdullāh sent a Nihm tribal force under the command of Sayyid Muḥammad al-Wazīr. Aḥmad's first victory was in the battle over this area; to it he sent a force of 'Amrān tribesmen, which was able to capture Sayyid Muḥammad and send him to Ḥajja, where rebel prisoners were collected. In retaliation, 'Abdullāh al-Wazīr sent his cousin, Sayyid Muḥammad ibn 'Alī al-Wazīr, to 'Amrān at the head of a column of the regular army. The column was easily defeated and plundered, although Sayyid Muḥammad was able to escape and make his way back to Ṣan'ā'. This desertion

43. 'Abdullāh al-Wazīr had been the primary Yemeni negotiator in the dispute with Saudi Arabia over 'Asīr and Najrān in 1934 and had won King Ibn Sa'ūd's respect.

44. Khadduri, "Coup and Counter-coup," p. 65.

by their leader and the obvious strength of the opposition led his soldiers to take the arms and money which had accompanied the column and join Aḥmad's cause.[45]

'Abdullāh al-Wazīr thereupon sent another column of soldiers of the regular army to take the main road to Ṣan'ā'. This column also fell under heavy attack, this time by 'Ans tribesmen. 'Abdullāh had counted heavily on the support of at least the Arḥab tribe in this district and had sent them a large amount of arms and money. The gifts, however, were refused by the tribal leaders, who told 'Abdullāh's agents they would accept them only if and when they were informed of the manner in which Imām Yaḥyā had died.[46]

When they learned of the failure of their military offensives, the revolutionaries began to make plans to defend only Ṣan'ā' against the approaching forces of Aḥmad. Sayyid Muḥammad 'Alī al-Wazīr went directly from his defeat at 'Amrān to Jabal Nuqum, the mountain which overlooks Ṣan'ā' in the east, along with Shaykh 'Alī Nāṣir al-Qarda'ī and a number of soldiers, to organize defenses there.

Aḥmad had, meanwhile, obtained the assistance of his brothers and other relatives.[47] At the time of the assassination, Sayf al-Islam Ḥasan had been in Ḥāshid territory, the area to which he had devoted his largesse and time. Sayf al-Islam 'Abbās, another favorite of the tribes, had been in Wādī Sirr. While Ḥasan was organizing the Ḥāshid, 'Abbās headed for the territory of the Arḥab, which tribes he gathered together for the march on Ṣan'ā'.

Meanwhile, Aḥmad's forces had begun their march to the capital; they were, however, considerably behind the fighters who had been organized by his brothers. Another addition to the growing force moving toward Ṣan'ā' was the Jadir tribesmen, under the leadership of another relative, Sayyid 'Abd al-Raḥmān ibn

45. Al-Jarāfī, *Al-Muqtaṭaf*, p. 262.

46. In the first public statements on the death of the Imām, announced in Ṣan'ā' and sent to leaders of tribes and governors throughout Yemen, the revolutionaries gave as the cause of Yaḥyā's death a " heart attack." The rumors of a violent death were now starting to make their way around the countryside, casting suspicion on the new government. See *ibid.*, p. 260.

47. There were some brothers and other relatives of Aḥmad's caught in Ṣan'ā' at the time of a revolution who were unable to come to his assistance: Yaḥyā, al-Qāsim, 'Alī, and Ismā'īl, all sons of the old Imām, and Muḥammad al-Badr, Aḥmad's own son. See *ibid.*, p. 261.

Aḥmad Hamīd al-Dīn. The latter attacked al-Rawḍa, a few miles north of Ṣan'ā', while tribesmen were also approaching the city from the south. Many of the latter were under the leadership of Sayyid 'Alī ibn Ḥamūd Sharaf al-Dīn, on whose support 'Abdullāh al-Wazīr had also counted heavily.[48] As the tribal fighters converged on Ṣan'ā' from all directions, one after another of the towns surrounding it fell.

The situation of 'Abdullāh al-Wazīr and his fellow revolutionaries was becoming increasingly desperate, for it was obvious that they would not be able to maintain a lengthy resistance to the forces arraigned against them. Nevertheless, in a last, rather futile gesture, they mounted the walls of the city and the turrets at the gates in order to throw a few last bombs on the tribesmen below them.[49]

On March 14, the troops and tribesmen of Sayf al-Islam 'Abbās, Sayf al-Islam Ḥasan, and other leaders marched into Ṣan'ā', bringing down the revolutionary government after only twenty-six days. It was not until March 19, however, that the major conspirators were taken prisoner, for when the fall of Ṣan'ā' appeared imminent, they made their way to the fort on Jabal Nuqum, where they were able to hold out for another five days. 'Abdullāh al-Wazīr, Jamāl Jamīl, and many of their coconspirators were captured and sent to Ḥajja for trial. One, the ever-elusive 'Alī Nāṣir al-Qarda'ī, was able to escape for a brief time, until he was apprehended by pursuing tribesmen and executed on the spot.[50]

Aftermath of the Revolt

Aḥmad, it may be noted, did not participate in the actual attack, siege, and capture of Ṣan'ā'. Although he had declared himself to be Imām Aḥmad soon after his flight from Ta'izz, it was not until March 15 that the 'Ulamā' of Ṣan'ā', recognizing the changed conditions, officially pronounced him to be the new Imām. During the trip to Ḥajja, Aḥmad had styled himself "al-Nāṣir li-Dīn Allāh" (He who aids the religion of God), and it was this title he kept as his Imamic one.[51]

48. The decision of Sayyid 'Alī to join Aḥmad was a great loss to 'Abdullāh, both militarily and in terms of prestige. Sayyid 'Alī, who had once been a candidate for the Imamate himself, apparently opted for Aḥmad after hearing of the manner in which Imām Yaḥyā had died.

49. For a complete description of the siege of Ṣan'ā', see *ibid.*, pp. 262–263.

50. *Ibid.*, p. 265.

51. *Ibid.*, p. 260; Sa'īd, *Al-Yaman*, p. 144.

The news of Aḥmad's victory was immediately telegraphed to the outside world, and recognition by other countries soon followed. The Arab League, then meeting in Beirut, to which Aḥmad sent a representative, recognized him as the legitimate ruler of Yemen on March 21, 1948. When recognition was granted by Great Britain on April 22, other states throughout the world followed suit.[52]

Inside the country, however, the aftermath of the revolution had yet to run its course. At Ḥajja, where the revolutionaries and their sympathizers had been collected, a trial began shortly after the final victory at Ṣan'ā'. The charges brought against the major conspirators were loosely grouped into four categories: (1) violation of the bay'a (which Aḥmad had received during the year 1938–1939); (2) " misleading the people of Yemen "; (3) dissipating and manipulating the state treasury; and (4) high treason. The trials lasted for about two weeks, resulting in death sentences for all the major conspirators and a variety of prison sentences for those whose roles were adjudged to be minor. The first of the death sentences, that imposed on 'Abdullāh al-Wazīr, was carried out on April 9, 1948.[53]

In order to obtain the allegiance, co-operation, and active assistance of many of Yemen's warrior tribes, Aḥmad exploited the age-old antagonism of the tribes toward city dwellers; he and his brothers used the argument that the city which had murdered the Imām must be punished. The tribesmen, therefore, had been promised they would be allowed to sack Ṣan'ā' and perhaps other cities. To many of these fighters, this was an opportunity to show the effete city dweller of Ṣan'ā'—to them, the epitome of decadent hedonism—the natural superiority of tribesmen in fighting ability, the only worthy attribute of a free man. Perhaps equally important, it gave them a chance to obtain some of the wealth which their imaginations had attributed to the residents of any large city.

The looting of Ṣan'ā' lasted for a number of days and was also permitted to a lesser degree in other towns that had evinced a leaning toward the revolutionaries, with the exception of Ta'izz. Imām Aḥmad had already decided that his residence would be there, and there was no sense in antagonizing its population

52. *The Times* (London), March 22 and April 22, 1948; al-Jarāfī, *Al-Muqtaṭaf*, p. 266.

53. Sa'īd, *Al-Yaman*, p. 144; al-Jarāfī, *Al-Muqtaṭaf*, pp. 265–266.

unduly. Before reaching his new capital, however, Aḥmad was forced to make a number of stops along the way from Ḥajja in order to restore law and order in the countryside, for the incidence of theft, highway robbery, and general lawlessness had increased markedly during the preceding month.[54]

Lessons Derived from the 1948 Revolt

The reasons for the failure of this first organized attempt to overthrow the established government of Yemen bear some analysis, for this revolution provided the first lessons for those, who, despairing of the Imām for leadership, would attempt repeatedly to modify the existing situation within Yemen. This is not to say that none of the reasons for the failure of this revolt were ever to be repeated; many of them played roles in other attempts. Nevertheless, Yemenis who saw no other way to bring reform to their country except through violence did learn something of the techniques of revolution from each attempt.

The major cause for opposition to the new regime was the brutal way in which the old Imām was removed from the political scene. Although he had been unaware of the developments within and without his kingdom which affected the loyalty of some of his subjects, there is no doubt that he retained among the majority of Yemenis a large personal following, due to his age, his piety, and the opposition to foreign interference in Yemen's affairs for which he was justly famous. The population at large, important tribal leaders, and other influential persons in the kingdom, as well as the outside world, were informed that he had died of natural causes. Had this been true, or if the revolutionaries had made a show of punishing those responsible for the actual killing instead of giving them government positions as obvious rewards for their action, many people who joined the counterrevolution might not have done so. When the news of Yaḥyā's murder became known, the support originally given to the revolution by many influential persons was withdrawn.

At this juncture, it was of equal importance that Aḥmad was able to escape a similar fate and make contact with powerful tribal forces in the north. When Aḥmad made his appearance and began

54. See, for example, Hoeck, *Als Ärztin unter Beduinen*, pp. 34–38; H. St. J. Philby, *Arabian Jubilee* (New York: John Day, 1953), pp. 191–192.

to organize a campaign against the new government, many of those who had heard of Yaḥyā's murder felt that Aḥmad had a legitimate cause and supported him. The assassination, therefore, provided a powerful motivation for those fighting against the new regime, and the inability of that regime to remove their major opponent from the scene meant that he could use this fact to stir up support for himself.

In addition, Aḥmad and his brothers were still in command of a good portion of the state's finances. These funds were enough to pay the tribesmen and portions of the army which sided with the counterrevolutionary forces. The rebels, on the other hand, never found the rumored fortune of Yaḥyā and therefore were unable to locate sufficient funds to pay their promised raises to government employees, the army which remained with them, and other salaried personnel. Their broken word in this respect decreased their prestige considerably.

Although a good portion of the army did not take any position at first, because each of the two primary antagonists had been a military leader, both sides were able to attract some trained military personnel eventually. The deciding factor, therefore, became the attitude of the tribesmen, whom Aḥmad was able to exploit and utilize more effectively than 'Abdullāh.

In addition to their other problems, there was considerable friction among the conspirators themselves. At first there was disagreement over which of them were to do what and where. Difficulties in traveling from Aden to Yemen meant that the rebels arrived belatedly in their assigned stations in the provinces, and fear over their colleagues' gaining the upper hand in the capital motivated many of them to leave their posts soon afterward. Within a few days, there were no members of the Free Yemeni Party in the provinces at all; the whole country except for the major cities was virtually abandoned to the counterrevolutionaries, who were free to roam without meeting any resistance.

Friction also arose among the conspirators of different religious beliefs; there was a general refusal among the Zaydi members of the revolution to delegate any of the important political posts to Shāfi'īs, perhaps for fear of alienating the 'Ulamā' who had given tacit support to the revolution. Oddly enough, the religious issue seems to have been temporarily forgotten by those determined to bring Aḥmad to the Imamate. When he himself moved through the Tihāma on the way to Ḥajja, he encountered no resistance, although his path lay through completely Shāfiʿī territory until he entered the mountains in the northeast.

The concentration of the revolutionaries on their own differences and the attempts of many of them to obtain individual positions of power prevented them from taking any effective actions as a group. The revolution was, in effect, paralyzed and did nothing but wait for the Arab League and other foreign powers to recognize it. Instead of undertaking a vigorous program of reform which would have increased their popularity in the progressive circles of the urban population, the rebels simply sat in the capital and allowed the counterrevolution to form around them.

Chapter V

OPPOSITION TO IMĀM AḤMAD

The adversaries of Imām Aḥmad may generally be said to have fallen into the same categories as those who had opposed his father: (1) progressive reformers interested in bringing changes to Yemen and (2) portions of the conservative elite who felt that their influence was being eroded through the Imām's concentration of power within his own family.

Imām Aḥmad allowed the introduction of some reforms for the benefit of the advocates of change, but the latter soon realized that his primary purpose was only to placate them. Therefore they continued to oppose him as vigorously as they had Imām Yaḥyā.

The conservatives, on the other hand, had additional grounds for discontent. In attempting to pacify the progressive elements and at the same time present an impressive international posture for the benefit of the British, Aḥmad invited a greater number of foreigners into Yemen than his father had ever dared to do. All conservative sectors of the population, including not only the religious circles but also many Zaydi tribes, became increasingly fearful of the effects these foreigners would have. In the final analysis, the fears were justified: foreign influences which were brought to Yemen did encourage and help the progressive opponents, who were eventually successful in bringing down the Imamate.

Aḥmad as Imām

The sanguinary circumstances surrounding his accession conditioned the character of Aḥmad's rule for many years afterward. In the first few months of his reign, he scarcely trusted anyone, for many of his father's most favored aides and members of prominent Yemeni families had been implicated in the revolt. As a result, Aḥmad was forced to handle personally an ever-increasing amount of detailed work which might normally have been delegated to subordinates. The fact that the people of Yemen had permitted his father to be assassinated was taken as a personal affront which he was never to forget; it prevented him from ever regarding any of his followers as trustworthy or from assuming that he had any personal popularity among the population at large, a belief not always substantiated by fact. In addition, the publicly expressed sympathy of the city of Ṣan'ā' for the revolutionaries embittered him; throughout his reign he was never to visit the capital, even though he continued to regard it as the most representative of Yemeni cities.[1]

Unlike Yaḥyā, the new Imām appointed a substantial number of Shāfi'īs to positions in his new administration in an effort to lessen Zaydi-Shāfi'ī hostility. When asked about his attitude toward Shāfi'īs by visitors, Aḥmad frequently voiced his belief that the two sects could govern and work with each other in peace and harmony; he often cited Ta'izz where he lived as an example, for it was governed by a Shāfi'ī 'āmil.[2]

The tradition in Yemen of granting amnesties and pardons on major state occasions, such as the Imām's accession to the throne and Muslim feasts, or even on the prisoner's own birthday, was used by Aḥmad to order the release of almost every one of the conspirators in the 1948 coup who had not been executed. By his generosity in issuing pardons, the Imām managed to "convert" many of these former revolutionaries to loyal subjects who devotedly served him thereafter; others took the new opportunity afforded them to engage in further revolutionary and anti-Aḥmad movements.[3]

Once Aḥmad believed himself to be in complete control of the internal situation, he set about implementing some of the reforms

1. Fayein, *Une française médecin au Yemen*, p. 48.

It has been said that Aḥmad may have feared to return, for he had permitted the city to be sacked and expected retribution. However, this does not reconcile with his astounding personal courage. Ṣan'ā' actually suffered a considerable economic blow when the government was moved to Ta'izz, and Aḥmad was often requested to return to it by prominent Ṣan'ānīs.

2. Aḥmad himself showed no favoritism toward Zaydis in his judicial decisions. On a number of occasions when he had decided against a Zaydi and an adviser or other presonality pointed out that he had decided for a Shāfi'ī, Aḥmad would call upon the entire assemblage to pray, and himself adopted the Shāfi'ī way of praying in order to demonstrate that he would show no favoritism for the adherents of his own sect.

3. Some of them naturally took the opportunity to leave Yemen and re-established or rejoined the Free Yemeni groups still operating in Cairo or Aden.

which he had promised the Free Yemenis in Aden in 1946. In so doing, he was careful to adopt only those reforms of which he personally approved, and few of these were quite what the progressive forces had in mind. Although somewhat more amenable to improvements and the assistance of foreigners in achieving limited reforms, Aḥmad's attitude was basically that of his father; he only expressed it in a more careful manner. He was once quoted as saying, "Ich scheue nichts so sehr wie Voreiligkeit." [4]

Many promises of improvements were made by Aḥmad under the pressure of criticism, but these proved to be only tactical retreats, for few of them were ever fulfilled. Shortly after coming to power he brought in large numbers of advisers from other Arab countries, primarily Palestinians, Syrians, Lebanese, and Egyptians. Some of these men were given important-sounding positions; all of them participated in drafting ambitious proposals for the improvement of nearly every phase of life in Yemen. For the most part, their work was ignored and in the end counted for very little. The reason in many instances was simply that the Imām could not be convinced of the necessity of a particular measure. Many economic reforms were drafted, and specific projects were even approved. Any such economic reforms, however, were bound to affect the welfare of some Sayyid family or other politically powerful group which was usually able to convince the Imām (through a variety of means, including faulty logic) that the proposals were not to the advantage of the Imām or the state treasury. Against Yemenis with such influence and whose interest were directly involved, the economic logic of the foreign advisers was ineffective, and even those few projects which had already begun to function were abandoned.[5]

The Opposition Reorganizes

The opposition forces which had participated in the 1948 attempted coup became inactive immediately after the death or imprisonment of many of their leaders and the increase in general

4. Pawelke, *Der Jemen*, p. 42.

5. Although Aḥmad was somewhat more receptive to the idea of exposing Yemen to twentieth-century techniques than Yaḥyā had been, it is probable that his primary motivation in permitting foreigners to assist his government was his desire to strengthen the state in order to better advocate its claim to the Aden Protectorates occupied by Great Britain. See below, Chap. VIII.

security measures throughout the country.[6] This state of truce continued for a few years while they apparently gave the new Imām a chance to prove his mettle and demonstrate the character of his new regime. The fact that Aḥmad had organized his first "government" of advisers along Western lines, establishing ministries and even assigning buildings for their use, was an encouraging sign to the reformists.[7] When foreign advisers were hired, it was generally expected that he would undertake further reforms and begin planning the economic and agricultural development of Yemen, in the process mitigating the oppressiveness of the previous regime.

As time passed and the expectations were not realized, however, the opposition organizations renewed their activities.[8] It was their claim that Aḥmad had deluded himself; he had created governmental departments and appointed prominent persons to head them, apparently believing that this was sufficient to quiet the objections of those who wanted a modern government. He had, however, failed to provide any of these new ministries with the funds and staff needed to carry out the least of their functions; most importantly, he had failed to give any of them authority to order projects started on their own initiative. The new officials had no idea how to proceed, for the Imām retained all the powers which would normally have been transferred to them. No one but the Imām could make decisions affecting affairs of state, and he personally regulated the disposition of nearly every item of business transacted by minor civil servants in other countries.[9] One

6. For a complete listing of the conspirators of the 1948 revolution and the sentences which they received, see Sharaf al-Dīn, *Al-Yaman*, pp. 329–330.

7. Some of the new ministries were housed in the properties of those who had participated in the 1948 revolution and whose possessions had been confiscated by the government. For the complete list of this first cabinet, see al-Jarāfī, *al-Muqtaṭaf*, p. 269.

8. Dating the renewal of opposition activity is difficult because of its clandestine nature in Yemen. It may be assumed, however, that by 1952 they had once again begun to organize and co-ordinate their activities. See, for example, 'Āfiyyah, *Adwā' 'ala Thawrat al-Yaman*, p. 131, concerning the "Yamani Union," established in Cairo by Muḥammad Aḥmad Nu'mān and Muḥammad Maḥmūd al-Zubayrī, both of whom participated in the 1948 and 1962 revolutions.

9. For many of the arguments which the progressives leveled at Aḥmad at this time, see Sharaf al-Dīn, *Al-Yaman*, pp. 331–332. Cf. Rāshid al-Barrāwī, *Al-Yaman wa al-Inqilāb al-Akhīr* (Cairo: Maktabat al-Nahḍa al-Maṣriyya, 1948), pp. 32–35, for the demands which had earlier been made of Imām Yaḥyā. Some of the similarities are striking.

traveler to Yemen who asked why the Imām concerned himself with these petty details was answered, " Avant lui, tous les Imams dont il descend ont gouverné comme ainsi. *Il se sentirait moins Roi* s'il ne gouvernait pas de la même façon qu'eux." [10]

Opponents within the Royal Family

In addition to opposition from the same groups who had killed his father, Imām Aḥmad also had a problem with certain members of his own family. He pardoned all those relatives, including his own son Muḥammad al-Badr, who had been in Ṣan'ā' and had submitted to the rebels in 1948, because he realized they had been placed under great pressure by the revolutionaries at that time. Despite this magnanimous gesture and the fact that his brothers had helped him to quell the 1948 revolt, not all of the royal family was necessarily united behind Aḥmad's leadership.[11]

Among the other candidates prominently discussed for the Imamate during the nineteen-thirties were some of Aḥmad's own brothers. The three whose names were most often mentioned were Ḥusayn, Ḥasan, and 'Abdullāh.[12] Ḥusayn had some reputation for his piety, but lacked the fierce determination and strong personality which are required of all who desire to become Imām. During the nineteen forties his candidacy was all but forgotten, and his death in 1948 at the hands of the rebels effectively eliminated him from future consideration. The candidacy of Ḥasan, as well as that of 'Abdullāh, continued. Ḥasan was renowned as a particularly zealous Zaydi, which made him an attractive choice to the 'Ulamā' and traditional circles; his fierce xenophobia and the respect he had among some of the powerful tribes in the north also added to his stature. 'Abdullāh was probably the most scholarly of Yaḥyā's sons and perhaps the most aware of the gulf which existed between Yemen and the outside world. The fact that he had inherited

10. Fayein, *Une française médecin au Yemen*, p. 47 (author's italics). The author reports that she received substantially the same answer on a number of occasions.

11. For example, Aḥmad's brother Ismā'īl, who had been made " Minister of Education," was arrested in early 1950 on charges of attempting to overthrow the government. (*The Times* [London], February 22 and 26, 1950.) He was apparently later released, for he met his death at the hands of a firing squad after the 1962 revolution.

12. For a complete list of Yaḥyā's sons, with a short sketch of their lives and roles during this period, see Appendix A.

his father's tendency toward parsimony and avarice, however, prevented him from ever attaining a large following among the Yemeni population.

It had been common knowledge immediately prior to 1948 that 'Abdullāh was the favorite son of Yaḥyā and had served his father as a general adviser on relations with foreign states. It was Ḥasan, however, who had the greatest political strength of all the princes.[13] The prominent positions granted to these two brothers in the first Advisory Council formed by Aḥmad demonstrated the importance which he placed on their support. Ḥasan became Prime Minister and 'Abdullāh, Foreign Minister. It seemed unlikely, however, that either of the two was completely willing to have the Imamate remain in the hands of their brother Aḥmad.[14]

THE REVOLUTION OF 1955

It is difficult to trace the activities of the opposition groups from 1948 to 1955, although there were periodic rumors of assassination attempts against Aḥmad during this period. Most opponents of Aḥmad stayed underground, fearing the wrath of the new Imām, who remained watchful for any signs of disloyalty. Finally, in March, 1955, an incident occurred which set off the first attempt to overthrow Aḥmad. It is doubtful that the revolt was very carefully planned, for there seems to have been no organized group of conspirators, as there had been in 1948. Instead it was originally the work of one man, although once the rebellion was started, others in opposition to the Imām, including both outsiders and members of the royal family, joined.

The revolt was precipitated by an incident which seemed minor at the time it occurred. On March 25, some members of the

13. Ḥasan's political prestige was so great that at the time of the counter-revolution it was rumored that there had been an agreement between him and Aḥmad to the effect that Aḥmad was to become the next Imām and designate Ḥasan as his successor in return for Ḥasan's support. See, for example, *The Times* (London), September 20, 1962. This is the obituary of Imām Aḥmad, and was probably written by Harold Ingrams, who repeats the same story in his book *The Yemen*, p. 76.

14. In 1952 it was reported that, following a quarrel over policy within the royal family, Ḥasan had fled to the mountains, where he had personal support. Although he must have returned to Ta'izz shortly thereafter, for nothing more was heard about his disaffection at this time, this was by no means the first instance of intrafamily feuds. See Ingrams, *The Yemen*, p. 83; *The Middle East Journal*, IV, No. 2 (April, 1950), 218.

Hawbān tribe in the village of al-Najda, which is located north of Ta'izz, attacked a group of government tax collectors, presumably as a protest against excessive taxation. Three of the tax collectors were killed. When the news reached Ta'izz, the *nā'ib* (governor) of the province and the Inspector of the troops stationed there, Colonel Aḥmad Yaḥyā al-Thalāyā,[15] requested permission to retaliate and attack the Hawbān tribe. Imām Aḥmad hesitated and then decided to send only a regiment trained specifically for the purpose of keeping order and enforcing tax decisions. Aḥmad Yaḥyā al-Thalāyā decided to use the situation as a pretext for rebellion against the Imām. He sent a message to Aḥmad asking him to abdicate because of his health and age.[16]

Al-Thalāyā sent a force to surround al-Urdī, the fort near Ta'izz where Aḥmad was staying, and Sayf al-Islam 'Abdullāh took this opportunity to ally himself with al-Thalāyā, apparently hoping that he would become the Imām; al-Thalāyā, a commoner, was ineligible. Besieged by approximately 600 troops, and under intense pressure, Aḥmad decided to yield active rule. He signed a document of abdication in which he said he was transferring power "from his right hand to his left hand." 'Abdullāh apparently took this to mean that power was being transferred from Aḥmad to himself, whereas it was Aḥmad's intention to take advantage of the fact that under Islamic law and precedent such an action is legally impossible, for the right hand is superior to the left.[17]

Sayf al-Islam al-Badr, hearing of his father's difficulties, fled to Ḥajja, the Ḥamīd al-Dīn's traditional stronghold. There he approached various tribal leaders and indicated that he required the support of their tribes to avenge an offense against the Imām.[18] To his assistance came the 'Āmil of Ta'izz, Muḥammad Aḥmad Bāsha (a Shāfi'ī), and many other important leaders.[19] At the

15. See above, Chap. III, footnote 2. Al-Thalāyā had been one of the Yemeni officers who had received training in Baghdad in the nineteen-thirties.

16. Sharaf al-Dīn, *Al-Yaman*, p. 384; Sa'īd, *Al-Yaman*, p. 260; Aḥmad Muḥammad Zayn al-Saqqāf. *Anā 'Ā'id min al-Yaman* (2nd ed.; Cairo: Dār al-Kitāb al-'Arabī, 1962), pp. 30–31.

17. Sa'īd, *Al-Yaman*, p. 260; Hickinbotham, *Aden*, pp. 177–181; *Arab World* (Beirut), April 12, 1955; al-Saqqāf, *Anā 'Ā'id min al-Yaman*, p. 33.

18. *Arab World* (Beirut), April 7, 1955.

19. Muḥammad Aḥmad was later made nā'ib of Ḥudayda as a reward for his assistance. See Sa'īd, *Al-Yaman*, p. 261.

head of some 8,000 loyal tribesmen, al-Badr marched on Ta'izz to attack the rebel troops under 'Abdullāh and al-Thalāyā.[20]

Before leaving Ḥajja, al-Badr cabled the Arab League, asking it for support against 'Abdullāh and the rebels. Meanwhile, the government of 'Abdullāh had cabled all Yemeni legations abroad the text of the old Imām's abdication and informed King Sa'ūd that 'Abdullāh was sending a delegation to Riyāḍ in order to explain to the King his viewpoint with regard to events in Yemen. In Cairo the conflicting telegrams and reports from Yemen to the Arab League occasioned the formation of a joint Egyptian-Sa'ūdī delegation to Yemen to investigate the reports.[21]

Meanwhile, in Ta'izz the Imām had been permitted to remain in his palace-fortress, which the rebels kept surrounded by troops. From there, Aḥmad sent a message to the insurgents asking that women and children be allowed to leave the palace. When rebel soldiers entered in order to escort the women and children out, the Imām gave them money and promised them a pardon if they would stay in the palace and fight for him; many did so. In order to mark this first success, the Imām ordered all the lights in the palace to be lit, which in Yemen signifies a victory. As a result, 'Abdullāh and al-Thalāyā soon were deserted by all but about forty of their troops. When the news reached the remaining insurgents that al-Badr was marching on Ta'izz at the head of a force of loyal tribesmen, and Aḥmad himself came storming out of the palace, sword in hand, 'Abdullāh and al-Thalāyā fled. Both were later apprehended trying to leave the country and sent back to Ta'izz, where they were beheaded, together with 'Abbās, another brother of Aḥmad and 'Abdullāh, who had apparently sided with the latter.[22]

After crushing the revolt, Aḥmad sent a telegram to the Arab League reporting that the situation in Yemen had returned to

20. *Arab World* (Beirut), April 6, 1955. The figure given is probably high.

21. *Ibid.*, April 5, 6, 7, and 8, 1955.

22. *Arab World* (Beirut), April 6, 12, 15, and 19, 1955ī al-Saqqaf, *Anā 'Ā'id min al-Yaman*, pp. 33–51.

'Abdullāh had no children, and his property was permitted to return to his mother and sister in Ṣan'ā'. An Arab News Agency report estimated that 'Abdullāh's fortune amounted to some nine million dollars in an American bank and one-half million pounds sterling in Egyptian banks, as well as extensive holdings in the Lebanese Railroad Company. This seems highly unlikely, however, for it has never been proved that any of the Yemeni royal family were very wealthy.

normal, and the joint Egyptian-Saʿūdi delegation still in Riyāḍ was disbanded. The Yemeni Legation in London issued an official communiqué in which it characterized the rebellion as "no more than a small military uprising that was promptly dealt with. Peace and order again reign in Yemen." A few days later it was learned that Aḥmad had proclaimed al-Badr the Heir Presumptive to the throne, obviously as a reward for coming to the assistance of his father.[23]

Aftermath of the Revolt

One of the immediate results of the 1955 attempted coup was the dismissal of Sayf al-Islam Ḥasan from his position as Prime Minister. He had been in Cairo at the time of the revolt, but nevertheless fell under suspicion for being in some way involved. However, at a press conference in Aden on April 14 he announced that he had been cleared of complicity in the revolt and was now proceeding to Bandung to represent his country at the Afro-Asian conference. When asked whether he had personally met with his brother, he said no, that he had been told to go directly from Cairo to Bandung. Five days later, however, it was learned that Aḥmad had dismissed Ḥasan from his post and made himself Prime Minister.[24] The Imām obviously still suspected Ḥasan of sympathizing with the revolutionaries, even if he could prove no active assistance; he was determined to keep his primary rival to the Imamate overseas, where opportunities for undertaking any domestic political activity would be limited.

The most important long-range effect of the unsuccessful coup was the rapid rise to favor of Aḥmad's son, Muḥammad al-Badr. By 1955 it had already become apparent that Aḥmad's health was not good and that he needed some trustworthy assistant. The important role al-Badr played in restoring Aḥmad to his throne probably removed many of the lingering doubts the Imām may have had concerning the personal fitness of his son for this position of trust. He thereupon assigned to al-Badr the posts of Deputy Prime Minister, Minister of the Interior, Commander-in-Chief of the Armies, and Minister of Defense.

Al-Badr, about twenty-five at this time, was well acquainted

23. *Arab World* (Beirut), April 7, 8, and 12, 1955.
24. *Ibid.*, April 15 and 20, 1955.

with the ideas of political reform then current in the Arab world. In an unsure and perhaps vain attempt to make himself appreciated, if not admired, by those Yemenis who wished to overthrow the Imamate, al-Badr had become the royal representative of these ideals of progress. He was to attempt to put into practice some of these ideas during the two brief periods when he was able to exercise leadership untrammeled by interference from his father; both experiments were to have disastrous results.

The country was relatively quiet after the revolt attempted in 1955. Punitive measures were insignificant except in the case of the principals, for the short duration of the rebellion meant that many people who might have joined if the movement had gained momentum were prevented from declaring their hostility to the regime. Thus they avoided implication and punishment.

Lessons Derived from the 1955 Attempt

The attempted coup of 1955 was largely an *ad hoc* affair; as the existence of a revolt became known, a variety of persons chose to side with the revolutionaries, no matter who they were, for reasons which often were no better than simple opportunism, as was undoubtedly the case with ʿAbdullāh. The leader of the revolt, Aḥmad Yaḥyā al-Thalāyā, however, did have serious plans to carry out a reform program in Yemen and cannot be considered an opportunist. Observers present at the time of the revolution have characterized al-Thalāyā as an intelligent and sincere reformer. That he had studied the abortive coup of 1948 and had determined not to make the same mistakes was demonstrated in his actions:

1. There was no attempt made on the life of Imām Aḥmad. The importance of the fact that the assassination of Yaḥyā had served to coalesce the counterrevolutionaries in 1948 was not lost on the much smaller group which participated in the 1955 attempt. The Imām was merely persuaded to sign a document of abdication in favor of ʿAbdullāh and then kept under guard.

2. There was a serious attempt, abetted by the fact that one of the prime movers of the attempted coup was an officer, to obtain the wholehearted support of the army for the revolutionary government. The short duration of the revolt, however, prevented al-Thalāyā's appeal for such support from having much effect.

Although the revolutionaries were careful to obtain the bayʿa for ʿAbdullāh, there were other important considerations which they did not take into account; these were to prove their undoing. Probably the most important factor to which the insurgents did not give sufficient attention was the character of Imām Aḥmad. In him, the rebels faced an exceedingly courageous and determined opponent. The fact that Aḥmad had survived several attempts on his life had given him an almost mythical reputation for indestructability.[25] He was called Aḥmad Yā Jinnāh, meaning "Aḥmad who is protected by the Jinn."[26] Consequently, merely surrounding his palace proved insufficient to keep him under control. Colonel al-Thalāyā's fear of committing the same blunder that the revolutionaries of 1948 had made in murdering Yaḥyā prevented him from taking further steps against Aḥmad.

In addition, the revolutionaries ignored the possible role of Aḥmad's son, Muḥammad al-Badr. This was a logical mistake, for few people would have thought that al-Badr would present any opposition to the new government. He had sided, although probably under pressure, with the 1948 rebellion and had been generally known as favorably inclined toward the introduction of reforms into Yemen. In addition, he was known for his soft living and self-indulgence and therefore was not seriously considered a threat by the leaders of the 1955 revolt. They did not believe that he possessed either the ability or the interest to maintain his father in power.

Aside from the revolutionaries' miscalculations concerning Aḥmad and his son, the most important factor in their downfall was the absence of a co-ordinated plan for the revolt. It was, in effect, the work of a very small group of military and civilian leaders located only in the district of Taʿizz, who simply took advantage of an opportunity which had fallen into their laps. Doubtless these men had been in secret opposition to the Imām for some time; there was not, however, an organized plot as in 1948. Consequently, they had no one to help them seize control

25. The story is told that in 1948, immediately after the abortive coup, Aḥmad had repaired a fountain on the road between Ṣanʿāʾ and Taʿizz which Yemeni tradition said would be the downfall of any Imām who mended it. See Hoeck, *Als Ärztin unter Beduinen*, p. 55.

26. (أحمد يا جنّاه); Jinn are the invisible demons who interfere in the lives of mortals and whose existence and efficacy are important causes of events in the everyday life of the average Yemeni.

of other parts of the country; and, as in 1948, this proved to be a deciding factor. Once more members of the royal family were free to solicit aid from their loyal retainers among the tribes. Because of the lack of planning and the short duration of the revolt, the revolutionaries were unable to obtain any popular support for their cause and therefore had to face the consequences of their attempted coup almost alone.

The revolt of 1955 was to be the last attempt to change the internal situation in Yemen by force in which the participants still accepted the necessity for retaining the Imamate, as well as most of its features. In both this attempt and the one of 1948, the purpose had been to remove the incumbent Imām and replace him with one who was thought to be more amenable to change. With the second failure, however, the progressive circles apparently decided that the Imamate itself was their greatest opponent; it was around this symbol that the counterrevolution had formed both times. The next attempts were undertaken with the purpose of eliminating the Imamate, as well as the Imām, and no thought was given to replacing Aḥmad with a more enlightened successor. Instead, the revolutionaries began planning to establish an entirely different type of government without a religious leader at its head.

The Opposition from 1955 to 1960

Dissident Yemeni elements in exile began to take greater interest in the possibility of effecting a change of regime in Yemen after hearing of al-Thalāyā's revolt. The Free Yemenis had never actually given up hope; there remained throughout the nineteen-fifties a group in Aden and another in Cairo concerned with bringing reform to their country under the leadership of the two grand old men of Yemeni opposition, al-Zubayrī and Nuʿmān.[27] In Aden, although *Ṣawt al-Yaman* had failed, a new paper, *al-Fuḍūl* (Superiority), had been founded in order to present the views of the Free Yemenis to their countrymen who left Yemen in order to search for employment in Aden.[28] In its issue of December 26, 1952, it had stated its primary belief:

27. Nuʿmān had escaped to Cairo in 1948, and al-Zubayrī joined him there after the Saʿūdīs released him from prison. He and the other members of the al-Wazīr delegation had been imprisoned by King ʿAbd al-ʿAzīz after the fall of the government they represented.

28. During the nineteen-fifties, *al-Fuḍūl* appeared twice a week with a circulation

> Yemen is independent, but the despotism of its rulers has created there a disastrous situation. . . . The number of Yemenis who have left their country in order to find liberty and a decent life now exceeds 1,250,000. The case of Yemen is the disaster of the Twentieth Century, and the true refugee of our time is the Yemeni.[29]

After al-Thalāyā's revolt, new manifestoes were published and new programs for economic development and other reforms were drafted.[30]

Progressive Opponents and Foreign Influence

Once the country had been put back under his firm rule, the Imām decided that it was possible once again to undertake a concerted program to drive the British from the Protectorates of Aden.[31] This decision and al-Badr's urging prompted him to invite into Yemen a number of Soviet and Egyptian advisers for a variety of military projects.

The progressive reformers both in and out of Yemen viewed the introduction of modern techniques as working toward their aims, regardless of the purpose for which they had been imported. They believed that the introduction of any modern methods and equipment to the Yemeni population would open the latter's eyes to the potential of modern techniques for eliminating the primitive conditions in their country. Earlier there had been a division of opinion among Free Yemenis on this subject. Some favored the introduction of any new ideas, while others argued that modern techniques and increased foreign assistance would only strengthen the Imām's position and delay far-reaching reforms. This latter group seems to have lost the argument in the nineteen-fifties.

---

of about 4,000 copies and carried heavily propagandistic articles against the rule of Imām Aḥmad. See Pawelke, *Der Jemen*, p. 51.

For other references to this newspaper, see, for example, J. J. Berreby, *La Péninsule Arabique* (Paris: Payot, 1958), pp. 129–130; al-Saqqāf, *Anā 'Ā'id min al-Yaman*, p. 139.

In addition, most of the papers in Aden were sympathetic toward Yemeni revolts and carried stories about them through the years.

29. As quoted in Berreby, *La Péninsule Arabique*, pp. 129–130.

30. For the new program of the Free Yemenis, see al-Saqqāf, *Anā 'Ā'id min al-Yaman*, pp. 80–83; Ḥasan Ibrāhim Ḥasan, *Al-Yaman* (Cairo: Dār al-Ma'ārif, Ikhtirnā Lak Series, No. 52, *ca.* 1958), pp. 178–181.

31. See below, Chap. VII.

Those who welcomed any change were evidently correct in their judgment, for it was within the ranks of the newly trained and equipped army that opposition was to be centered in the next few years.

Imām Aḥmad was aware of the opposition toward his government which existed in progressive Arab circles and the potential effectiveness of the propaganda organs of Jamāl 'Abd al-Nāṣir's revolutionary Egypt if they were turned against him. Consequently, he took advantage of the opportunity presented by the signing of the United Arab Republic Agreement between Egypt and Syria, and its provision for additional members, to ally himself with 'Abd al-Nāṣir and thus avoid becoming the target of the type of propaganda campaigns which were then being carried out against the kings of Jordan and Iraq.

There had been rumors of assassination attempts on the Imām's life at least twice during 1958, and Aḥmad's failing health had made it difficult for him to control fully all the activities of government, a fact which allowed more and more power to slip into the hands of Muḥammad al-Badr. The latter liked to consider himself a progressive leader, and he sympathized with 'Abd al-Nāṣir's regime openly. It was, therefore, also partially due to his urging that Aḥmad decided on the loose association with the U.A.R.

In this association, however, Aḥmad was careful to retain a veto with regard to all decisions affecting Yemen. In the formal organization—the United Arab States—each member was permitted to keep its own government, armed forces, and diplomatic representation independent of the other. A Supreme Council was formed with a number of subordinate bodies for the co-ordination of defense and foreign, economic, and cultural policies. Although Aḥmad strictly controlled the amount of influence which this agreement gave to the Egyptians, he did permit a small number of Egyptian educational and military missions to come to Yemen in order to train Yemenis—if only for the purpose of demonstrating that he had not signed merely for the purpose of keeping Egypt's revolutionary philosophy and propaganda out of Yemen.

These limited training missions which Aḥmad permitted to assist him in developing his army were, however, to prove an additional impetus toward revolution. By early 1959, outright opposition to the Imām in the ranks of the army had become so blatant that leaflets and pamphlets signed by the "Free Yamani Army Officers" were said to be circulating within Ta'izz itself.[32]

Conservative Opponents

By this time, too, conservative elements within Yemen were beginning to disapprove openly of the activities of Muḥammad al-Badr and the introduction of large numbers of Egyptians and other foreigners. The Imām was said to be receiving messages from tribal leaders, prominent Sayyids, and the 'Ulamā' asking that he limit the activities of his son, which they felt were leading to the destruction of the independence of Yemen and turning it into an Egyptian colony.[33]

Al-Badr's Reforms

At this critical time, when the traditional holders of political power were becoming annoyed at the increased dependence of Yemeni foreign policy on the assistance of outsiders and the army was beginning to show signs of the revolutionary influence exerted on it by Egyptian and Soviet Bloc trainers, Aḥmad fell ill. He left for Rome to obtain medical care in April, 1959, and during his stay there nearly all governmental business came to a standstill.[34] It was, however, necessary that some administrative activities continue, and Aḥmad had only one person whom he felt he could

32. *The Middle East Journal*, XII, No. 2 (Spring, 1958), 193; *New York Times*, November 21, 23, and 16, 1958; *al-Jarīda* (Beirut), January 31, 1959, as quoted in *Oriente Moderno*, XXXIX, No. 2 (February, 1959), 132.

33. *Filastīn* (Jerusalem, Jordan), June 8, 1958, as quoted in *Oriente Moderno*, XXXVIII, No. 7 (July, 1958), 644. It should be noted that this is a Jordanian paper and King Ḥusayn was at odds with 'Abd al-Nāṣir. Nevertheless, because of the xenophobic character of the traditional political forces in Yemen—that is, the Sayyids and the tribal leaders—their opposition to this foreign assistance is not unlikely.

34. This illness was probably caused by some type of narcotic poisoning, due to Aḥmad's intake of drugs in order to reduce the pain of arthritis from which he was suffering. The fact that the medicines were administered in some cases by people not qualified to do so may have brought on the poisoning. See Ingrams, *The Yemen*, p. 108.

It is worth adding that there was no historical precedent for this action of Aḥmad. According to Zaydi theory, the community of believers cannot be without an Imām; the departure of Aḥmad, therefore, could be considered illegal and even heretical. Zaydi theologians argued that Zaydi prayers throughout the period of his stay outside Yemen were invalid. This prolonged absence naturally displeased the 'Ulamā' and conservative Zaydi circles and increased their dislike of Aḥmad's policies in general.

trust with any power—his son al-Badr. Perhaps, too, Aḥmad thought that this might be a good opportunity for al-Badr to learn something of the complexities of administering Yemen.

During the Imām's absence, al-Badr took the opportunity afforded him by his increased authority to introduce some of the "progressive" reforms about which Arab nationalists were talking at that time. He began a reform of the civil service and a design for an over-all plan using the development programs and ideas formerly drawn up by foreign experts; he also set up a representative council composed of seven members under the chairmanship of Qāḍī Aḥmad al-Siyāghī, who had been acting as governor of Ibb and was known for his progressive attitudes.[35]

It appeared that al-Badr wished to assert his claim to succession by demonstrating that he was capable and willing to introduce reforms and that he was worthy of the support of those groups who were committed to the overthrow of the Imamate. In order to increase his support, al-Badr decided to concentrate on the army. He assumed that an army which had been trained by Bloc and Egyptian experts would be progressive in outlook and would support someone with programs such as his. During Aḥmad's stay in Rome, the old Commander of the Army, 'Alī ibn Ibrāhīm, was forced to resign and was replaced 'Abd al-Qādir Abū Ṭālib, a colonel. At the same time, a number of other officers lost their positions, but it is unknown whether this was due to their having participated in the distribution of leaflets in January or because al-Badr found them to be too reactionary for his purposes.[36]

Alienation of the Tribes

The slackening of governmental authority which came about as a result of Aḥmad's departure gave several groups in Yemen an opportunity for settling old grudges. Some troops mutinied for higher pay, and a number of tribal leaders decided to settle tribal disputes by force; lawlessness, in general, increased markedly. Al-Badr promised the soldiers more money and, in an effort to cope with the rapidly deteriorating situation in the northern

35. *The Times* (London), May 29 and June 18, 1959. Sa'īd, *Al-Yaman*, p. 313, gives its membership.

36. *The Times* (London), May 29 and June 18, 1959; and *L'Orient* (Beirut), May 30 and June 4, 1959, as quoted in *Oriente Moderno*, XXXIX, No. 6 (June, 1959), 644.

tribal areas, began to pay a subsidy to the chiefs of some member tribes of the Ḥāshid and Bakīl confederations. Later in the summer there were further outbreaks among the army, for al-Badr had no funds with which to pay the 25 per cent increase he had promised,[37] and general rioting broke out in Ta'izz and other cities. Al-Badr finally cracked down, using the time-honored threat of the interference of the northern tribes, whose loyalty he had just purchased. An Egyptian was made director of public security, and the army, undoubtedly under the command of Egyptian trainers, was brought into Ta'izz. There were some executions of rebellious army officers, and some money was finally released in order to pay the overdue salaries of the soldiers.[38]

In August, 1959, the Imām returned from Rome, considerably better in health. Almost immediately after his return, the political situation also improved. With his customary ruthlessness, Aḥmad condemned the few leaders he deemed responsible for the disturbances to lose their heads, and a wave of arrests and imprisonments swept the country. Within the month, he ordered a purge of the liberal reforms which al-Badr had instituted.

Considerably worried by the large amounts of money which his son had spent, he canceled the subsidies to the tribes of the north and attempted to get back from the recipients some of the money which had been used as bribes.[39] This attempt to regain the funds spent by al-Badr was to prove to be Aḥmad's most disastrous error of internal policy; its effects were particularly extensive and materially assisted the revolutionaries in gaining tribal support in 1962.

Although subsidies had been paid to a number of tribes, the largest amount went to the powerful Ḥāshid confederation. Aḥmad's first attempts to retrieve the monies led to a number of small disturbances in the north, creating a potentially explosive situation. In an effort to solve the problem, the Imām invited the

37. Ingrams, *The Yemen*, p. 109.

38. *The Middle East Journal*, XIII, No. 4 (Autumn, 1959), 442; *New York Times*, August 18, 24, and 25, 1959; Ingrams, *The Yemen*, p. 110.

39. Aḥmad had paid the troops who surrounded his fortress in 1955 fifty riyals each in order to get them to serve him instead of the revolutionary leaders. When he had firmly re-established himself, he promptly went around to each soldier and fined him fifty riyals for having participated in an attempted *coup d'état* against "their Imām" and the legitimate government, and collected these fines without difficulty. See: Pawelke, *Der Jemen*, p. 115.

paramount shaykh of the Ḥāshid, Shaykh Ḥusayn ibn Nāṣir al-Aḥmar, and his son Ḥamīd al-Aḥmar, to visit him in al-Ḥudayda in late 1959. Under a safe-conduct guarantee and as guests of the Imām, the two men went to meet him. During the talks, designed to settle the problem amicably, a heated discussion took place. Aḥmad, in a burst of rage at the insubordination of the tribal chief, ordered that he and his son be decapitated. Regrettably for Aḥmad (who almost invariably rescinded such orders made in anger after his temper cooled), and unfortunately for his guests, the order was immediately carried out.[40]

The Ḥāshid and other tribal leaders were incensed at this breach of tribal law; the custom of safety for a guest within the house of his host had been broken, not to mention the specific Imamic guarantee of safe-conduct. This action alienated from the Imām most major tribes in the north, where the traditional support of the Zaydi Imāms lay. It naturally set off a wave of tribal uprisings, and the Imām was forced to rush regular army troops from the southern frontier to the north in order to quell the more serious outbreaks.[41]

Tribal Revolt of 1960

The situation throughout the country was now becoming almost unmanageable. During nearly all of 1960, there were incidents of terrorism, acts of civil disobedience (the first in Yemen's history), and similar opposition activities in Ta'izz, Ṣan'ā', al-Ḥudayda, Dhamār, and other towns. Troops clashed with citizens in a number of places, and increased numbers of leaflets and pamphlets advocating the overthrow of the government were seen throughout the country.[42]

40. For a partial account of this important incident, see Ingrams, *The Yemen*, p. 110, and the references given below, footnote 41.

41. Sharaf al-Dīn, *Al-Yaman*, p. 405; *Le Monde* (Paris), October 14–15, 1962; and British Broadcasting Corporation, *Summary of World Broadcasts*, Part 4 (*The Middle East*), January 30, 1960, as quoted in *The Middle East Record 1960* (Tel Aviv: The Israel Oriental Society, n.d. [c. 1962]), p. 395.

42. Imām Aḥmad held the Free Yemenis in Aden responsible for all opposition and sent a protest to the British authorities there. The latter claimed they could do nothing, for although the exile groups were making plans and printing their literature in Aden, the actual acts of sabotage and violence were being committed in Yemen. Aḥmad, not unnaturally, took this reaction as another indication of the British policy of furthering their own position in south Arabia and decreasing the power of the Imām.

At the same time, it was becoming increasingly obvious that the Imām's health had again deteriorated. There were reports that the administration of the country was nearly at a standstill, as officials refused to discharge their duties without the Imām's approval, which the latter was often unable to give. The illness of the Imām, combined with the weakness of al-Badr's administration, led to an increase in the independent actions of the various political and tribal factions.[43]

In April, 1960, it was reported that many tribes of the Bakīl confederation had joined in a general uprising; although some chiefs and their followers were forced to flee to Aden by the campaigns the army carried out against them, the rebellion continued to spread. A request by the Imām that certain chiefs of the Khawlān, another important and powerful tribe of central and northern Yemen which was in revolt, meet him in al-Sukhna for talks was refused. It was specifically stated in their refusal that the reason was the actions taken by the Imām with the Shaykhs of the Ḥāshid, an indication of the extent to which the Imām's authority in tribal matters had been diminished.

By June other powerful tribes had joined in the revolt, and all now refused to surrender new hostages to the Imām. Regular army columns were sent out, and with the aid of some tribes who remained pro-Imām, an attempt was made to crush the Khawlān rebellion. The power of the Khawlān and the nature of their terrain, however, was such that it was nearly impossible to carry the campaign to complete victory. The Imām finally decided to negotiate with the leaders, sending an aged politician experienced in settling tribal disputes, al-Qāḍī Muḥammad al-Shāmī, now over seventy.[44] A tentative peace was apparently established, for accounts of the difficulties disappeared from the newspapers; the tribal issue, however, was by no means settled.

Aḥmad's continuing difficulties with the northern tribes who normally supported his rule led him, in December, 1960, to restore the possessions of the Wazīr family. Although some members of

43. *Aden Chronicle*, April 14 and May 19, 1960, as quoted in *The Middle East Record 1960*, pp. 393–394.

44. *Fatāt al-Jazīra* (Aden), April 22, May 1, June 3, 17, and 23, 1960; *Aden Chronicle*, April 21 and June 16, 1960; the last-named issue also reported that al-Badr had requested support from Cairo to suppress the Khawlān rebellion and had been refused. The above are all quoted in *The Middle East Record 1960*, p. 395.

the family had been pardoned in 1956, their property, said to amount to over 3,000,000 riyals in value, was still sequestered by the government. This move was one part of an attempt to rally all the Sayyids of Yemen to the side of the Imamate against what Aḥmad considered, with some justification, a serious threat to its existence from the northern tribes.[45]

By this time many of these tribes, including the powerful Ḥāshid confederation and most of its allies, were disillusioned with Aḥmad's ability to supply the traditional leadership expected from a Zaydi Imām. With the illogic born of their despair over Aḥmad, they seized upon the one factor which differentiated them from the Sayyid Ḥamīd al-Dīn house—their Qaḥṭānī ancestry, as opposed to the 'Adnānī ancestry of all Sayyids, whom they now despised as a class in positions of authority over them. Consequently, they started a movement in 1959 to elect a new Imām.[46] If the larger tribal federations were to go into outright opposition to the rule of the Hāshimite Imāms and even elect among themselves a Qaḥṭānī Imām, Aḥmad would need allies. The most logical ones were his fellow Sayyids, especially the more powerful ones, even though some of them had formerly opposed his and/or his family's rule. Undoubtedly it was for this reason that Aḥmad tried to obtain the co-operation and support of prominent families formerly in disgrace, such as the Wazīrs, and unify the Sayyids, all of whom had a personal interest in seeing the Imamate and their privileges maintained.

THE OPPOSITION FROM 1961 TO 1962

1961 Assassination Attempt

In January, 1961, the Imām was involved in an automobile accident in which he suffered a number of injuries. In Aden it was

45. *Al-Ahrām* (Cairo), December 19, 1960, quoted in *Oriente Moderno*, XLI, No. 5 (May, 1961), 224; *al-Ahrām* (Cairo), December 25, 1955, quoted in *Oriente Moderno*, XXXVI, No. 1 (January, 1956), 46.

46. Although it was their pre-Islamic ancestry which now served to unify them, the traditions of the Zaydi faith, no matter how closely connected with the Sayyids and the Imām, could not be completely ignored by these tribesmen. It seems likely that they would have settled for another Sayyid more to their own choosing, such as Ḥasan, if only the now despised Aḥmad were eliminated.

For an account of the movement to elect a new Imām in the Arab press, see *The Middle East Record 1960*, p. 395.

reported, perhaps too hopefully, that the accident had been another attempt on the Imām's life. The next authentic effort to assassinate Aḥmad came soon after, in March, when he and Muḥammad al-Badr went to al-Ḥudayda in order to participate in the official opening of the Russian-built port of Aḥmadī.[47] The Imām was to undertake an inspection tour of the General Hospital at al-Ḥudayda at the same time and receive an X-ray examination because of his recent accident. The usual security precautions were taken; members of the Royal Guard were sent in advance to see to the safety of the Imām. The man in charge of security at the hospital was Lieutenant Muḥammad ibn 'Abdullāh al-'Alfī, who informed the Royal Guards that the hospital could not accommodate the entire retinue of Aḥmad. When the Imām arrived, several princes and some bodyguards were locked out of the hospital and forced to remain in the grounds by al-'Alfī.

The Imām went first to visit some of his guards who had been injured in the automobile accident and then started downstairs to the X-ray room. At that point, two appointed assassins, Lieutenant 'Abdullāh al-Laqya, a twenty-eight-year-old soldier of the Ḥudayda Fire Brigade, and Lieutenant Muḥsin al-Hindwāna, forty-one-year-old army officer, opened fire on the Imām and his party, while Lieutenant al-'Alfī fired from the opposite direction. Although the revolutionaries later claimed that the Imām was struck by twelve bullets, he was not killed; he threw himself to the floor and feigned death.[48]

The assailants, leaving Aḥmad for dead, left the building and engaged in a brief but fierce exchange with the aroused guards outside. The three were, nevertheless, able to escape from the hospital and its grounds. Al-'Alfī ran to a guest house near the palace, where a passing soldier saw him and reported his suspicious actions to the Royal Guards, now searching the city. When they arrived, at first he attempted to do battle;[49] then, seeing the number of guards who opposed him, he committed suicide. Al-Laqya and al-Hindwāna were both arrested and later executed for their part in the attempted assassination.

47. *The Times* (London), April 3, 1961; *New York Times*, March 27, 1961; *Christian Science Monitor*, April 8, 1961.

48. Others in the party were also wounded, including Ismā'īl ibn Qāsim and Ḥasan ibn 'Alī, both nephews of the Imām.

49. In this fray, al-'Alfī only succeeded in killing a judge of the Ḥudayda Sharī'a Court, as well as injuring some onlookers.

Others were also implicated in the plot, and the Imām's guards were able to trace several conspirators. Because their immediate connection with the assassins could not be proved at their trial, some were only relieved of their posts, while others received short prison sentences. Among these suspected plotters were 'Abdullāh al-Sallāl, at the time Director-General of the Port of al-Ḥudayda, who was dismissed and transferred to Ṣan'ā'; Muḥammad al-Ra'īnī, Director of the Airport of al-Ḥudayda; and Sayyid Ḥusayn al-Muqaddamī, Director of the Hospital. The latter two were arrested and interned at the Washha Prison.[50]

The Imām was taken back to the palace and examined by an American Navy doctor whose ship was in the harbor at the time. The Imām's personal physician, an Italian, and a Soviet doctor were called in, and later additional doctors were flown in from Italy. Aḥmad had been hit by about five shots, the most important of which struck him in the thigh and smashed his femur; he also apparently suffered a slight head injury as a result of throwing himself to the floor.[51]

Rivalry of Ḥasan and al-Badr

Although it was reported shortly thereafter that the Imām was making a speedy recovery, it soon became apparent that the latest assassination attempt had seriously affected his ability to deal with the uncertain state of affairs in Yemen. He was again forced to delegate some powers to al-Badr; worried by the way his son had handled affairs in the past, however, he also summoned his brother Ḥasan from New York.[52] Immediately rumors sprang up to the effect that Aḥmad was considering abdicating in favor of either al-Badr or Ḥasan. The fact that Aḥmad had called in Ḥasan pleased the more conservative of Yemen's political groups, for he was known to be orthodox and had not alienated himself from the tribes. Because of his long absence from the country, he had in fact had no chance to alienate anyone and therefore

50. They were both released from prison by the revolutionaries headed by al-Sallāl in September, 1962.

51. Sharaf al-Dīn, *Al-Yaman*, pp. 379–381; Ingrams, *The Yemen*, pp. 111–113; *The Times* (London), April 1, 3, and 6, 1961; *New York Times*, March 28 and April 1, 9, and 11, 1961.

52. Ḥasan, after his dismissal as Prime Minister, had been made Yemen's permanent delegate to the United Nations in New York.

had the approval of many groups, including some Shāfi'īs. Al-Badr, on the other hand, was considered by the conservative and orthodox circles as being too weak, too amiable, erratic, and prone to foreign influences.

It seems reasonable that Aḥmad should fear al-Badr's weakness, for he had demonstrated his inability to manage internal affairs with a firm hand during Aḥmad's absence in 1959. The radicalism al-Badr exhibited at that time also gave Aḥmad reason to believe that giving the rule to his son might ultimately put an end to the long period of Zaydi rule in Yemen. Eventually, however, he decided to favor al-Badr again; there seems to be no reason other than the fact that he was his son. Ḥasan was delegated to supervise in a general way al-Badr's activities during the latter's new term of apprenticeship.[53]

Following a relatively quiet period immediately after the assassination attempt, there was another spate of bombings in Ta'izz, Ṣan'ā' and al-Ḥudayda. Pamphlets directed against both Ḥasan and al-Badr were seen. During this time, Aḥmad's condition improved considerably, and by August he felt strong enough to rule the country himself. Consequently, he sent Ḥasan to represent Yemen at the Belgrade Conference of Neutral Nations, and al-Badr went off to Zürich and Rome for medical treatment. Neither one of the two rivals for the Imamate was, therefore, in Yemen when Aḥmad made an important speech, broadcast over Ṣan'ā' Radio in October, 1961. In this talk the Imām admitted indirectly that considerable pressure had been placed on him by tribal chiefs, the 'Ulamā, and other prominent personalities to make some provision for Yemen's future; the implication was that it was time to put an end to the wrangling and decide on his successor.[54]

In his speech Aḥmad specifically said, "Follow our son Muḥammad al-Badr." Although he thereby made it clear that his son was his deputy, he did not abdicate, as was first reported, nor did he refer to al-Badr as Crown Prince (Waliyy al-'Ahd).

53. *New York Times*, June 26 and 28, 1961.

54. It seems strange that the Zaydi notables, who formerly had been opposed to any prior designation of an heir, should make such a request. One can only assume that either the Imām was lying about this pressure or the Zaydi notables had become so worried over the state of affairs in the country that they felt only a public announcement by the Imām concerning his successor would stave off civil war.

Ḥasan's position was not clarified by the speech, and it may be assumed that his assignment to represent his country overseas again was another maneuver by Aḥmad to get his popular brother out of the country and limit the amount of support he could attract. Shortly thereafter, Aḥmad asked al-Badr to come back to Yemen.[55]

Last Attempts at Reconciliation

In December, 1961, after the dissolution of the U.A.R., Aḥmad wrote a poem in which he gave his own candid views about Arab socialism and the reform movements with which Jamāl ʿAbd al-Nāṣir was associated. Aside from his genuine dislike for ʿAbd al-Nāṣir and his policies, Aḥmad's main motive in writing the poem was his hope that this clear demonstration of his belief in Zaydi Islam and his rejection of Arab socialism as a perversion of the true religion would cause the Zaydi tribes, whom he had so badly disaffected, to support him again. It was, of course, also aimed at the ʿUlamāʾ and Zaydi notables, displeased with the large number of foreigners the Imām had brought into the country.

This action quite naturally precipitated the Egyptian leader's breaking off ties with Yemen and the start of a Radio Cairo campaign against the Imām designed to help the opposition groups who wished to bring revolution to the country. Al-Zubayrī was introduced on the Voice of the Arabs as "the leader of the Yemeni liberation movement in Cairo." Others who were to hold prominent positions in the postrevolutionary government of 1962 were also brought to the fore: Muḥsin al-ʿAynī and ʿAbd al-Raḥmān al-Bayḍānī.[56]

During the next few months, Cairo's propaganda began producing results; there were demonstrations throughout Yemen

55. *Oriente Moderno*, XLIII, No. 3 (March, 1962), 235–236; *The Times* (London), October 14 and 16, 1961.

56. During the nineteen-fifties, Imām Aḥmad sent a group of about forty young Yemenis abroad for additional education. Most of these, like their counterparts of the nineteen-thirties, soon joined the ranks of the opposition. Many of them achieved cabinet rank in one or more of the many Republican cabinets of 1962–1965. One of these was al-ʿAynī, who in the years prior to the revolution of 1962 had been at one time personal secretary to Muḥammad al-Badr and a schoolteacher in Aden. Under the Republic, he was alternately Foreign Minister and Ambassador, either to the United Nations or the United States, until 1966.

Other data on both these individuals can be found in Ingrams, *The Yemen*, pp. 124–125.

against the Imām; processions in various cities were held in which 'Abd al-Nāṣir's picture was prominently displayed; and student riots and other disturbances took place.[57]

At the same time, tribal unrest in the north showed no signs of decreasing. The Imām, in order to demonstrate that he would not tolerate any more insurrection from the tribes, had villages of one of the weaker tribes, the Qamā'ira, destroyed. In August, however, the Imām decided to try a different approach; in order to obtain the support of the tribes, he divorced one of his wives of long standing to marry the daughter of one of the tribal chiefs from the north.[58]

In an attempt to placate progressive forces at the same time, a hurried program of reforms was introduced.[59] The government announced the formation of a new planning council, a program for village co-operatives, and other reforms; many of these bore a resemblance to those being proposed for Yemen by Radio Cairo at the time. As had been the case in the past, however, little was actually done to implement the promises, for they were obviously announced only in direct answer to the regime's critics.

Whether or not these conciliatory gestures would have had the desired effects will never be known, for on the night of September 18, 1962, Aḥmad died quietly in his sleep;[60] it was the same

57. *The Middle East Journal*, XVI, No. 3 (Summer, 1962), 372; *Christian Science Monitor*, August 11 and 21, 1962; *New York Times*, August 12, 1962; *Frankfurter Allgemeine Zeitung*, September 11, 1962.

58. *Daily Telegraph* (London), September 20, 1962.

59. This announcement came soon after a series of talks was begun over Radio Cairo by al-Bayḍānī, in which he outlined a program for a Yemeni Republic based on the principles of Arab nationalism, social justice, the development of the economy, and other progressive features.

60. When it was announced that the Imām had died naturally, there was much skepticism expressed by observers of the Middle East and those who had some acquaintance with Yemeni history. The past record of the Imamate would lead many observers to assume that the Imām had died a violent death, as had so many of his forebears, including his father. Therefore, it was immediately assumed by many that he had fallen victim to another assassination attempt by poison or some more violent means and that his manner of death had been covered up by his son al-Badr in order to avoid adding to the disturbed state of affairs.

Although the actual cause of death was still unknown in 1966, three likely causes have been advanced: (1) Cerebral hemorrhage, *Le Monde* (Paris), September 23–24, 1962; (2) Lung congestion, Brown, "The Yemeni Dilemma," p. 349; (3) Ahmad's constitution was simply no longer strong enough to take the accumulated diseases and wounds from which he had suffered for a number of years. It is known that he had arthritis, and it was said that one of the bullets which had

day that Cairo broadcast a prediction that revolution was coming to Yemen. The next day al-Badr announced Aḥmad's death and the fact that the 'Ulamā' and notables of the country had agreed on his succession to the Imamate; Muḥammad al-Badr took the patronym "Al-Manṣūr Billāh," (the victorious, by the will of God).

The Opposition under Muḥammad al-Badr

Although the new Imām retained all the old members of the former government in their posts, his first announcements re-emphasized his general predilection for reform. He announced a policy of "positive neutrality, non-alignment, and treaties and cordial relations with everyone." [61] Three days later, a general amnesty was announced for political prisoners; exiles and refugees were requested to return home; taxes were canceled for the remainder of the year; feudal mortgage laws (requiring prison terms for debtors) were abolished; and pay increases were announced for the army.[62]

It was soon obvious, however, that these published goals were not deemed sufficient by those whose self-assigned task was to bring reform to Yemen. The U.A.R. government treated the new Imām and his government with extreme coolness, and the Free Yemenis, from their office in Cairo, sent messages to al-Badr asking that he establish a "democratic government" with no special privileges for interest groups in Yemen.[63] The young Imām was perhaps dismayed by the cool reception he had received from Cairo, where he had undoubtedly hoped to find support. In an effort to impress Jamāl 'Abd al-Nāṣir with his sincere desire to introduce changes along the Egyptian model, al-Badr announced further reforms. Among these was a decree establishing municipal councils, which would restore to villages and towns some local authority, of which they had been deprived for many years, as

---

been fired at him in the 1961 assassination attempt was still in his body at the time of his death, *The Sunday Times* (London), September 23, 1962.

If death was from natural causes, as the author personally believes, the identity of the specific final cause is not particularly important. Its basic general cause was certainly to be found among the many illnesses and generally deteriorated state of Aḥmad's health, a result of the many attempts on his life in preceding years.

61. *Washington Post*, September 20, 1962.

62. *Ibid.*, September 23, 1962.

63. *Le Monde* (Paris), September 23–24, 1962.

well as a decree establishing a Consultative Council. The latter was to be composed of forty members, of which twenty were to be elected and twenty appointed.[64] The effects of these decrees were never to be learned, for in the night of September 26 a new *coup d'état* was launched in Ṣan'ā'.

Imām Muḥammad al-Badr, although not possessed of the strength of character or the incredible personal courage with which Aḥmad was blessed, was partially a victim of circumstances, for he came to power at the very moment when the most carefully plotted plan to overthrow the Imamate was coming to fruition. At the same time, his own sympathies for the reformers and his fumbling attempts to bring changes to Yemen also contributed to his downfall.

'Abdullāh al-Sallāl, the leader of the *coup d'état*, had been involved in various attempts to bring reform to the government of Yemen in the past; for his role in the attempted revolution of 1948, he received a sentence of over seven years in Nāfi' Prison in Ḥajja; the attempt in al-Ḥudayda in 1961 meant his dismissal from his post as Director of the port. Muḥammad al-Badr, soon after al-Sallāl's release from prison in 1956, had him and his confrere, Ḥamūd al-Jā'ifī, reinstated in the army. Later al-Badr appointed al-Sallāl Commander-in-Chief of his personal bodyguard.

Although al-Badr purposefully tried to stay close to reform elements in Yemen and even knew that such officers as al-Sallāl and al-Jā'ifī were prone to revolt, these facts would not explain how al-Badr first met the two officers. It may be that during the revolution of 1948 one or both of them were responsible for permitting al-Badr to live, for other members of the royal family were executed at that time. It may have been as repayment of a personal debt that al-Badr had these two men reinstated. In any case, it is certain that after 1956 there was a close relationship between them, and upon al-Badr's succession, al-Sallāl was appointed Commander-in-Chief of the Royal Guards. In this capacity, for the first few days of the new regime, he enjoyed a position equivalent to that of Chief of Staff and became responsible for nearly all military equipment and supplies for the kingdom.

Even before al-Badr had announced most of his reforms, conservative political forces within Yemen began to exert pressure

64. *Daily Telegraph* (London), September 25 and 26, 1962.

on the new Imām. Al-Badr's initial pronouncement and his past reputation as a reformer seriously disturbed many tribal leaders, orthodox Zaydi circles, and conservative advisers who had served Aḥmad. Many at first declared themselves for al-Badr, perhaps in order to stave off a civil war and with the hope that they could then apply pressure upon him, but al-Badr's early statements were far too radical for them. They began a campaign to convince him of the folly of speaking and acting in this way, arguing that this would only further alienate already disaffected conservative groups. It was doubtless argued that if al-Badr gave in to demands for reform, he would be " less of a king " than his forebears.

The threat of facing concerted Zaydi oppositions to his rule from the start impressed al-Badr. On the Friday after the death of his father, he capitulated to this pressure and announced, in a speech given in a Ṣan'ā' mosque, that he was going to rule Yemen as had his father and his grandfather before him. Privately he doubtless hoped to be able to introduce reforms anyway, but the slowness and vagueness with which they were later enumerated demonstrate the control his advisers had over him.

The Revolt of 1962

Al-Sallāl and others, who may or may not have been waiting until the new Imām had an opportunity to reveal the way in which he intended to govern the country, became genuinely alarmed; they decided that revolution was now the only alternative. In order to obtain arms and equipment, however, they needed permission from the Imām to move them from depots outside the city. The revolutionaries, headed by al-Sallāl, who seems to have had the confidence of the Imām,[65] made the most of an unexpected opportunity. The decision to make al-Badr Imām had by no means been accepted by everyone; among the conservative tribal leaders of the north, there was a movment to bring back Ḥasan and make him Imām, and the latter's supporters lost no time in making preparations for his return.

65. It has been argued by one authority that al-Sallāl was an unconscious agent of Jamāl 'Abd al-Nāṣir. His usefulness was due solely to his relationship with al-Badr and the latter's willingness to listen to him. It is likely that this group of revolutionaries had been receiving at least moral support from Cairo, judging from its official reaction to the news of the death of Aḥmad and the accession of al-Badr. At least some truth must be granted to this assertion; al-Sallāl made good use of his friendship with al-Badr in the next few days. See Ingrams, *The Yemen*, p. 122.

Emphasizing the threat that Ḥasan presented to al-Badr and his desire to introduce reforms, al-Sallāl and his fellow plotters were able to convince al-Badr that he should undertake some defensive action against the (largely imagined) threat which his uncle represented. They recommended that sufficient motorized strength to protect the palace from any assault be dispatched to its vicinity. Although wary at first, the new Imām was finally convinced that it would be a wise action to take, and he gave permission for al-Sallāl to transfer some arms and mechanized equipment from the fortress outside Ṣanʿā' closer to the palace.

During the night of September 26, tanks and other armored equipment made their laborious way from al-Urdī to the palace grounds. As soon as they were in position, the plotters started shelling the palace, in which al-Badr was still holding meetings. Because of the location of the palace with respect to the old city walls it was not, however, possible to bombard the building effectively; Imām al-Badr was able to escape from the barrage and make his way north to some loyal tribes.

It is worth pointing out that the revolutionaries of 1962 took their lesson concerning the role of the Imām as a focus of counter-revolution from the experience of their 1955 counterparts, and not from the example of 1948. There was a concerted effort by the press and propaganda media of the now revolutionary Radio Ṣanʿā' as well as those of the U.A.R. to convince the Yemeni population and the world at large that the Imām was, in fact, dead and had not escaped the fate intended for him by the plotters; this remained true even after it had become reliably established that the Imām had, in fact, successfully escaped.

If one is to judge by succeeding events, this was perhaps the logical thing to do; the Imām was soon joined in the mountains of the north by his uncle Ḥasan and by all the members of the royal family who had been able to escape assassination at the hands of the revolutionaries. Although the revolution at first had at least the tacit support of the many tribes who had been alienated by Imām Aḥmad and his policies, this soon changed. Their fierce xenophobia was aroused by the presence of Egyptian troops in support of the Republican regime; moreover, the fact that it was a new Imām, al-Badr, who was actually present and leading the campaign brought many of them back to the cause of the Zaydi Imamate.

PART III: EXTERNAL AFFAIRS

CHAPTER VI

FOREIGN RELATIONS UNDER IMĀM YAḤYĀ

In the field of foreign relations, Imām Yaḥyā saw as his first duty the need to prevent his newly independent state from suffering the fate of the Arab countries of the Levant, that is, administration or occupation by European powers. Consequently, in order to avoid any such foreign interference in Yemen's affairs, he adopted a policy of nearly absolute isolationism. His experiences with the Ottomans had helped to convince him of the need for this policy; their occupation and administration of the country had showed him that foreigners, even those with whom Yemen shared a common religion, could never take an unselfish interest in his country. The Porte's main purpose had been to exploit Yemen and its people for its own benefit. Clearly, any of the European countries could only be worse, for they were not even Muslim. Therefore, all influences of other powers must be prohibited from entering Yemen.

Although Yaḥyā achieved to a remarkable degree his goal of isolationism, gaining thereby considerable stature among the other Arab states, the policy was not wholly feasible. Yemen, like most other states, was not economically self-sufficient and needed to import many items which she did not herself produce: petroleum products, textiles, weapons, and an indispensable minimum of machinery and other manufactured items. In addition to Yemen's economic needs. Yaḥyā had one other goal which took precedence over his desire for insularity: his wish to recapture all those lands which his ancestors had once ruled as a part of a " greater Yemen." These territories extended from the mountains of 'Asīr on the Red Sea, directly north of present-day Yemen, to the coasts of Ḍūfar on the Arabian Sea to the southeast.

Such grandiose ideas of " historic and natural " Yemen led naturally enough to conflicts with the *de facto* rulers of the territories claimed, that is, the small principality of 'Asīr and Saudi Arabia in the north and Great Britain in the south. Because of his conflict with Britain, Imām Yaḥyā sought assistance from another European power—Italy—which was then engaged in commercial and political rivalry with the British in the Red Sea area. Throughout his campaigns to balance the Italians against the British, however, the Imām still managed to keep the influences of these powers negligible in the internal affairs of Yemen.

YEMENI–SAUDI ARABIAN RELATIONS

During the years when nearly the entire Arabian Peninsula formed a portion of the Ottoman Empire, there was no need for exact frontiers between the various subdivisions. The desert terrain and the nomadic way of life of the majority of the inhabitants of the peninsula made the exact delimitation of boundaries difficult and largely unnecessary. At the end of World War I, however, when the Empire was divided among numerous smaller potentates, these formerly irrelevant frontiers took on greater significance, and the lack of any exact boundary between Yemen and the area that later became Saudi Arabia finally resulted in a war between them.

Dispute over 'Asīr

The immediate cause of the conflict was 'Asīr, a small principality immediately north of Yemen on the Red Sea coast. Under the Ottoman Empire, it had been administered as a *qā'immaqāmiyya* within the Wilayat of Yemen, although it was in fact two separate areas governed by different families. The northern portion was ruled by the 'Ā'ids, formerly subject to the Wahhabi rulers of the Najd; the southern portion was ruled by al-Sayyid Muḥammad al-Idrīsī of the Idrīsī house.[1]

The Idrīsī was in almost constant rebellion against the Porte and was often allied with the Imāms of Yemen against Ottoman occupation, even though there were territorial disputes between them. When Yaḥyā achieved autonomy within the Empire, the Idrīsī territories were retained by the Porte, and the Idrīsī persisted alone in his hostility to Ottoman rule. As a result, he became the

1. The family's history extends back to 1837, when al-Sayyid Aḥmad al-Idrīsī, a learned man who founded a religious order, died at Ṣabyā, a town in 'Asīr. In the twentieth century, his descendants, long the spiritual rulers of the population in the area, claimed temporal power in addition to their spiritual authority, taking the title of Amīr of 'Asīr, as well as Imām of the Idrīsī sect.

first Arab ruler to join the Allies during World War I; in April, 1915, he signed an agreement with the British by which they recognized his independence, guaranteed him protection from attack (on his coastal cities), and provided him with a subsidy as well as armaments. At the end of the war, the British demonstrated their appreciation for the Idrīsī's attitude by turning over to him the towns and surrounding territory of al-Ḥudayda and al-Luḥayya, which they had taken from the Empire, but which Imām Yaḥyā believed to be a part of historic Yemen. This action, quite naturally, incensed Yaḥyā, who thereupon planned to regain these territories.[2]

Shortly after the war, the two rulers of ʿAsīr became involved in a dispute. Shaykh Ḥasan ibn ʿĀ'id appealed to Ibn Saʿūd, then Sultan of the Najd, for support; the latter, willing to accept the pretext for expanding his domains, sent his son Fayṣal in 1920 to annex these highland portions of ʿAsīr. The new arrangement was recognized by Muḥammad al-Idrīsī in a treaty drawn up in the same year.[3]

Upon the death of Muḥammad al-Idrīsī, the rule passed to his eldest son, Sayyid ʿAlī, then only eighteen years old, who proved to be a weak and ineffectual ruler. Soon after his accession, Imām Yaḥyā took advantage of this weakness and the internal divisions in the Idrīsī house to annex the entire Tihāma area and its ports as far north as Maydī and also to threaten the cities of Jizān and Ṣabyā. Sayyid ʿAlī fled to Aden, and his uncle, Ḥasan ibn ʿAlī, proclaimed himself the new Imām and Amīr; he appealed to Ibn Saʿūd to support his claim, in accordance with the terms of the 1920 treaty.[4]

The Sultan of Najd was only too happy to have another excuse

2. H. St. John Philby, *Arabia* (New York: Charles Scribner's Sons, 1930), p. 239; Ameen Rihani, *Around the Coasts of Arabia* (London: Constable, 1930), pp. 166–167.

For further historical background of the Idrīsī sect, its connection with the Sanūsī of North Africa, its genealogy, and so on, see al-ʿArshī, *Bulūgh al-Marām*, pp. 105–112; Philby, *Arabian Highlands*, pp. 471–473; Rihani, *Around the Coasts of Arabia*, pp. 149–169.

3. Philby, *Arabia*, p. 276; Saʿīd, *Al-Yaman*, p. 76; Arnold J. Toynbee, *Survey of International Affairs 1925*, Vol. I, *The Islamic World since the Peace Settlement* (London: Oxford University Press, 1927), pp. 320–323; and, especially, A. J. Toynbee, *Survey of International Affairs 1928* (London: Oxford University Press, 1929), p. 320.

4. Toynbee, *Survey 1928*, pp. 319–320.

to extend his own influence in the southwestern corner of the peninsula, and his troops quickly occupied Ṣabyā and Jīzān. Sayyid ʿAlī, however, had not given up his claim to the throne; a civil war ensued, with Imām Yaḥyā now supporting ʿAlī because of the former's fear that the Wahhabi monarch was encroaching on territories he considered to be his own. Wahhabi power carried the day, the Ḥasan al-Idrīsī was established as the ruler of a truncated ʿAsīr.

In so doing, he was forced to accept what amounted to a Saudi protectorate over his territories; the Sultan of Najd, ʿAbd al-ʿAzīz ibn Saʿūd, guaranteed him his throne, his then current frontiers, and full powers of internal administration (but not foreign policy); what remained of the Idrīsī's lands was to be annexed to Ibn Saʿūd's domains upon Ḥasan's death. This agreement was formalized in the Treaty of Makka signed October 21, 1926, between Ibn Saʿūd and Ḥasan.[5]

Relations between Yemen and the Saudi monarch became somewhat strained as a result, but Ibn Saʿūd assured the Imām that he had no intention of recovering the territories lost by the Idrīsī before the date establishing his protectorate; this mollified Yaḥyā to some degree. Nevertheless, the Imām believed that large portions of territory rightfully belonging to him were included in ʿAsīr. He sent out troops occasionally to occupy small villages and valleys on the border between the two countries, causing Ibn Saʿūd to distrust his intentions.

In order to strengthen his legal claim to ʿAsīr, Ibn Saʿūd forced Shaykh Ḥasan to sign a new treaty with him in October, 1930. The Idrīsī was left with nothing except the purely nominal title of sovereign, all of his prerogatives having been taken over by ʿAbd al-ʿAzīz ibn Saʿūd. Ḥasan, as might be expected, began to plot revenge.

His plan was based on co-operation with ʿAbdullāh, the Hāshimite King of Transjordan; together they were to make a two-pronged attack on the Ḥijāz from the north and south, driving out Ibn Saʿūd. During the summer of 1932, the attack from the north was begun under the leadership of Ibn Rifāda, Shaykh of

5. Sharaf al-Dīn, *Al-Yaman*, p. 278; Brémond, *Yémen et Saoudia*, p. 93; Rihani, *Around the Coasts of Arabia*, p. 168.
For the text of this treaty, see Toynbee, *Survey 1925*, pp. 584–586.

the Bālī tribe. The attack was repelled and the tribesmen driven back into Transjordan. Shaykh Ḥasan did not make his move until November. Wahhabi reinforcements rushed into ʿAsīr, and Ḥasan was completely defeated; the Saudi troops occupied Ṣabyā, and the Idrīsī fled to Yemen, which had remained neutral during the conflict.[6]

Saudi-Yemeni War

The Imām intervened with Ibn Saʿūd for Sayyid Ḥasan, and a conference on the matter was held in Maydī in March, 1933. The talks broke down over Yaḥyā's insistence that the Idrīsī be reestablished in his old position. In May, Imām Yaḥyā ordered his troops into ʿAsīr and the Oasis of Najrān, the ownership of which was also disputed between the Wahhabi monarch and Yemen.[7]

Yaḥyā was evidently not interested in any negotiated settlement at the time, for he arrested Ibn Saʿūd's emissaries and held them as hostages. Hostilities between the two sides began about the middle of November, 1933; the fighting was not, however, pursued with much vigor by either army at first, and it was interrupted frequently for further fruitless discussions. On February 17, 1934, representatives of Yemen and Saudi Arabia met in Abhā. There the Saudis listed their conditions for peace. The Imām rejected them immediately and reiterated his claim to both the Oasis of Najrān and ʿAsīr.

In April, Ibn Saʿūd finally decided that he had had enough of Yaḥyā's procrastination and expansionist aims and sent him an ultimatum. At the same time, he ordered his army, under the leadership of his two sons, Saʿūd and Fayṣal, to be deployed and made ready to attack if the ultimatum were not answered within two days. A sandstorm of exceptional violence cut off all wireless communications between the two opposing sides, and the Saudi troops, having received no orders to the contrary, attacked Yemen on April 5.

The Tihāma army, under Fayṣal, encountered only limited resistance and was able to march into al-Ḥudayda within three weeks. The other army, under the command of Crown Prince

6. Sharaf al-Dīn, *Al-Yaman*, pp. 283–284; Brémond, *Yémen et Saoudia*, p. 104; Saʿīd, *Al-Yaman*, p. 84.

7. For background on the Najrān dispute, see al-Jarāfī, *Al-Muqtaṭaf*, p. 244.

Sa'ūd, was hindered in its march by the terrain and made only limited progress toward Ṣan'ā'.

The speed with which Fayṣal had managed to penetrate so far south stirred to action the European powers which had interests in the area. British, Italian, and French warships soon appeared off al-Ḥudayda. The British Arabist H. St. John Philby has claimed at this point, " Ibn Sa'ud had now developed habits of caution entirely out of keeping with the rest of his career . . . (for) Faisal received, with understandable dismay, his father's orders not to advance beyond Hudaida on any account, while Sa'ud was also bidden to remain where he was." [8]

It seems evident, however, that Ibn Sa'ūd's moderation was inspired by the concern which the European powers demonstrated over the possibility of the Wahhabi monarch's controlling the whole of the Arabian Peninsula except for the British Protectorates.

Treaty of Ṭā'if

Although he had previously demanded conditions which were practically identical with those imposed upon Shaykh Ḥasan al-Idrīsī earlier, the Saudi King now changed his mind and declared that the acceptance of the conditions which he had listed at the Conference at Abhā would be sufficient. The Yemenis, whose military inferiority to the Saudis had been dramatically revealed, had already declared their willingness to accept these conditions. Consequently, on May 20, 1934, a " Treaty of Muslim Friendship and Arab Fraternity " was concluded between Yemen and Saudi Arabia, under the watchful eye of a conciliation committee of representatives from other Arab states. The treaty was called the Treaty of Ṭā'if, after the village south of al-Ḥudayda where it was signed. According to its terms, the disputed areas of Najrān and 'Asīr were to become fully incorporated sections of the Saudi Arabian Kingdom.[9]

Although King 'Abd al-'Azīz ibn Sa'ūd's moderation was doubt-

8. H. St. John Philby, *Sa'udi Arabia* (London: Ernest Benn, 1955), p. 323.

9. A complete account of the complex series of events, meetings, negotiations, and agreements which preceded this war over 'Asīr and Najrān has not been attempted here. For further details, see Foreign Ministry of the Government of Sa'ūdī Arabia, *Bayān 'an al-'Ilāqāt bayna al-Mamlaka al-'Arabiyya al-Su'ūdiyya wa al-Imām Yaḥyā Ḥamīd al-Dīn* (Makka: Umm al-Qurā Press, 1934); Brémond, *Yémen et Saoudia*, pp. 97–116; Sharaf al-Dīn, *Al-Yaman*, pp. 276–301; Sa'īd, *Al-Yaman*, pp. 76–113; Philby, *Arabian Jubilee*, pp. 184–188.

less due in this instance to foreign pressure, Imām Yaḥyā attributed it to the King's magnanimity and good will. In assuming this, he had the precedent of Ibn Sa'ūd's genuine disinterestedness and eminently fair decision concerning a minor border dispute of two years earlier.[10]

After the delimitation of the border by a binational commission,[11] relations between the two monarchs were probably the best in the Arab Middle East. Ibn Sa'ūd and Imām Yaḥyā remained on excellent terms,[12] and the good relations between their respective countries outlasted not only the death of Yaḥyā and the accession of Aḥmad but also the death of King 'Abd al-'Azīz in November, 1953. Indeed, their international policies, especially on Arab affairs, may fairly be said to have coincided through the revolution of 1962, which removed Muḥammad al-Badr from temporal power, for it was the Saudi Kingdom which provided the major support for the Royalist side in the ensuing civil war.[13]

YEMENI-BRITISH RELATIONS

Great Britain first occupied Aden in 1839 and soon thereafter began to establish alliances with the various petty rulers of the immediate hinterland of her new possession. Nevertheless, throughout most of the nineteenth century her occupation of these areas seemed temporary. During this period, the anarchic situation in the Yemeni highlands and the later Ottoman occupation prevented the Imāms of Ṣan'ā' and the governors of Aden from dealing directly with one another or obtaining an understanding

10. Quincy Wright, "Arbitration of the Aaroo Mountain," *American Journal of International Law* XXXIII (1939), 356–359; Sa'īd, *Al-Yaman*, p. 82; Philby, *Sa'udi Arabia*, p. 322. Cf. sources in footnote 9, above.

11. Philby, *Arabian Jubilee*, p. 187. For a more complete account of Philby's travels along the new boundary, as well as a description of the make-up of the Boundary Commission and how its decisions were made, see his *Arabian Highlands*, pp. 213–565, *passim*.

12. Nevertheless, Imām Yaḥyā seems to have still believed that 'Asīr belonged to him, for a Yemeni school textbook of 1940 divides Yemen into three areas: (1) independent Yemen, (2) 'Asīr (under Saudi occupation), and (3) Ḥaḍramawt and 'Umān (under British occupation). See Lambardi, "Divisioni amministrative del Yemen," p. 143.

13. But, the Saudi government was notably more receptive to foreign assistance in the development of its domestic resources, especially oil. In addition, both of Ibn Sa'ūd's successors, Sa'ūd and Fayṣal, undertook more active roles than Yemeni rulers on the international scene generally, and in inter-Arab affairs specifically.

of one another's policies, objectives, and character. It was not, therefore, until 1902–1904, when the British and Ottoman authorities co-operated in defining the frontier between their respective spheres of influence, that the Imāms had any real idea of what the objectives of the British were.

The fact that a European power, in occupation of what the Yemenis still considered "the eye of Yemen," now had decided to take it upon itself to establish Yemen's frontiers convinced Imām Yaḥyā that the British wanted to occupy Yemeni soil permanently. During World War I there had been minor contacts between Yemen and Great Britain; these were initiated by the latter as part of its attempt to obtain another Arab ally against the Ottoman Empire. The Imām, however, despite his opposition to the Porte's hegemony, would not ally himself with an infidel against a Muslim state. Because he had been able to make the Porte recognize his autonomy before the war, it is possible that the Imām hoped that the Ottoman Empire would be able to evict the British from Aden and that it would eventually fall under his control.

Situation at the End of the War

After the war, the British and the Yemenis finally faced each other without intermediaries, for the British remained in Aden and Yaḥyā became independent and responsible for the Arab territories north of Aden (Yemen).

According to the terms of the Armistice of Mudros, British troops were permitted to enter areas occupied by Ottoman troops during the war in order to assist and supervise the evacuation of wartime garrisons. After this task was completed, the British turned over some of them, including al-Luḥayya, to their wartime ally, the Idrīsī of ʿAsīr; they temporarily retained, however, the port of al-Ḥudayda—the major port of the old Wilayat.[14] The Imām was particularly annoyed by these actions on the part of the British, for it meant that he was effectively cut off from the sea. Because he felt himself to be in an excellent military position, he was determined to regain these ports.

Great Britain, at the conclusion of hostilities, was officially prepared to recognize Yaḥyā's independence in all internal and

14. Brémond, *Yémen et Saoudia*, p. 89.

external matters concerning the sanjaqs of Taʿizz and Ṣanʿāʾ. But British opinion was divided on the question of how far these territories were to extend. Most officials in Aden apparently believed that when the Ottoman Turks left Yemen, the boundary line established in 1902–1904 was voided and the underlying reason for Britain's treaties with the tribal shaykhs of the interior had also disappeared. These men felt that except for a small strip of hinterland directly behind the port of Aden, the remainder of the Protectorates should be allowed to revert to their previous ruler. In general, the assumption was that they would return to Yemeni suzerainty.

The formulators of English policy did not, however, agree. They decided that the Imām should recognize the 1902–1904 boundary and the special British-protected status of the shaykhs. The Imām was required to recognize these agreements, so the argument went, because as a successor state to the now defunct Ottoman Empire, Yemen automatically became responsible for all treaties which applied to the old Wilayat. While the British were willing to undertake negotiations, these must be preceded by Yaḥyā's recognition of British rights in the Protectorates and the frontier treaty.

It was argued that if Great Britain were to relinquish the Protectorates there might be serious repercussions throughout her colonial empire. Such an action would be tantamount to admitting that the Imām's claims to the territories had always been valid and that England had been in illegal possession of them. It was, therefore, decided that Britain would give consideration to the Imām's claims only if he recognized the old Ottoman frontier and entered into treaty relations of some sort with England.

Assertion of Yemeni Claims

In order to come to some agreement with the Imām, the British in August, 1919, sent Lt. Col. Harold F. Jacob, First Resident Assistant at Aden, with some assistants, from al-Ḥudayda to Ṣanʿāʾ in order that discussions should be held. Jacob had hardly crossed the Tihāma, however, when he was captured by the Quḥra tribe near Bājil and "detained."[15] This incident was final proof to the

15. The Quḥra tribe may have felt that Jacob's mission was in preparation for British occupation of the Tihāma in order to cede their territories to the Imām, a possibility which the Idrīsī had gone to great lengths and expense to present

Imām that he was in a very strong position. He had first seen a small Ottoman and Yemeni force keep the British at bay in Aden throughout the war; then he had seen that the British were incapable of bringing about the release of one of their own diplomats from the hands of one of the minor Tihāma tribes. To the Imām, the Ottoman Turks were a European power, and a strong one at that; yet he and his tribesmen had been able to defeat them, bring them to the bargaining table, and obtain recognition from them of his special position before the war. He concluded, therefore, that the British could be handled with equal ease.

Consequently, in 1919 the Imām's troops invaded a number of frontier districts and principalities of the Western Aden Protectorate: Ḍāliʿ, Quṭayb, Shuʿayb, ʿAlawī, Bilād al-Ajʿūd, and portions of the Amīrī, Upper Yāfiʿī, ʿAwdhalī, and Subayḥī shaykhdoms.[16] Although the Imām sincerely believed that these territories rightly belonged to him, his immediate purpose behind this occupation was to compel the English to release al-Ḥudayda to him.

When the British did evacuate al-Ḥudayda in 1921, however, they ceded it to the Idrīsī. The Imām thereupon concluded that they were unconcerned about the loss of the portions of the Protectorates which his troops had occupied, and he began to establish his own administration in them. Nevertheless, he continued to consider the port of al-Ḥudayda of far greater importance to Yemen than the Protectorate areas. When a neutral observer of the situation visited the Imām in 1922 and attempted to get the Imām and the British to come to some sort of agreement, he found Yaḥyā willing to agree to a trade with the English —the port of al-Ḥudayda in exchange for the territories he had occupied.[17]

The British, when this proposition was relayed to them, seemed

---

in its worst light. The Imām, somewhat embarrassed, sent the former Wālī, Maḥmūd Nadīm, to intercede. As a result of negotiations, 4,000 Turkish pounds, and the gift of some horses, he was able to secure Jacob's release. Jacob returned to al-Ḥudayda empty-handed after four months. See Harold F. Jacob, *The Kings of Arabia* (London: Mills and Boon, 1923), pp. 202–225.

16. Al-Wāsiʿī, *Tārīkh al-Yaman*, p. 262; al-ʿArshī, *Bulūgh al-Marām*, pp. 92–93; al-Jarāfī, *Al-Muqtaṭaf*, p. 227; Toynbee, *Survey 1928*, p. 312; M. V. Seton-Williams, *Britain and the Arab States* (London: Luzac, 1948), pp. 197–198.

17. Ameen Rihani, " Ibn Saud und Imam Jahia," *Europäische Gespräche*, VII, No. 7 (July, 1929), 342.

unable to decide on which, if any, course of action to take. Their inaction and indecision further convinced the Imām of the strength of his position. While the British procrastinated, Yaḥyā attacked and succeeded in occupying the entire Tihāma region and ejected the Idrīsī from Yemen. As a result, he now held al-Ḥudayda and the portions of the Protectorate. To the British, the Yemeni occupation of the Tihāma and its ports undoubtedly proved to be an economic blow, for some of the trade with Yemen which formerly passed through Aden was now diverted to these ports. Primarily, however, it was a political blow, for it considerably reduced the territory of their old ally, the Idrīsī, who was soon to fall victim to Sa'ūdī claims to 'Asīr. No official British protests were heard, however.

Negotiations

The English authorities were still determined to obtain the Imām's recognition of their position and now decided to try to achieve this goal through diplomacy. After several British negotiating teams had gone to Yemen without results, the Ambassador to Saudi Arabia, Sir Gilbert Clayton, was dispatched to Ṣan'ā' in 1926. The Imām, displaying a willingness to negotiate, welcomed him.

The British, for the first time since the occupation of the Protectorate territories six years before, now demanded that Yemen evacuate all the land which she had occupied since the close of the war.[18] The Imām refused and offered essentially the same terms that he had proposed in past talks; he would consent to British retention of the port and its immediate hinterland as long as friendly relations were maintained between his country and Britain. He also would consent to a continuation of the *status quo* in those Protectorate areas which the British considered essential to their interests in the port of Aden, provided that the inhabitants of these areas were guaranteed freedom and security of communications and allowed to act " with justice," that is, apply and obey the Sharī'a. He agreed not to send troops into Laḥij, another border state, and other districts which were unoccupied, but he refused to withdraw from those which he already occupied.[19]

18. Jacob, *The Kings of Arabia*, p. 240; al-'Arshī, *Bulūgh al-Marām*, pp. 93–94, 226 ff.; Toynbee, *Survey 1928*, p. 312.
19. Jacob, *The Kings of Arabia*, p. 240; Ingrams, *The Yemen*, p. 65.

H. St. John Philby is undoubtedly correct when he says the Imām was seeking

> from the British Government the cession of Dhali' and other parts of the Aden Protectorates of which he was in *de facto* possession as a *quid pro quo* for the desired friendly agreement, and it would perhaps have been politic on the part of the British Government to have given up an area which was, and is, of no practical value to it, in return for friendly relations which would have had some moral, if not material value.[20]

Britain refused to recognize the ancestral claim of the Zaydi Imāms to the territories included in the Protectorates.[21] Yaḥyā was unwilling to negotiate on what he considered to be his legal right, and the Clayton mission ended in failure.

THE AGREEMENT WITH ITALY

After the unsuccessful termination of these talks, Yaḥyā turned his attention to searching for foreign powers to help him in his dispute with Great Britain. He first attempted to obtain Turkish support for his position, but when this failed, the Imām was forced to look farther afield for assistance.[22] In 1926, he con-

20. Philby, *Arabia*, p. 334.

21. The legitimacy of the Imām's claim to all the Protectorates as part of "historic Yemen" naturally contains some flaws. Whatever the situation may have been in pre-Islamic and early Islamic times, certainly the medieval Imāms rarely ever managed to control these areas effectively. Until the seventeenth century, the Zaydi Imāms were largely confined to their historic seat at Ṣa'da where the first Rassī Imām is buried. During the period after the first departure of the Ottomans, the Imāms did not control all the areas they claimed. Portions of the territories over which they had been the accepted sovereigns declared themselves independent by the early eighteenth century. Nevertheless, despite the legal validity or invalidity of their claims, the important fact was that the Imāms seriously entertained these ideas and acted on them. The purpose of this study is not to decide whether the claims of the Zaydi Imāms were historically accurate; it is an attempt to explain the behavior of the Imāms in the twentieth century.

For a short summary of the history of the Zaydi claims, see Toynbee, *Survey 1928*, pp. 310–312.

22. In 1923 and again in 1936, the Imām sent special envoys to the Grand Assembly in Ankara declaring his loyalty to the Turks and requesting assistance. The Turks were far too busy with other problems to concern themselves with Yemen and gently ignored the Imām's communications. See al-Wāsi'ī, *Tārīkh al-Yaman*, p. 277; al-'Arshī, *Bulūgh al-Marām*, p. 96; Brémond, *Yémen et Saoudia*, p. 90.

sented to receive the Italian Governor of Eritrea, and before the year was out Italy and Yemen had signed a Treaty of Friendship and Commerce.[23]

This treaty was the first recognition by a European power of the " full and absolute independence of Yemen," as well as Imām Yaḥyā's position as King. Because it was signed while Yemen was in possession of the disputed areas of the Aden Protectorates, Yemenis have since argued that the treaty implied Italian recognition of their right to these territories. In signing this treaty, Italy may very well have meant to recognize Yemen's claim to all the lands it then occupied, for the actions of the Italian government at this time were most certainly undertaken with the intention of decreasing or containing British influence in the area near the Red Sea where Italy itself had colonial ambitions.

The Imām was delighted that he had succeeded in finding a European ally to aid him in his conflict with Britain and hoped that by emphasizing his friendship with the Italians he would be able to obtain a better bargain from the former. In 1927, Italy's pre-eminence among the European powers in influence in Yemen was marked by a visit by Sayf al-Islam Muḥammad, Qāḍī Muḥammad Rāghib ibn Rafīq, and other Yemeni officials to Rome in order to meet Benito Mussolini. As a result of this visit, a supplementary aid agreement was negotiated, in which Italy agreed to give Yemen economic and technical aid, as well as arms and other military equipment, including aircraft.

23. Italian interest in the Red Sea area extends back into the nineteenth century, when Italy first established itself on the east African coast and finally occupied Eritrea, directly across the Red Sea from Yemen. Although its actual acquisitions were located exclusively on the African continent, Italy's explorers and commercial agents were also busy on the Arabian Peninsula, and the Italian government's representatives in Eritrea were well aware of the importance which Yemen could play as a result of its strategic location. The Civil Commissioners of Eritrea had for many years recruited Yemenis for their army and as laborers, and throughout much of the Ottoman occupation the Italians maintained strong consular representation in Yemen.

During World War I, the Imām had good reason to be suspicious of the Italians, who during their Libyan campaigns allied themselves with the Idrīsī because of their exaggerated idea of the connection between the Idrīsī movment in 'Asīr and the Sanusī movement in Libya. After this cause for friction was eliminated by the waning of Idrīsī power, Italian influence with the Imām increased as Italy undertook a campaign to cultivate his friendship in order to retain its influence in the eastern Red Sea coast. Imām Yaḥyā, for his part, was happy to listen to Italian overtures, for he was much more concerned about British penetration into what he considered his rightful sphere of influence than he was about the Italians.

The understanding between the Italians and Yemenis did not, however, override the Imām's basic prejudice against having permanent foreign diplomatic representatives in his country. Consequently, Italy had to use other means for extending its influence inside Yemen, and soon Italian technicians, engineers, and other professional men, particularly doctors, were found in large numbers in the capital and other cities.[24] Many of these men had strong political convictions and worked to spread Italian Fascist ideas in the country in order to establish a political atmosphere sympathetic to the commercial and political aims of Mussolini in that part of the world.[25]

BRITISH COUNTERMEASURES

Worried by the Imām's new alliance with the Italians and the latter's increased interest in the Red Sea, the British finally decided to act more decisively with respect to Yemeni occupation of parts of the Protectorates. They would first force the Imām's troops out of these areas and then renew negotiations for a settlement.

In the spring of 1928, the defense of Aden was transferred to the hands of the Royal Air Force, which set out to "restore British prestige" in the area by evicting the Imām's troops. A rash of minor hostilities had broken out, and the R.A.F. used these as an excuse to bombard occupied towns and villages as well as cities actually in Yemen. These attacks proved very effective, and by late 1928 the Imām had evacuated all but minor pieces of territory on the southern side of the 1902–1904 frontier.[26]

24. Cesare Ansaldi, the first doctor sent to Ṣan'ā' in 1929, established the first modern hospital there and became, in addition, the personal physician of the Imām. See Ansaldi, *Il Yemen*. He was later replaced by Dr. Emilio Dubbiosi, who was followed by Dr. Passera. Other members of the medical staff of the Missione Sanitaria Italiana a San'a during the nineteen-thirties were: Dr. Luigi Merucci, Dr. Carlo Toffolon, Dr. Deferri, Dr. T. Sarnelli, Dr. Vittorio Rossi, Dr. Danino, Dr. Favetti; many of the latter also wrote about their own experiences in Yemen, or the results of research which they undertook at the time, for medical and other journals.

25. There is little doubt that, despite their politics, these medical men were conscientious workers, and not virulent propagandists. Although they tried to influence many army officers, they are best known for their introduction of smallpox vaccination and the good reputation which they created among the people of Yemen for European medicine in general.

26. Bernard Reilly, *Aden and the Yemen* (London: Her Majesty's Stationery Office, 1960), pp. 20–21; J. A. Chamier, "Air Control of Frontiers," *Journal of*

New Negotiations

The Imām, although at a loss to understand British policy, again indicated a willingness to open negotiations. He wrote to his friend Colonel Jacob that he still hoped for an honorable redress of his grievances and sent a representative to Aden for preliminary talks. The Resident at Aden was given power to negotiate with the Imām on the basis that the latter recognize the old Anglo-Turkish frontier, in which case Britain would recognize the independence of Yemen. Negotiations dragged on, marred periodically by small border incidents, all to no avail.

By 1930, the British were again convinced of the necessity of coming to some agreement with the Imām. The Soviet Union had recognized Yemen in 1928, and the loss of prestige and trade which Britain felt she was suffering as a result of increased Soviet and Italian interests in Yemen led once more to the dispatch of Lt. Col. Jacob to Ṣan'ā'.[27]

---

the Royal Central Asian Society, XXI, Pt. 3 (July, 1934), 407–408; al-'Arshī, *Bulūgh al-Marām*, pp. 188–190; al-Jarāfī, *Al-Muqtaṭaf*, p. 239; Brémond, *Yémen et Saoudia*, p. 100.

27. In early 1928, when relations with Great Britain were severely strained over the situation in the Protectorates, Yemeni officials sought out the Soviet representative in the Ḥijāz, asking that diplomatic and commercial relations between the two countries be established.

As a result, G. A. Astakhov and other Soviet officials arrived in al-Ḥudayda in May (1928), followed soon after by an additional Soviet ship carrying a variety of goods. On November 1, 1928, a ten-year Treaty of Commerce and Friendship was signed; after the exchange of ratifications in June of 1929, Yemeni-Soviet trade relations were established on a regular basis.

The Soviets enjoyed an immediate success in their trade with Yemen, due no doubt to their artificially low prices. As far as the Yemenis were concerned, the treaty had its desired effect: it caused considerable concern in Great Britain (and the Western countries generally). By 1931, the amount of Soviet goods supplied to Yemen totaled almost 22,000 tons, consisting of such items as kerosene, sugar, soap, timber, flour, cement, and agricultural and other heavy machinery.

The Soviet Union also began to provide medical aid, and initial steps toward the establishment of cultural relations were taken. These seem to have been fruitful, for Soviet sources report that a Soviet film unit made a motion picture in the country in 1929.

By the middle nineteen-thirties, however, Soviet interest appeared to have waned. Their only representative in Yemen was a woman doctor, F. Yaskolko; the trade mission and all other officials had already returned to the Soviet Union. It has been reported that a connection with the " purges " of the mid-nineteen-thirties may be responsible; however, whether the failure of these missions to achieve more notable results led to the imprisonment (and perhaps death) of the officials involved, or whether the " purges " eliminated the officials responsible for imple-

Jacob found the Imām still hoping for successful negotiations. However, the Imām would not agree that Britain's claim to the Protectorates was stronger than his. In Imām Yaḥyā's view (based on Zaydi belief), he could not relinquish or alienate any territory; this would constitute an impairment of his religious authority and his sovereignty. However, the Imām was willing to adhere to the *status quo* without future hostilities, if England agreed to do the same. More specifically, "He [the Imām] asked for formal recognition of his proprietary and reversionary rights in the Yemen, including Aden . . . [and] asked the immediate privilege of appointing kadis, or magistrates, to dispose of all *religious* matters in these areas." [28] This implied an acknowledgment of the Imām's religious suzerainty over the Protectorate states, as well as his right to levy the *zakat* (alms) and some recognition of his claims to the Protectorates as a whole.

Colonel Jacob advised the Imām that Great Britain could not sanction this, for it had no such jurisdiction, although Jacob also points out in his book that "for many years past our proteges, when aggrieved with the rulings of their own kadis, had repaired to the Arab Appellate Courts at Zabid or Dhu Jibla, lying across the Anglo-Turkish border." [29]

Jacob advised the Imām also that all claims on Aden itself were impractical and that he should reduce his demands somewhat. As a result of Jacob's advice, the Imām mitigated them to the extent that the British Government need only recognize his reversionary rights to the Protectorates. In the view of the British, the Imām had not yet limited the amount or character of his prerogatives sufficiently to satisfy their requirements, and again nothing came of the talks.

Division in British Opinion

Colonel Jacob was deeply disappointed. It was his opinion that most of the Imām's demands could be met with little difficulty

---

menting the original policy, has not been established. (Soviet interest was, of course, later revived: see below, Chap. VII, "Agreements with 'the Bloc.'")

A. Ye. Ioffe, "Early Soviet Contacts with Arab and African Countries," *Narody Azii i Afriki*, No. 6 (1965), pp. 57–66, as quoted and translated in *The Mizan Newsletter*, VIII, No. 2 (March–April, 1966), 89–90.

28. Harold F. Jacob, "The Kingdom of Yemen: Its Place in the Comity of Nations," *Transactions of the Grotius Society*, XVIII, *Problems of Peace and War* (1933), 141–142.

29. *Ibid.*, p. 142.

and that the British position in the Protectorates was pointless, expensive, and illogical.

The primary arguments of those British officials who favored the retention of the Protectorates were: (1) the British government could not break faith with its "protégés," that is, the various tribal shaykhs with whom it was in treaty relations and to whom it paid an annual subsidy; and (2) the division between the Shī'a Zaydis and the Sunni Shāfi'īs was irreconcilable, and therefore there was no point in subjecting the predominantly Shāfi'ī Protectorates to the domination of a Zaydi overlord. It is also likely that many of the British were unalterably opposed to relinquishing any portion of the Empire per se and used the above reasons as rationalizations.

Jacob, in his discussion of British policy at the time, legitimately points out the fallacious logic behind the first reason. Great Britain had done little or nothing in the Protectorates since 1839; it had not even managed to establish a minimum of public security there. In one of the few instances in which Britain had attempted to guarantee the safety of the caravan routes, the Imām had been so delighted that he sent a telegram of congratulations.[30]

The policy of dealing with the innumerable petty shaykhs was in itself pointless, for

> It is the tribesmen who plan tribal policy, and not the tribal shaykhs, who are figure heads, and are often deposed. The tribesmen have never adequately shared the benefits of the doles paid by Aden. If, as has been mooted, certain engagements with our proteges may be revised, and the doles which we give decreased, we shall see dissatisfied tribesmen going over to the Imam. Before, during, and after the Great War several of them have corresponded with Sana to get better terms. It is our doles, not ourselves that allure the proteges, and an idle dream to believe that an Arab prefers British rule to that of a Moslem King.[31]

Jacob went on to point out that

30. However, when the same tribe again interfered with legitimate commerce, the British advised the aggrieved merchants to find another route to take. "The Imam, in similar circumstances, would have planted a punitive force there, and quickly restored order." *Ibid.*, pp. 143–144.

31. *Ibid.*, p. 139.

> [This] protection of ours is not wholly pleasing to these tribesmen, except in so far as it prevents their coming under the sway of an Arab ruler who would enforce taxation.[32]

At the time of his writing, Jacob said that the British government had not as yet conquered the Protectorates and claimed that it did not desire to annex the area, did not wish to expend the men nor money in order to administer it properly, and yet was unwilling to give it up to the Imām.

The argument on religious grounds has, on the surface, more merit. It should be added, however, that the differences between the Sunnis and Shīʿas in south Arabia are less important than in other areas. Aden had been under the Government of India, where there also existed a Sunni-Shīʿa split within the Islamic community, and, as a result, many of its administrators applied their experiences in India to the situation in Aden. Consequently, the religious differences between the two sects were sometimes overemphasized by British officials in Aden.

Jacob's arguments produced no change of viewpoint either in London or Aden, and the recommendations he made were not accepted. His main point, that the Imām's claims "to the Yemen as a whole would materialize *only* if, and when, we should have abandoned the country," was ignored.[33]

Anglo-Yemeni Treaty of 1934

While Yaḥyā was advancing his claims to the Protectorates in the south, he had also begun to extend his authority in the north and northeastern border areas: ʿAsīr and the Oasis of Najrān. Here he encountered increasingly determined opposition from King ʿAbd al-ʿAzīz ibn Saʿūd of Saudi Arabia. Imām Yaḥya's knowledge of the effectiveness and power of British forces (especially the R.A.F.) made him aware of the dangers of fighting a war on two fronts at the same time. In order to avoid this, he realized he would have to come to some sort of an agreement with one or the other of his opponents.

> Great Britain was obviously far more powerful than the Arab Bedouin King of Saudi Arabia, against whom the

32. *Ibid.*

33. Jacob, "The Kingdom of the Yemen," p. 142. For Jacob's views on the treaty with Yemen, see pp. 131–153, *passim.*

> Imam felt he had a reasonable chance of success if it came to hostilities. . . . Great Britain, therefore, would have to be placated, at least temporarily, and this could only be done by putting his claims to the Aden Protectorate into cold storage, which he proceeded to do and he approved a draft of the Treaty to be negotiated at Sana and welcomed the Mission led by Sir Bernard Reilly to conduct the negotiations, which were brought to a satisfactory conclusion in 1934.[34]

The "satisfactory conclusion" was the Treaty of Friendship and Mutual Cooperation, signed on February 11, 1934, by Sir Bernard and Qāḍī Muḥammad Rāghib ibn Rafīq.[35]

This treaty was to be of great importance in future Anglo-Yemeni relations and for an understanding of the foreign policy of the Yemeni Imāms after its signing. It consists of seven articles, and much of its content is devoted to definitions. Article 7 sets its life at a period of forty years and provides that, should there be doubts concerning the interpretation of any portion of the treaty, the two parties will rely on the Arabic text. It is Article 3 which has caused immense controversy and much misunderstanding and is, therefore, worth quoting in full:

> The settlement of the question of *the southern frontier* of the Yemen is deferred pending the conclusion, in whatever way may be agreed upon by both high contracting parties in a spirit of friendship and complete concord, free from any dispute or difference, of the negotiations which shall take place between them before the expiry of the period of the present treaty.
>
> Pending the conclusion of the negotiations referred to in the preceding paragraph, *the high contracting parties agree to maintain the situation existing in regard to the frontier on the date of the signature of this treaty*, and both high contracting parties undertake that they will prevent, by all means at their disposal, any violation by their forces of the above-

34. Hickinbotham, *Aden*, p. 69.

35. Great Britain, *Parliamentary Papers, 1934*, Treaty Series, No. 34, Cmd. 4752; as quoted in J. C. Hurewitz, *Diplomacy in the Near and Middle East* (2 vols.; Princeton: D. van Nostrand, 1956), II, 196–197. The Arabic text may be found in: al-'Arshī *Bulūgh al-Marām*, pp. 234–236; Fakhrī, *Al-Yaman*, pp. 191–193; Sa'īd, *Al-Yaman*, pp. 72–74; Sharaf al-Dīn, *Al-Yaman*, pp. 320–322.

> mentioned frontier, and any interference by their subjects, or from the side of that frontier, with the affairs of the people inhabiting the other side of the said frontier.[36]

The Arabic text of the treaty uses the word *ḥudūd* where the English text uses " frontier," and the difficulties which have arisen over this treaty are based on the interpretation given to these two words.

In Arabic the word *ḥudūd* is the plural of *ḥadd*, which although it commonly has the same meaning as frontier in English, has a different concept at its root. The Arabic root Ḥ-D-D from which the word for frontier is derived means to hone or sharpen, and therefore secondarily to delineate or mark off, demarcate. The noun *ḥadd* means the edge of a sword or knife, the sharpness of which is all-important. But this edge itself is nearly invisible. Consequently, Arab thought on the subject of delimitation concentrates on the area between two opposing forces, not the line itself. Western concepts of territorial sovereignty, however, concentrate on the actual frontier which separates the domains of two countries or rivals.

A perfectly logical and valid reading of the Arabic text of the treaty, specifically those portions italicized above, would be: " the question of the southern Yemeni area." Should there be any doubt about whether to read the text in this way, the opening article could be referred to in order to dispel any remaining doubts: " the King of Great Britain . . . acknowledges the complete and absolute independence of His Majesty the King of Yemen, the Imam, *and his kingdom* " (emphasis added). The addition of these words is normally unnecessary according to Western concepts of sovereignty, wherein the word *king* alone implies a kingdom or area over which the king is in fact sovereign. Moreover, the Arabic word *mamlaka* has the additional connotations of empire, as well as royal power or sovereignty.

Consequently, the Yemenis and Imām Yaḥyā read the treaty as they wished; to them it meant that the status quo of the regions on the old Anglo-Turkish frontier separating independent Yemen from the Protectorates would be maintained. The fact that there was nowhere in the treaty a specific renunciation of the Imām's claim to sovereignty over these areas—indeed, there was an implied

36. Hurewitz, *Diplomacy*, pp. 196–197. (Emphasis added.)

recognition of it—only served to strengthen this belief. The British, on the other hand, read the text to mean specifically the frontier which had been demarcated between the former Ottoman Wilayat of Yemen and their Protectorate areas.

The fact that an article so loosely worded was permitted to pass and be ratified by both parties concerned indicates the depth of the disagreement between them. The vague wording permitted each side to interpret the article in question as it desired and then later to base its attitude and policies on this interpretation.

Great Britain's Forward Policy

Administratively, Aden and that portion of its hinterland under British control had been under the Government of India Office (The Bombay Presidency) ever since 1839. Because of a number of changes affecting India and its subdivisions, the lines of command and responsibility with respect to Aden became confused and contradictory, and it was decided to remedy this situation. The first steps for the removal of Aden from India's jurisdiction were taken in 1928. In 1937, a British Order in Council put Aden and the Protectorates under the direct control of the Colonial Office in London; the port of Aden became a Crown Colony, and the Protectorates became a part of the Colony for administrative purposes.[37]

From the point of view of the British Government, the Order in Council and its effects on the new Colony were the natural result of political evolution. In fact, however, it indicated an awareness of the delicate political situation which existed in the Red Sea area (where Italian influence was steadily increasing) and a realization that if they were going to be able to keep this area under their " protection " and jurisdiction, the British would have to take some measures to create a peaceful internal situation.

Insufficient funds and staff had prevented the small group of political officers in Aden from ever establishing internal security in the Protectorates. Tribal wars were handled on a purely *ad hoc* basis, and, indeed, it was not even considered worthwhile to fully administer the hinterland until 1934, when the treaty was signed with Yemen. At that time, the Imām is said to have asked pointedly

37. Herbert J. Liebesny, " Administration and Legal Development in Arabia: Aden Colony and Protectorate," *The Middle East Journal*, IX, No. 4 (Autumn, 1955), 385–388.

whether the British intended to take any steps toward protection of travelers and commerce in the Protectorates. Undoubtedly uppermost in his mind was the fact that much of Yemen's trade passed through Aden, and now that he was in treaty relations with Britain, it should do its part in assuring the safety of his trade when it passed through British-controlled territories. The fact was that once caravans passed the last Yemeni police post, they entered "the most dangerous part of Arabia," for there was an almost total lack of security in the Protectorates.[38]

The major British negotiator, Sir Bernard Reilly, promised the Imām that something would be done about the security of the trade routes, and this pledge was apparently interpreted by the British to mean that they "were committed to a forward policy of the protection of travellers who passed through tribal territory." [39] Ironically, it was precisely because of this need for public security and the protection of legitimate commerce that some Englishmen had advocated giving these tribal areas to the Imām. Such an action would spare Britain the expense of (1) subsidies needed to pay off marauding tribesmen and rebellious shaykhs and (2) training the personnel and purchasing the equipment needed to do such a large policing job effectively.

In 1937, the British government began a campaign to achieve a truce among some 1,300 to 1,400 tribes, clans, and other tribal subdivisions whose feuding had disturbed conditions in the Eastern Aden Protectorate for as long as anyone could remember.[40] Once this step was accomplished, the British began to appoint political officers for the Protectorates, whose duties and functions were outlined in the special treaties which the various shaykhs signed with the British. These political officers were to provide "advice" on all matters except those concerning the Muslim religion, that is, on economic improvements, agriculture, health, communications, and the like, but especially in the training of tribesmen for security forces under the command of British officers.[41]

Although Yaḥyā is said to have originally intimated to the British that they should establish a minimum of public security

38. Hamilton, *The Kingdom of Melchior*, pp. 58–59.

39. *Ibid.*, p. 59.

40. The justly famous "Ingrams' Peace," named after Harold Ingrams, the man responsible for its establishment. See Ingrams, *Arabia and the Isles*, pp. 223–311.

41. Liebesny, "Administration," pp. 388–389; Reader Bullard, ed., *The Middle East* (3rd ed.; London: Oxford University Press, 1958), p. 103.

in their districts so that commerce could pass between the city of Aden and Yemen unimpeded by banditry, he regarded the measures which they took in the Eastern Protectorate, far from the Yemeni-Aden trade routes, as completely unjustified. In his view, the establishment of public security was permissible; but the British, by setting up an administration and appointing political officers, had directly contravened the terms of the Treaty of 1934. The Imām construed these activities as an attempt to change "the situation existing in regard to the frontier." The fact that the British had, in the meantime, radically increased their estimate of the size of the Protectorates from 9,000 square miles to "approximately 42,000 square miles" considerably disturbed the Imām and reinforced his belief that the "frontier situation" had been violated.[42]

The British were aware of the Imām's attitude toward their "forward policy," but chose to ignore it. In the process, they sacrificed any good will which the Imām may have had toward the British position in Aden. Great Britain undoubtedly felt that her national interest and world commitments, particularly her investments in the Far East, demanded surer control of the districts around Aden, especially in view of the prewar situation in the Red Sea area. At the same time, it would seem that British policy makers hoped that if they were to provide for proper internal security and administration in these areas, the tribes might lose one of the primary reasons for preferring the Imām's rule. Great Britain might even be able to get the tribes to join in a loose confederation if they saw the benefits of "enlightened" British rule.[43]

The Imām was aware of the potential consequences of organized administration in the Protectorates and was determined that the new British policy should not succeed. He immediately set about creating disturbances in those areas in which Britain had recently signed the new truces and treaties—the northern Ḥaḍramawt and

42. *The Statesman's Yearbook* (London: Macmillan). Cf. the data given for the size of the Protectorates in the years 1918–1931 and those given for the years 1932–1939. There is not a single work by any of the British colonial officers during this period which admits or attempts to explain this astounding growth in the size of the Protectorates.

43. The idea of tribal confederation had been broached earlier and soon abandoned as being unattainable, considering the state of affairs which existed at the time. See *The Times* (London), March 17, 1931. The same idea was again suggested in 1954, when another federation scheme was announced.

the Shabwa district; he seemed particularly concerned about the latter, for he vigorously maintained that its status had not been decided by the old Border Commission and that it was unquestionably located within the confines of Yemen.[44] These incidents were the first of the type of frontier disputes which characterized Anglo-Yemeni relations until the revolution of September, 1962.

The pattern for future negotiations and discussions between the two parties on incidents such as these is seen in this first example. An Aden Frontier Officer was dispatched to Ṣan'ā' in order to negotiate with the Imām over the settlement of the dispute. The Imām insisted upon his legitimate rights, claiming first that the disputed area had always been under Yemeni suzerainty, and second that the British had violated the terms of the 1934 treaty by attempting to change the existing situation "on the frontier." The mission proved futile, although the commerce of the region was resumed. As was to happen so many times in the future, both sides agreed to negotiate on a specific incident, reiterated their previous positions, refused to compromise their positions; and the talks came to nought.

WARTIME FOREIGN RELATIONS

The outbreak of World War II produced greater willingness on the part of Great Britain to consider the Yemeni side of the issue, and the "forward policy" was temporarily put into abeyance. Britain was forced to take the political effect of Italian propaganda into account in her dealings with the shaykhs and tribes of the Protectorate, as well as with the Imām, for any untoward incident was considerably magnified by Italian broadcasts and redounded to the discredit of Great Britain.

When the war started, Yemen declared her neutrality, despite her recent renewal of the treaty with Italy, because of her dependence on overland shipment from Aden for the bulk of her imports. But it would seem reasonable that Imām Yaḥyā's sympathies lay with the Axis powers for most of the war, in the hope that somehow the British would be evicted from Aden by an Axis victory.

Aware of the increasing Italian influence inside Yemen, the British decided in the late nineteen-thirties to offset this propa-

44. Ingrams, *Arabia and the Isles*, pp. 292 ff.; D. van der Meulen, *Aden to the Hadhramaut* (London: John Murray, 1947), pp. 94 ff.; Hamilton, *The Kingdom of Melchior*, pp. 127 ff.

ganda advantage. An opportunity was presented by the request of the Imām for an eye specialist, and in 1937 the Aden government arranged with the Church of Scotland Medical Mission in Shaykh 'Uthmān to send a medical mission to Ṣan'ā'.[45] Later, in 1940, after repeated requests to the Imām for permission, Miss Freya Stark was allowed to travel to Ṣan'ā', where she carried on an active anti-Fascist, anti-Italian campaign. Although Miss Stark claims to have smuggled her projector and films into Yemen, the Imām was aware of her intentions, and there can be no doubt that unless he had approved of her mission, she would never have obtained entry to the country.[46] Consequently, it is apparent that the Imām was conscious of the disturbed political situation in the world, and he at least wished to have both sides of the dispute heard.

Although Italian propaganda was able to influence British policy with respect to Yemen and the Protectorates, it was less successful in Yemen itself. The Italians never succeeded in wholly swaying the Imām's policy in their favor, and he even actively discouraged their attempts to recruit Yemenis for service in the armies of Somaliland and Eritrea, probably because of the economic pressure which the British were able to exert.[47] He continued to treat individual Italians with special consideration, how-

45. This mission, headed by Dr. P. W. R. Petrie, who was accompanied by his wife, remained in Yemen until 1943. Dr. Petrie, under his own name and the pseudonym William Robertson, wrote a number of interesting articles on his experiences. (See the bibliography.)

46. Freya Stark, *East Is West* (London: John Murray, 1945), pp. 22–34; Freya Stark, *Dust in the Lion's Paw* (London: John Murray, 1961), pp. 17–40.

47. Indeed, the Italian successes in Eritrea and Ethiopia (and in the League of Nations as well) were probably the major reason for Imām Yaḥyā's decision to sign the Treaty of Arab Brotherhood and Alliance on April 29, 1937.

Concerned that Italy had become the major power in the Red Sea area, the Imām cast about for a new ally. Unwilling to turn to Great Britain, the Imām accepted the one offer of friendship available to him—the recently signed (April 2, 1936) Arab Treaty between Iraq and Saudi Arabia. Article 6 of this treaty read: " Yaman, brother in religion and language, shall be invited to adhere to the Pact, which is also open to all independent Arab states."

King 'Abd al-'Azīz ibn Sa'ūd, after settling his dispute with the Imām, had embarked on a campaign to improve his relations with all the principalities and states which bordered his realm. As part of his program to become the rallying point of pan-Arab sentiment, he had visited Baḥrayn, Kuwait, and finally Iraq. As a result of his efforts, the Treaty of Arab Brotherhood and Alliance, which pledged mutual assistance against aggression by a foreign country (Article 4), had been signed. Yemen, the only other independent Arab country at the time, had been invited to join from the outset. The Imām, however, hesitated, for at first

ever, receiving many of them as they fled from the British occupation of Ethiopia, Eritrea, and Somaliland in 1941.[48]

By 1942, the British position in the Red Sea area was very much improved, and their concern over Italian propaganda lessened considerably. It was only after the defeat of Field Marshal Rommel's forces in North Africa that the Imām decided that the Axis powers were not going to be the victors. On February 26, 1943, he finally ordered the arrest and internment of all Italians and Germans who had been operating on Yemeni soil, as well as the severance of diplomatic relations with the Axis states—a largely symbolic gesture.[49]

Throughout the war, the border between Yemen and the Protectorates had remained quiescent. Only one relatively serious incident took place in 1943–1944, when the Yemeni government posted a small force on the Protectorate side of the frontier near the sea opposite Perim, an island in the straits governed by Aden. Negotiations followed, and the Imām succeeded in prolonging them for over sixteen months while he tried to obtain the support of the United States, Egypt, and Saudi Arabia. He eventually withdrew his troops, but only after an ultimatum had been issued by the British.[50]

Once the Italian threat in the Red Sea area had disappeared and its position was assured, Great Britain continued with its "forward policy" in the Protectorates. During the years 1944 and 1945, five of the states of the Western Aden Protectorate agreed by "advisory treaties" to accept the "advice of the Governor of Aden" on administrative affairs: the Faḍlī, Lower Awlāqī, Lower Yāfi'ī, as well as the Sharīf of Bayḥān and the Amīr of Dāli'.[51]

he saw no purpose to his accession. It was undoubtedly the actions of the Italians during the years 1935–1936 that finally brought about his signing in the spring of 1937.

48. One prominent example was an Italian officer, Amadeo Guillet, who took charge of the Imām's cavalry and became his intimate friend, receiving the Arabic name of 'Abdullāh al-Radā'ī. After the war, he became Italian Minister to Yemen and was Italian Ambassador to Jordan in the early nineteen-sixties.

49. *The Statesman's Yearbook*, 1944, p. 704.

50. Reilly, *Aden and the Yemen*, pp. 23–24.

51. Liebesny, "Administration," pp. 389–390; Doreen Ingrams, *A Survey of Social and Economic Conditions in the Aden Protectorate* (Eritrea: The Government Printer for the British Administration, 1949), pp. 170–172 (the text of the Bayḥān agreement is given on pp. 178–179); *The Middle East 1963* (10th ed.; London: Europa Publications, 1963), p. 59.

By the time World War II had come to a close in Europe and the Far East, Imām Yaḥyā had aged considerably and was no longer able to direct a concerted effort against the latest British "changes" in the status and size of the Protectorates.[52] The British, however, had good cause to mourn the passing of Yaḥyā, for after the brief civil war which raged in Yemen upon his death, his son and successor Aḥmad was to take up the Yemeni campaign to regain the Protectorates with a fierce and unrelenting vigor.[53]

YEMENI-AMERICAN RELATIONS

Although there had been one semiofficial contact between the United States and Yemen while the latter was still under Ottoman administration, relations between the two countries were of little significance to either during the reign of Imām Yaḥyā.

52. By the end of the war, British figures for the size of the Protectorates had undergone another increase: they were now said to include approximately 112,000 square miles. Cf. *The Statesman's Yearbook* for the years 1939 to 1945.

53. See, for example, Sir Tom Hickinbotham, Governor of Aden from 1951 to 1956: "It was a sad day for Anglo-Yemeni relations when Ahmad came to his father's throne. Harsher than his father, with little of the old man's political wisdom, his long residence in the south of the Yemen in close contact with the Protectorate and the Colony made him jealous of their progress and determined to revive his country's historical claims as soon as possible." (Hickinbotham, *Aden*, p. 75.) Also, Sir Bernard Reilly: "In February, 1948, a tragedy occurred in Sana, the sequel to which had evil consequences both for the Yemen and the Aden Protectorate. . . . [The new Imam's] accession marked the beginning of a period of increasing tension between the British and the Yemen Governments." (Reilly, *Aden and The Yemen*, p. 25.)

There is marked unwillingness or inability on the part of the various British officials to recognize the intimate connection between their "forward policy" and the reactions of both Imāms Yaḥyā and Aḥmad. In all their accounts, they fail to see that the Yemeni actions about which they complain so bitterly were all determined by actions which they themselves had taken. None of them, for example, ever mentions the twelvefold increase in the size of the Protectorate areas. In a chronological narrative such as Sir Bernard's it is obvious that there is a very close connection between British actions and Yemeni counteractions, yet the author seems totally unaware of it.

It may be admitted that there is some question about the legality of the Yemeni claims. Nevertheless, it is quite specious to argue, as the British have done, that Yemeni administrative changes on their side of the border (including the construction of new police posts) were examples of Yemeni unwillingness to abide by their own arguments concerning the status of the frontier. The Yemenis could and did argue that the English had begun the policy of undertaking administrative and military changes on their side of the frontier, and they therefore felt constrained to do likewise.

The Imām, however, was apparently fully aware of the policies of the United States and the increasing influence Americans wielded in international affairs. It was President Woodrow Wilson's assertion of the interest of the United States in seeing the independence of small nations protected which first attracted the Imām's attention. As a result he wrote a letter on December 22, 1918, to President Wilson, in which he requested recognition of Yemen's full independence, as well as his own position as Imām and King.[54]

Nothing came of this request, however, and relations between the two countries remained on a purely private level throughout the nineteen-twenties and thirties. Nevertheless, Imām Yaḥyā attempted once again, in 1927, to obtain recognition from the United States by proposing a treaty wherein his independence and position would be recognized. The Department of State, however, decided against entering into formal relations with Yemen, giving as its reason the fact that it had not as yet decided on its attitude toward the status of the nonmandated former Ottoman territories in the Arabian Peninsula.[55]

The primary contact between the two countries in the interwar period was a private one. At the request of a wealthy American philanthropist, Charles R. Crane, who had become fascinated by the country, an American engineer, Karl S. Twitchell, was sent to Yemen to investigate its mineral wealth and provide technical assistance in the building of roads, experimental farms, and a bridge, as well as distributing such gifts as farming and industrial machinery, in addition to a variety of other projects. These apparently completely altruistic expeditions, which lasted from 1927 to 1932, at which time both Crane and Twitchell changed their area of interest to Saudi Arabia, paved the way for several other American groups to attempt to enter Yemen for their own eco-

54. Department of State, Despatch No. 241 (Aden), 13 January 1919.

55. United States, *Papers Relating to the Foreign Relations of the United States, 1927* (3 vols.; Washington: U.S. Government Printing Office, 1942), III, 825–827.

Undoubtedly Imām Yaḥyā's primary motivation in requesting American recognition at this time was the possibility of using it as a lever against Great Britain. He had already obtained recognition of his independence and position as King of Yemen from one state, Italy, while he was in possession of extensive areas of the Protectorates to which he laid claim. Undoubtedly he hoped to do the same with the United States. Whether or not the reason given by the Department of State was the real one, it enabled the United States to avoid becoming embroiled in the Anglo-Yemeni border dispute at this time.

nomic gain.[56] All such attempts failed, however, for Imām Yaḥyā remained convinced throughout his reign that he should not allow any of Yemen's natural resources to fall into the hands of foreign concessionaires or exploiters. He remained extremely cautious in dealing with all business interests which approached him.[57]

It was not until after World War II, in 1945, that the United States took the first step toward opening diplomatic relations with Yemen. This was precipitated by the request of the Imām's government, presented by al-Sayyid Ḥusayn al-Kibsī to the American Consul in Cairo, in May of 1944, that the United States intercede in Yemen's border dispute with Great Britain over the Protectorates. In order to investigate for itself the conditions then prevailing in southwestern Arabia, the United States sent the Consul at Aden, Harlan B. Clark, to Yemen in March, 1945. At that time, Imām Yaḥyā once again requested American recognition, as well as American aid for the development of his country.[58]

Establishment of Formal Relations

Clark's report on his trip, together with the increase in American private interests intent on gaining economic concessions, prompted

56. Crane (1858–1939) had been president of the Crane Company, the Chicago valve and process-control manufacturing firm. He had filled a number of special diplomatic assignments during the nineteen-tens, including (with President King of Oberlin College) the King-Crane Commission report on Palestine. His interest in Yemen was due to a meeting with Charles K. Moser, the American Consul in Aden in 1910, who had been sent to Yemen at that time in order to investigate the death of an American traveler. As a result of Moser's stories about Yemen, Crane decided to visit the country himself, and it was he who returned from seeing the Imām carrying the latter's proposal for the draft treaty between Yemen and the United States. Possessed of considerable personal wealth, he undertook to finance by himself the surveys and projects undertaken by Karl Twitchell.

Karl Twitchell described his purpose and activities in his own work, *Saudi Arabia* (3rd ed.; Princeton: Princeton University Press, 1958).

Accompanying both Crane and Twitchell to Yemen as interpreter and assistant was a young Syrian, Captain Nazīh Mu'ayyad al-'Aẓm, who later published his own very informative book on the country: *Riḥlat fī Bilād al-'Arabiyya al-Sa'īda min Miṣr ilā Ṣan'ā'* (2 vols.; Cairo: Maṭba'at 'Isā al-Bābī al-Ḥalabī wa Shurakāh, n.d.).

57. An American anthropologist visiting the Imām reported that the latter thought very little of the idea of permitting foreigners to operate concessions, no matter how good the terms offered might sound. See Coon, *Measuring Ethiopia*, pp. 226–228. A German diplomat quotes Imām Yaḥyā as having once said the equivalent of, "lieber Grass fressen, als diesen Ausländern eine Konzession geben." Pawelke, *Der Jemen*, p. 42.

58. Harlan B. Clark, "Yemen–Southern Arabia's Mountain Wonderland," *The National Geographic Magazine*, XCII, No. 5 (November, 1947), 631–672.

the State Department to review its policy on Yemen. It was finally decided to recognize Yemen as an independent country in the spring of 1946, and a diplomatic mission set out for Ṣan'ā'. This mission was headed by William Eddy, the American Minister to Saudi Arabia, who had the title of Envoy Extraordinary and Minister Plenipotentiary to Yemen, and included among others Harlan Clark. Colonel Eddy presented the Yemeni Foreign Minister, Qāḍī Muḥammad Rāghib ibn Rafīq, with the often requested letter recognizing the "complete and absolute independence of the Kingdom of Yemen."

Negotiations were opened between the American mission and a Yemeni team composed of the Foreign Minister and Qāḍī 'Abd al-Karīm Muṭahhar, the Imām's personal secretary, in order to draw up a routine treaty of friendship and commerce. The talks were interrupted, however, by Sayf al-Islam Ḥusayn, the Imām's particularly pious son, who protested against the phrase "subjects of His Majesty the King of Yemen in the United States, and nationals of the United States of America in the Kingdom of Yemen shall be received and treated in accordance with the requirements and practices of generally recognized international law."

Prince Ḥusayn voiced the obvious objection of the religious community, claiming that this would create a regime of "capitulations," like that formerly extant in the Ottoman Empire. The American negotiators regarded it as essential, however, that American citizens in Yemen not be subjected to traditional Islamic law as practiced among the Zaydis, and the talks were broken off. The Imām finally overruled Prince Ḥusayn's objections. The talks were reopened, the objectionable phrase was retained, and the agreement was completed on May 4, 1946, and duly ratified.[59]

Imām Yaḥyā, although desirous of obtaining official recognition for his country and his own position therein, never felt the necessity of exchanging diplomatic representation with countries with whom he signed treaties. Consequently, no American mission

59. Richard H. Sanger, *The Arabian Peninsula* (Ithaca: Cornell University Press, 1954), pp. 248–271, describes the progress and adventures of this first official mission, of which he was a member.

For the text of the agreement, see United States Department of State, *Treaties and Other International Acts Series*, No. 1535 (Department of State Publication 2688), Washington, D.C., 1946.

was established in Yemen, even though the new American Minister to Saudi Arabia, now also accredited to Yemen, appeared in Ṣan'ā' in September, 1946, in order to present his credentials to the Imām.

Membership in the United Nations

In July, 1947, Sayf al-Islam 'Abdullāh, one of the Imām's more international-minded sons, appeared in New York City in order to seek admission for Yemen to the United Nations. Backed by the other Arab states and challenged by no important power (for neither the East nor the West appeared to have any reason to object to Yemen's admission), Yemen was successful in obtaining membership and international recognition from the world organization—further insurance, in Yaḥyā's view, for the continued existence of the Zaydi state in its present form.[60]

'Abdullāh established himself in New York in an unofficial legation and thus became Yemen's second permanent representative outside Yemen.[61] In addition to his duties as Yemen's first representative to the United Nations, 'Abdullāh also worked to increase trade between the United States and his country, saw to important purchases of needed equipment, and carried on negotiations with American business groups concerning development projects for Yemen.[62]

60. It became the fifty-sixth member on September 25, 1947. It seems likely that the Imām had his doubts about joining the United Nations, as he had about joining the Arab League, for fear that they would interfere in his internal affairs. Perhaps assured by al-Kibsī and 'Abdullāh that this was not the case and had not been with the Arab League, the Imām consented to join for the reasons cited and in order to avoid unpleasant criticism from other Arab states.

61. The first had been Ḥusayn al-Kibsī when he represented the Imām at the Arab League meetings in Cairo in 1945.

62. Clark, "Yemen," p. 672; Sanger, *The Arabian Peninsula*, p. 276.

Although it is possible that the Imām fully intended to undertake some development projects at this time, perhaps because he had become aware of the growing opposition to his reign, it seems more reasonable to assume either that these plans were the creation of 'Abdullāh (who may still have cherished ideas of becoming Imām upon his father's death) or that they were announced in order to appease opposition sentiment, and it was not intended that they actually be implemented.

CHAPTER VII

FOREIGN RELATIONS UNDER IMĀM AḤMAD

Throughout the reign of Imām Aḥmad, Yemen's foreign relations were similarly centered around the conflict with the British over the Aden Protectorates. Unlike Imām Yaḥyā, Aḥmad was willing to establish diplomatic links with several countries and became considerably involved with some of them. Like Yaḥyā, his primary motivation in making contact with third countries was the hope that they would help him in his dispute with Great Britain, and he similarly attempted to limit their influence within Yemen itself.

He was, however, less successful than his father in keeping out foreign and modernizing influences, for during his rule many modern ideas were widely disseminated throughout the other Arab countries. The growth of new means of communications meant that Yemen could no longer remain immune to these ideas, and inroads were made on the traditional Yemeni way of life by all foreign visitors and advisers, whether Arab or non-Arab. Aḥmad's preoccupation with the British, however, made him less aware of the dangers of these foreign influences, which eventually proved to be the undoing of the Imamate in 1962.

RELATIONS WITH GREAT BRITAIN

Immediately after the abortive revolt of 1948, the dispute with Great Britain over Aden and the Protectorates remained quiescent while Imām Aḥmad attended to the internal problems which faced his new regime. As soon as he felt firmly ensconced in his position as Imām, however, he resumed his father's policy of attempting to obtain British recognition of Yemen's claims to the Protectorates.

Imām Aḥmad's Attitude toward the British

The new Imām's belligerency toward the British was increased by his conviction that they had been at least indirectly responsible for his father's death and the revolution. This belief was based on the tolerant attitude of the British toward the exiled Yemeni groups in Aden and the Adeni authorities' obvious favoring of Shāfi'īs there in the expectation that these strengthened Sunni groups could be used to oppose the Zaydi Imām. The fact that Ḥusayn al-Kibsī sent a telegram to the Arab League threatening to seek foreign support if the League did not recognize the revolutionary government further bolstered Aḥmad's conviction that the British were behind the revolt.[1]

Imām Aḥmad's dislike of the British was increased by the fact that they had taken new steps to increase their influence in the Protectorates in the last years of his father's life. During his own period as governor of southern Yemen he had seen the English increase the size of the Protectorates from a total of 9,000 to over 112,000 square miles.

It was Imām Aḥmad's belief that the authorities in Aden acted independently of the government in London and that the policies of Aden's Governor did not have the full approval of the British Foreign Office. Consequently he often sent his protests over frontier incidents directly to London. At the end of 1948, however, Aḥmad decided to face his opponents directly without a London intermediary: he invited the Governor of Aden to visit him at Ta'izz, at which time he proposed that direct negotiations be established between Aden and Yemen.[2] Nothing came of these talks, however, because the Imām changed his mind in the course of them, deciding that the authorities in Aden were not worthy of attention and it would be better to deal directly with London.

The 1950–1951 Agreement

A frontier incident in the Najd Marqad area during March to September, 1949, prompted the Governor of Aden to write to the Imām suggesting that permanent boundary marks be placed on the frontier. The Yemenis replied by requesting compensation for their losses in the fighting before any talks could be held and reiterating their claims concerning Bayḥān and the Najd Marqad areas. In December, 1949, the Governor of Aden wrote that

1. This telegram was so worded that it could be interpreted to mean that the British had already agreed to give al-Kibsī limited support. See Sa'īd, *Al-Yaman*, pp. 138–139.
2. Reilly, *Aden and The Yemen*, p. 27.

"[because] the status quo referred to in the Treaty of Sana (1934) was specifically defined as the status quo as regards the frontier, the British representative would not be authorized to discuss any matter relating to administrative developments on the Protectorate side of that frontier." [3] However, the Governor added that while the government would not accept the payment of compensation as a precondition for negotiation, it would be willing to entertain the complaint in the light of the results of the proposed meeting regarding the frontier.

The Imām did not respond to the Governor of Aden, but instead again turned to the Foreign Office and informed it that he would not negotiate with Aden concerning a settlement of the Najd Marqad affair, although he was willing to deal with Britain. It was eventually agreed to hold an Anglo-Yemeni conference in London to discuss Najd Marqad, Shabwa, the frontier in general, diplomatic relations, and economic and trade relations. The talks opened on August 28, 1950, and lasted until October 12, when an agreement was reached for a *modus vivendi* between the two governments.[4]

A wide divergence of views on the status of the Protectorates still remained, however, and the agreement soon became a dead letter. The situation along the frontier remained unchanged. The new series of border incidents begun in 1949 continued through the nineteen-fifties and sixties. It is unnecessary to enumerate them here. The underlying cause for all of them was the same; as the British expanded their influence among the semi-independent tribal shaykhs of the Protectorates and sought to bring these rulers closer together, the Yemeni government used its influence in the area to see that this plan did not succeed. Provincial governors and other Yemeni agents on the northern side of the frontier became involved in controversies over landownership with British-supported shaykhs on the other side, and these inevitably led to the involvement of the two protecting powers.

Renewal of the "Forward Policy"

In 1952, the British government succeeded in extending its influence by obtaining advisory treaties with additional princi-

3. *Ibid.*, p. 30.

4. This agreement was approved by both governments in January, 1951, and later published. It is quoted in full in *ibid.*, pp. 31–33.

palities in the Protectorates. Treaties were signed by the Upper ʿAwlāqī Shaykh and the ʿAwdhalī Sultan, and a joint advisory and protectorate treaty was accepted by the Sultan of Laḥij, the largest and most important of the West Aden Protectorate states.[5] By January, 1954, enough tribal allies had been secured in this manner for the Commissioner in Aden, Sir Tom Hickinbotham, to announce that the British government was going to sponsor a scheme for a formal federation of the separate shaykhdoms of the Eastern and Western Protectorates.[6] Most of the tribal chiefs, who were nominated by their followers but subsequently had to receive the approval of the Governor of Aden, "agreed in principle though the details of any scheme which would be generally acceptable would have to be worked out."[7] Britain had obviously embarked on a policy which, although intended to improve the social and economic conditions in the Protectorates, also revealed her increasing dominance in political affairs there.[8]

Imām Aḥmad took violent exception to these measures, which aimed at the amalgamation of the numerous small shaykhdoms and principalities in the Protectorates into a strong political unit under the control of a non-Yemeni and non-Arab power. He was now convinced that the British intended to remain in Aden forever, thereby eliminating Yemen's reversionary claim to that territory. In the next few years the Yemeni government undertook an intensified campaign of bribery, infiltration, and propaganda; it took advantage of age-old feuds to set tribe against tribe and leader against leader in the Protectorates. Britain's

5. *The Middle East 1963*, p. 59; Liebesny, "Administration," p. 390.

6. *The Times* (London), January 8, 1954; Hickinbotham, *Aden*, pp. 164–168. This announcement constituted a resuscitation of a similar earlier proposal, characterized by Colonel Jacob as "impractical" and abandoned by the British in the early nineteen-thirties. Jacob pointed out that a tribal confederation would only perpetuate tribalism, and not create the nationalism which the Imām would favor. Perhaps recalling Jacob's objections, the new scheme spoke of a "federation." See *The Times* (London), March 17, 1931; Jacob, "The Kingdom of the Yemen," pp. 144–145.

7. Reilly, *Aden and the Yemen*, pp. 37–38; see also Saʿīd, *Al-Yaman*, pp. 189–190.

8. One commentator has remarked, "This led to an increase in her administrative personnel of 3,000% as compared to the number in 1934, naturally creating uneasiness in Yaman. . . ." See George Lenczowski, *The Middle East in World Affairs* (3rd ed.; Ithaca: Cornell University Press, 1962), p. 579.

"forward policy" was the immediate cause for this more concentrated Yemeni opposition to British rule in the Protectorates.[9]

RELATIONS WITH OTHER COUNTRIES

Meanwhile, in early 1955, there occurred inside Yemen another major attempt to change the government by revolution. Once the perpetrators of the coup had been dealt with, Imām Aḥmad, following his father's example, began a search for powerful friends in order to aid Yemen in its dispute with Great Britain.

Agreements with "The Bloc"

The U.S.S.R. was the obvious opponent of Great Britain and the entire Western alliance. It had already supported Syria diplomatically in the United Nations and was now assisting Egypt, both economically and militarily. No doubt Imām Aḥmad was also able to recall the shock with which his father's first association with the Soviet Union had been greeted by his traditional enemy. So it was that Yemen turned first to the Soviet Union; by November, 1955, a friendship pact had been signed between the two countries.[10] In the new agreement, the Soviets offered

9. Nevertheless, the role of the "forward policy" in creating this ever more virulent opposition to the British program in south Arabia was not clear to the English. For example, it was still possible in 1957 for the correspondent of *The Times* (London) to attribute Britain's unpopularity in this area to its association with the creation of the State of Israel. See *The Times* (London), January 29, 1957.

Others, however, were aware that this was a totally illogical rationale; see Jean-Jacques Berreby's letter of rebuttal to the editor of *The Times*, February 2, 1957.

10. *New York Times*, November 23, 1955.

The Soviet Union had an ambivalent attitude toward Yemen. Soviet writers during the nineteen-fifties emphasized the fact that the Imāms were opposed to British policy in south Arabia and that Aḥmad followed an "anti-imperialist" line by his refusal to join military compacts such as the Baghdad Pact. For this reason, these writers generally treated the Imām and his policies with sympathy, although at rare intervals one would point out some of their more reactionary characteristics. See, for example, *Komsomolskaya Pravda*, June 10, 1956; *Sovetskaya Rossiya*, February 15, 1959; *The Mizan Newsletter*, Vol. V, No. 1 (January, 1963), 30–31.

Various reasons have been advanced for the willingness of the Soviet Union to assist Imām Aḥmad economically and militarily. In addition to the anti–United States motivation already indicated, these were:

(1) The desire to control the Straits of Bāb al-Mandab. As evidence, some writers have pointed to the postwar request by the Soviet Union for a trusteeship over Eritrea, as well as the rumored Soviet fortifications at Shaykh Sa'īd.

(2) The use of Yemen as a "jumping-off-point" for Soviet efforts to obtain

to provide Yemen with industrial plants, factories, and technical and economic assistance in return for a variety of Yemen's agricultural products, primarily coffee and tobacco.[11]

Still not satisfied that he had sufficient diplomatic and military aid with which to intimidate the British, Imām Aḥmad sent his son Muḥammad al-Badr on an extensive tour of Eastern Bloc countries between May and September, 1956; among al-Badr's stops were Moscow, East Berlin, and Prague. As a result of this trip, Yemen signed a variety of pacts establishing diplomatic relations, trade and payments agreements, and friendship, economic, and technical-assistance treaties with members of the Soviet Bloc. Moreover, Yemen recognized Peking as the legitimate government of China, with which it also established diplomatic relations while receiving economic and technical assistance.[12] Yemen's drift toward the Communist Bloc continued through early 1957, as an arms agreement with the Czechoslovakian government was revealed.[13]

Relations with the United States

It was Aḥmad's attempt to gain international support for his anti-British policies which increasingly turned him toward the nations of what was then known as "the Bloc." But Aḥmad had

---

greater influence in East Africa. As evidence, one writer has pointed to the publication in *Izvestiya*, on June 10, 1962, of a proposed air route between India and the Malagasy Republic (formerly Madagascar), with Yemen shown as an intermediary stop. See *New York Times*, July 30, 1963.

In the opinion of the author, the Soviet Union's primary motive for assisting Yemen at this time was its desire to diminish the influence of Great Britain in a strategic area of the Arab world. While it is quite likely that longer-range policy objectives may have been present (as indicated by Soviet policy during the civil war following the September, 1962, revolution), it would appear that from its support of Imām Aḥmad during the nineteen-fifties the Soviet Union expected only intangible benefits. These included added prestige and whatever political propaganda could be used with the nations of Afro-Asia in general, and the Arab world in particular, as a result of supporting an Arab cause against the power and wishes of Great Britain. These could, of course, and perhaps were expected to, result in diplomatic support for other Soviet objectives.

11. *The Times* (London), January 14 and March 6, 1956.

12. Wolfgang Bartke, "Die Beziehungen der VR China zum Nahen und Mittleren Osten," *Der Ostblock und die Entwicklungsländer*, No. 16 (July, 1964), pp. 143–144.

13. *The Times* (London), June 11 and 24, 1956; *New York Times*, May 5, July 6 and 17, and August 22, 1956, January 10, 1957; *Le Monde* (Paris), July 6, 1956; *Middle East Journal*, XI, No. 1 (Winter, 1957), 91; *Oriente Moderno*, XXXVI, Nos. 6 through 12, *passim.*

learned from the experience of his father that close relations with anti-British powers often entailed dangers to Yemen's traditional government and policies nearly as great as those represented by Britain itself. Consequently, Aḥmad associated his country with additional powers, if only to mitigate the influence of those he had chosen to help him with his primary objective.

Among the nations with which Imām Aḥmad decided to have closer relations was the United States—not only the most obvious opponent of the Soviet Union and its allies but also the richest country in the world, from which extensive foreign economic assistance might be obtained. Indeed, shortly after the United States recognized Aḥmad's government—a step it had shown some hesitancy in taking [14]—the Imām requested that the United States provide some foreign aid, under the terms of "Point Four," as well as technical assistance.[15] The United States, however, was unwilling to provide the kind and amount of assistance which the Imām had expected, and nothing came of the requests. Nevertheless, the re-establishment of diplomatic relations in 1950 permitted the entry into Yemen of a number of American scientific missions and expeditions.[16]

14. The United States announced its recognition of Aḥmad's government on February 14, 1950 (*Department of State Bulletin*, XXII [27 February 1950], 326), but did not receive the Yemeni diplomatic representative until December, 1950. *Department of State Bulletin*, XXIII (18 December 1950), 970.

15. *The Times* (London), January 6, 1951.

16. A United States Navy Medical Mission, permitted to enter Yemen, surveyed health conditions and undertook zoological studies. See Harry Hoogstraal and Robert E. Kunz, "Yemen Opens the Door to Progress," *The National Geographic Magazine*, CI (February, 1952), 213–244. (The more technical reports are to be found in a variety of Navy Department Publications.)

Undoubtedly the major expedition to enter Yemen was that of the American Foundation for the Study of Man, which went for the purpose of undertaking archaeological and paleographic investigations on the remains of the pre-Islamic kingdoms. Because of misunderstandings between the government and the leaders of the expedition, and especially the latter's seeming indifference to Yemeni sensibilities, the group was forced to leave the important site of Mā'rib suddenly in 1952 without having completed its work. As a result of the ill feelings which had been engendered, the Yemeni authorities were less than enthusiastic about permitting other foreign expeditions into the country for scientific purposes, and Yemen became almost as closed to scholars and scientific investigators as it had been prior to Aḥmad's succession.

This was extremely unfortunate: significant sites which contain extensive ruins of the ancient pre-Islamic kingdoms—of inestimable value for a proper study of the history of this area—have been rendered worthless for archaeologists or completely destroyed by the civil war which raged in these regions after the revolution

At the same time, many American speculators and financiers were convinced that oil was to be found in commercial quantities in Yemen. Consequently, American economic interest as a potential market as well as profitable investment opportunity was very high. Probably the longest-lived and most enticing opportunity for such investors was the often renegotiated concession for the exploration and development of mineral resources, particularly oil, first granted to a German firm in 1953. In 1955, this concession was taken over by the Yemen Development Corporation (organized by Walter S. Gabler and George E. Allen); in 1959 it went to the American Overseas Investment Corporation (organized by W. Angie Smith III and Shelby Owens), and finally in 1961 to John W. Mecom's Houston Independent Oil Company. Of these owners, only the first and the last appear to have undertaken any actual operations in Yemen.[17]

---

of 1962. It is known, for example, that certain sites were bombed or razed with artillery barrages; similarly, many of the fine pieces of sculpture and bronze work, as well as royal inscriptions, which had been discovered and stored in the small museums of Mā'rib and San'ā', have disappeared and found their way into private collections or been completely destroyed.

For the American accounts of the expedition and its work, see Wendell Phillips, *Qataban and Sheba* (New York: Harcourt, Brace, 1955); Richard L. Bowen and Frank P. Albright, *Archaeological Discoveries in South Arabia* (Baltimore: Johns Hopkins Press, 1958).

17. The concession was first granted at a time when the Imām appeared to have a distinct preference for German firms, and it was perhaps for this reason that C. Deilmann Bergbau, the original concessionaire, was selected. Despite the fact that the Deilmann firm actually began work on a number of projects (notably around al-Salīf), its concession was canceled under strange circumstances and given to the Yemen Development Corporation. It was not until John W. Mecom obtained the concession that actual operations were again undertaken. In fact, Mecom was the only one to actually begin drilling operations: he spudded his first well (dry, as were all the others) by July, 1961, and continued his operations through the revolution of 1962 until finally moving his operations to the Gulf region in 1963. On this long and complex concession history, see:

C. Deilmann Bergbau period:

A. M. Stahmer, "Erdölpartner Jemen," *Zeitschrift für Geopolitik*, XXIV, No. 1 (November 1, 1953), 615–616.

Stephen H. Longrigg, *Oil in the Middle East* (2nd ed.; London: Oxford University Press, 1961), p. 321.

Yemen Development Corporation period:

The Middle East Journal, X, No. 1 (Winter, 1956), 76.

New York Times, November 23 and 28, 1955.

Life, XXXIX (December 5, 1955), 51–52.

American Overseas Investment Company period:

The Middle East Journal, XIV, No. 1 (Winter, 1960), 86.

Longrigg, *Oil in the Middle East*, p. 321.

On an official level, Yemen opened a permanent diplomatic establishment in Washington, D.C., in 1951 and finally permitted the United States to do likewise on March 16, 1959, in the city of Ta'izz;[18] in fact, an American representative of the diplomatic corps had resided in Ta'izz for some time prior to the actual opening of the legation.

Although American recognition of Yemen was due largely to Yemeni desires for legal acknowledgment of the status of the Imām within the kingdom and its present frontiers, American interest in the country was due to two factors, both basically non-Yemeni in origin. The first of these was the proximity of Saudi Arabia, where American economic and military stakes were extensive. The second was in response to the obvious interest shown in Yemen by the Bloc nations after 1955, opening the possibility of increased Communist influence in the peninsula.

Until the close of World War II, American concern for the peninsula remained small. After the war, however, the economic interests of the United States there increased sharply. This was due primarily to the vastly increased amount of private investment in the oil reserves of Saudi Arabia; by the mid-nineteen-fifties this investment amounted to over a billion dollars in the infrastructure and facilities needed for the extraction, refining, and marketing of the petroleum. In addition, American interests, in co-operation or conjunction with British companies, also extracted and marketed the oil reserves of Kuwait, as well as the lesser but still important sources located in Baḥrayn, Qaṭar, and later the Trucial Coast.

At the same time, the United States had also invested in the construction and maintenance of military facilities in Saudi Arabia, especially in such installations as al-Ẓahrān Air Base, which were intended to provide not only for the defense of the Middle East as a whole but also for the important oil reserves and installations of the whole Gulf region which were essential to the energy supply of Western Europe and Great Britain.

The extensive economic and military aid which Aḥmad and al-Badr brought to Yemen as a result of their desire to force the

Department of State, Despatch No. 131 (Taiz), 18 November 1959.
John W. Mecom period:
Platt's Oilgram (New York), March 1 and July 20, 1961, *et seq.*
Oil and Gas Journal (Tulsa), April 3 and July 31, 1961, *et seq.*
18. *Department of State Bulletin*, XL, No. 1033 (13 April 1959), 538.

British to compromise on the issue of the Protectorates was supplied almost solely by the Soviet Union and the Eastern European states. This aid, and the Soviet and other Bloc technicians needed to administer it, created opportunities for making of Yemen an instrument in the fulfillment of Soviet foreign-policy objectives in the Middle East and East Africa which could not be ignored. If only to know the extent of this influence, it was thought wise to have American diplomatic and economic interests represented. Certainly the establishment of a pro-Soviet state on the peninsula could have serious repercussions for other states, especially Saudi Arabia; it would most certainly provide a base for political propaganda and perhaps also for outright assistance to other groups dedicated to bringing revolution to the relatively backward nations of the peninsula.[19]

It should not be forgotten that Yemen's strategic location was an important factor: nearly all American trade with the Gulf, as well as a large portion of the oil exports of this area (both to American allies in Europe and to North America itself), is carried in ships through the Suez Canal via the Red Sea. A militarily strong Yemen, especially one subject to Communist influence, could seriously interfere with this Western trade.

In view of the possible consequences of American indifference to the situation in Yemen, it was not surprising that the United States sought an economic and political foothold in the country. Whereas in the early nineteen-fifties the Imām desired American economic assistance and the United States had been reluctant to commit large amounts to the backward kingdom, now the immense sums offered by the Bloc provided the needed funds, and the Imām only desired a minimal American presence as " insurance " against a too-great dependence on the Bloc. In order to counter the increased influence of the Bloc, the United States now undertook to convince Yemen that it needed a foreign-aid program. By mid-1957 the Department of State, perhaps with too much optimism, claimed that " promising discussions " were taking place.[20]

19. Undoubtedly the best example of the changed attitude of the United States government at this time is provided by Allen W. Dulles, Director of the Central Intelligence Agency. In remarks made before the United States Chamber of Commerce in Washington, D.C., on April 28, 1958, Dulles outlined at length the amount and significance of Bloc aid to Yemen. (*New York Times*, April 29, 1958.)

20. *The Middle East Journal*, XI, No. 3 (Summer, 1957), 308; *New York Times*, June 11 and September 5, 1957.

These discussions, however, remained unproductive for the time being, for it was not until January, 1959, that the United States provided Yemen with any aid. In this instance, some 15,000 tons of surplus grains and other foodstuffs were sent to relieve the effects of a severe drought.[21]

In succeeding months, additional American aid programs were announced, and by December, 1959, a U.S. Overseas Mission was attached to the Legation in Ta'izz. In the years that followed, additional projects were inaugurated, and further food and medical supplies were granted when natural disasters or the situation required them.[22]

Relations with Other Arab States

Probably the most important result of the unsuccessful coup of 1955 was the increased prominence it gave to Muḥammad al-Badr in internal and external affairs. Al-Badr apparently considered himself to be the royal representative of the progressive views of the younger Arab generation with which he associated himself. He, like them, was impressed with the success of the reforms of the Egyptian revolution under Jamāl 'Abd al-Nāṣir, as well as the latter's diplomatic accomplishments vis-à-vis the British, and wished to emulate him as far as possible. He doubtless urged his father, whose health was failing at the time, to develop friendlier relations with 'Abd al-Nāṣir. Aḥmad, however, did not trust the revolutionary Egyptian and feared the effects of his ideas in Yemen. Nevertheless, the growing prestige of 'Abd al-Nāṣir in the Middle East and the increasingly bad relations between Yemen and Great Britain and between Egypt and

21. *The Middle East Journal*, XIII, No. 3 (Summer, 1959), 302; *L'Orient* (Beirut), January 30, 1959, as quoted in *Oriente Moderno*, XXXIX, No. 2 (February, 1959), 132; *Department of State Bulletin*, XL, No. 1025 (16 February 1959), 246–247.

22. Department of State, *Treaties and Other International Acts Series*, 4286, 4346, and 4413 (1959), Washington, D.C.; *Department of State Bulletin*, XLIV, No. 1130 (20 February 1961), 271.

Undoubtedly the major project undertaken by the United States was the construction of a modern road connecting al-Mukhā with Ṣan'ā' via Ta'izz. Construction work began in late 1960 and continued through the revolution of 1962 as a result of a new agreement signed with the Republican government in January, 1963. (This latter agreement provided for additional projects, the most notable of which was the John F. Kennedy Memorial waterworks system for Ta'izz.) (*The Middle East Journal*, XIII, No. 4 [Autumn, 1959], 442.)

Great Britain led to a short-lived but interesting agreement among Yemen, Egypt, and Saudi Arabia. King Sa'ūd was also unhappy with Great Britain because of a dispute over the Buraymī Oasis in the eastern part of the Arabian Peninsula; the basically anti-British pact was signed in Jidda by the three rulers on April 2, 1956.[23]

DEVELOPMENTS OF THE LATE NINETEEN-FIFTIES

Early in 1957, Imām Aḥmad attempted to make use of his new allies to bring pressure upon the British, whom he charged with provocative military action in the Protectorates. He called a meeting of the Jidda Pact and asked Egypt and Saudi Arabia to condemn British actions; he also requested that the United States intervene in the dispute with Great Britain. Moreover, he tried to obtain the moral support of the United Nations and the Arab League by lodging formal protests there. Nothing ever came of these requests for aid. For the first time, Imām Aḥmad permitted foreign newsmen to interview him in order that he might put his views of the situation in south Arabia before the world.[24] He emphasized that the British were violating the 1934 treaty by continuing with their plan for a federation of the Protectorates. The failure of the press, the world organizations, and other Arab states to come to his assistance undoubtedly convinced Aḥmad that he would have to solve the issue alone.

Negotiations with the British

Increased Yemeni incursions into the Protectorates and maneuvers by her diplomats to stir up the tribes in these areas finally led the British again to consider talks with Yemeni officials in order to find some way of settling the border dispute. Although

23. *Al-Ahrām* (Cairo), April 22 and 23, 1956, as quoted in *Oriente Moderno*, XXXVI, No. 5 (May, 1956), 325. This treaty served its intended function in that the three signatories did not join the Baghdad Pact, then under discussion in Middle Eastern capitals. Its primary purpose, of creating a viable alternative to the Baghdad Pact, was not achieved, for the revolutionary regime in Cairo had little in common with the two kingdoms. The only use made of the treaty came in 1962, when both Egypt and Saudi Arabia invoked its mutual-defense clause in order to justify their support for the Republican and Royalist factions in the civil war which followed the September revolution.

24. *The Times* (London), February 1, 1957; *New York Times*, February 3 and 4, 1957.

the British seemed unimpressed by Aḥmad's efforts to marshal his new allies against them, for they remained firmly attached to their previous position, the frequent frontier incidents and the reports of large arms shipments from the Soviet Union to Yemen produced a response in August, 1957. The British authorities sent an invitation to al-Badr to visit London and discuss the border dispute there. The talks lasted for ten days during November, but the lack of a formal communiqué at their conclusion indicated that once again neither side had moved from its previous position.[25]

Visit to the Eastern Bloc

Imām Aḥmad and his son concluded that they had not obtained sufficient foreign support to inspire the British to compromise. Consequently, immediately after the talks ended, al-Badr made another trip through the Bloc countries: Rumania, Poland, Yugoslavia, the Soviet Union, and finally the People's Republic of China. On his return, al-Badr boasted that he had signed ten pacts with four Communist countries. These were a new series of agreements establishing diplomatic relations and economic, technical, and military assistance. The real purpose behind these visits was demonstrated most clearly by the communiqué issued after al-Badr's stop in China: he obtained from the Peking government an unequivocal affirmation of its support for Yemeni claims to the territory held by the British.[26]

Alliance with Egypt in the United Arab States

Imām Aḥmad knew that he could count on the moral support of other Arabs, including Jamāl 'Abd al-Nāṣir, now the most important figure in Arab politics, for his claims against the British in Aden. He realized, however, that they were not interested in seconding any military adventure against the British. He also knew that the revolutionary Arab states were probably more than willing to see his government overthrown by internal revolt. This knowledge and his sensitivity to the domestic pressure then building up against him inspired Aḥmad to undertake an ingenious diplomatic maneuver. When he heard of the union of Syria and Egypt in early February, 1958, he cabled 'Abd al-Nāṣir and asked

25. *The Times* (London), November 10, 22, and 28, 1957.

26. *New York Times*, December 24, 29, and 31, 1957; January 10, 12, 14, and 16, 1958.

permission for Yemen to join the new federation. The United Arab Republic leader, who had specifically requested other Arab states to adhere to the new union, could do little but accept.[27]

Yemen's connection with the U.A.R. was extremely tenuous, however, and no effort was made to link the former's internal economic and political life to Egypt's as thoroughly as was the case with Syria. Imām Aḥmad displayed great skill in solving the problems he had created by associating the most traditional and conservative of all Arab countries with the most progressive, for the agreement he signed permitted Yemen to preserve its independence and internal administrative structure intact.[28] In implementing the terms of the federation, Aḥmad was quite reserved: Egyptians were not allowed to travel to or in Yemen unless they had specific advance permission from the proper authorities. As a result, few Egyptians actually went to Yemen. Most of those who did went for the purpose of training the army, which Aḥmad obviously felt he could still control, regardless of foreign influences.

The Imām at this point obviously believed that Eastern Bloc assistance held fewer dangers for his regime than did Egyptian aid. In the case of Russian and Chinese technicians, a considerable cultural difference had to be overcome; the fact that they were not Arabs and could not speak Arabic provided an effective barrier between them and Yemeni citizens. This barrier did not exist in the case of Egyptians, whom Aḥmad barely trusted. By paying lip service to Arab unity, however, and nominally recognizing 'Abd al-Nāṣir's pre-eminence in Arab affairs and even joining in an association with him, Imām Aḥmad avoided becoming a target for one of Radio Cairo's propaganda campaigns.[29]

27. *New York Times*, February 3 and March 9, 1958. 'Abd al-Nāṣir's prestige was at this time extremely high among progressive Arab political circles, partly due to his "victory" at Suez in 1956. Al-Badr's predilection for 'Abd al-Nāṣir's pan-Arabism and other vague political ideals naturally led him toward closer ties with Cairo. His visits to Egypt were frequent, and they provided him with an opportunity to express publicly his approval of Arab solidarity, positive neutralism, and other slogans then current. There is little doubt that al-Badr was important in bringing about this federation of the U.A.R. and Yemen in the United Arab States.

28. For the text of this treaty, see Ṣalāḥ al-Dīn al-Munajjid, *Al-Yaman wa al-Muttaḥida* (Beirut: Dār al-Kitāb al-Jadīd, 1962), pp. 12–17. (Related documents, pp. 21–32); *Oriente Moderno*, XXXVIII, No. 3 (March, 1958), 205–206.

29. Imām Aḥmad was doubtless aware of similar campaigns carried on against King Sa'ūd and King Ḥusayn of Jordan. Even in Yemen it was no longer possible

Confederation in the Protectorates

In the meantime, Imām Aḥmad pressed his plan to extend his influence into the Protectorates. His agents' actions on the frontier again prompted a meeting between the Yemenis and the British in July, 1958—this time on the neutral ground of Ethiopia. The results were the same as in the London talks: neither side was willing to compromise.[30] Unfortunately for Aḥmad, his policy was beginning to have repercussions among the shaykhs of the Protectorates. The increased military power of the Yemeni government was apparently worrying these shaykhs, for in meetings with Great Britain over the plan for federation they showed a greater willingness to enter into some sort of agreement.

Britain had, in the intervening time, taken steps to make the terms of the agreement more palatable to the shaykhs. The emphasis was now on confederation rather than federation, although the latter word continued to be used; each of the tribes and shaykhs would be able to retain considerable autonomy. The idea of complete political unity in southern Arabia, for which the British had originally hoped, was now considerably modified. In February, 1959, the new Federation of the Amirates of the South was announced; the name was later changed to South Arabian Federation.[31]

Imām Aḥmad's Concern with the Bloc

At the same time, Aḥmad apparently became concerned over the possibility of subversive activities by the Soviet Bloc technicians whom he had invited into the country. Expressions of apprehension over the growth of this influence had already been voiced by 'Abd al-Nāṣir in 1958; specifically, the latter feared the effects which the Soviet military installations reportedly being built on the Red Sea coast would have on the Suez Canal trade. At that time, the Egyptian leader is said to have informed Muḥammad al-Badr that Aḥmad's truculence concerning the British in Aden and his use of Soviet equipment and trainers to undertake a

---

to prohibit radios (as the government had in the past), for inexpensive transistors were easily available.

30. *The Times* (London), July 12, 1958.

31. *The Times* (London), February 4, 1959, and July 17, 1962; *The Sunday Times* (London), February 15, 1959; Hickinbotham, *Aden*, pp. 162–174; Ingrams, *The Yemen*, p. 106.

military adventure against them would not be supported by Egypt.[32]

Although an attempt by the United States to establish a mission in the middle of 1957 had been rebuffed by Aḥmad, the latter's serious concern about the activities of the Soviets in his country led him in early 1959 to pay greater attention to United States efforts to establish an International Cooperation Administration (I.C.A.) mission in Yemen. Soon American wheat, flour, and animal foodstuffs were on their way there. Permission was also granted for the stationing of permanent diplomatic representatives in Ta'izz.[33] Following his father's policy, Aḥmad was counter-balancing one powerful foreign country's influence by also dealing with its primary adversary.

But Aḥmad's health had worsened, and during his visit to Italy for medical treatment he was forced to hand over the reins of government to his son al-Badr. The latter took the opportunity to initiate some reforms, all of which were canceled on Aḥmad's return. After studying al-Badr's changes, some of which were based on Bloc models, Aḥmad became more worried about Soviet Bloc influences in the country and accepted new Western offers of assistance. He signed a number of new agreements with Western groups, such as the United States Overseas Investment Corporation and the West German government, while rebuffing aid offers from Cairo.[34]

DEVELOPMENTS OF THE NINETEEN-SIXTIES

In the summer of 1960, another attempt at Yemeni-British *rapprochement* was tried—again with no success. Immediately

32. Jamāl 'Abd al-Nāṣir was at this time negotiating with the British over the Suez War reparations, expanded trade, and other matters; consequently he did not wish to see the talks fail. See especially *New York Times*, August 31, 1958, and *The Times* (London), March, April, and May, 1958, *passim* on the alleged Soviet fortifications.

33. *The Sunday Times* (London), April 12, 1959; *The Middle East Journal*, XIII, No. 2 (Spring, 1959), 192; *L'Orient* (Beirut), January 30, 1959, quoted in *Oriente Moderno*, XXXIX, No. 2 (February, 1959), 132; *The Times* (London), June 3, 1959.

34. *L'Orient* (Beirut), June 20, 1959, quoted in *Oriente Moderno*, XXXIX, No. 7 (July, 1959), 555; *U.S. Foreign Service Despatch*, No. 131 (Taiz), November 18, 1959; *New York Times*, August 25 and November 18, 1959; *The Times* (London), May 29, August 18 and 23, 1959. It was even reported that the Imām had asked a number of Communist technicians and advisers to leave Yemen, although these reports probably contained a bit of wishful thinking.

thereafter further amounts of Communist Bloc aid were introduced into Yemen, conspicuously displayed and used. At the same time, further United States attempts to ingratiate itself with the Imām were rewarded by an agreement to have the I.C.A. construct a road between al-Mukhā and Ṣan'ā', similar to the Chinese project to build a road from al-Ḥudayda to Ṣan'ā'. In early 1961 additional Soviet-sponsored projects were agreed upon, the most important being the construction of a new harbor for al-Ḥudayda, to be called Aḥmadī.[35] Other pacts were also signed with North Korea and Yugoslavia.[36]

Then, late in 1961, an event occurred which pleased Aḥmad immensely; Syria withdrew from the United Arab Republic. Never having fully trusted 'Abd al-Nāṣir, Aḥmad took this as an indication that other Arab states had begun to have doubts concerning 'Abd al-Nāṣir's plans for Arab socialism. Emboldened, Aḥmad decided to express his own views on the subject. He composed a poem, now famous, in which he condemned the policies and ideology of 'Abd al-Nāṣir, declaring them to be incompatible with the tenets of Islam.[37] The Egyptian leader, who had never appreciated Aḥmad's unwillingness to act on any of the principles of the United Arab States and by this time may have been on the verge of effecting a break with Yemen himself, terminated the U.A.S. on December 26, 1961.[38]

The rupture between Yemen and Egypt following the publication of Aḥmad's poem probably sounded the death knell for Aḥmad's regime. There was nothing left to prevent 'Abd al-Nāṣir from aiding Yemeni revolutionary groups, and Egyptian assistance to the rebels was not long in coming. On January 22, 1962, Radio Cairo opened a scurrilous campaign against the Imām, identifying him with imperialism and accusing him of trying to reinstate

35. This project was desperately needed if Yemen were to be able to carry out its own trade with other countries, for its harbors had long ago been allowed to silt up, making lighters and human labor the only possible means of unloading imports. Obviously, this harbor improvement project would make Yemen less economically dependent on Aden and Great Britain.

36. *The Middle East Journal*, XV, No. 1 (Winter, 1961), 68; XV, No. 2 (Spring, 1961), 210.

37. The poem was first published outside Yemen in *Al-Ayyām* (Aden) on December 9, 1961. See also al-Munajjid, *Al-Yaman*, pp. 35–51, for the text.

38. *The Times* (London), December 27, 1961; and *New York Times*, December 27, 1961.

colonialism in the Arab world.[39] Aḥmad, belatedly realizing his error, made a futile effort to prevent any break in diplomatic relations between the two countries,[40] but the Egyptian government was no longer interested in postponing the downfall of the Ṣan'ā' regime.

Throughout the major part of 1962, there seems to have been a hurried attempt inside Yemen to placate the reinvigorated progressive groups, but during the latter part of the summer there was an increasing number of incidents of violence directed against the regime. Nevertheless, the old Imām, Aḥmad, was able to die in peace on the eighteenth of September. He left behind such a turbulent state of affairs, in part inspired by the vitriolic attacks of Radio Cairo, that his son and successor, al-Badr, was able to withstand the tide for only one week.

One is forced to conclude that Aḥmad's foreign policy, and especially his near monomania concerning the British and the Aden Protectorates, was a major cause for the September, 1962, revolution. If Aḥmad had not felt the need to secure outside assistance at any cost in order to threaten the British, he might never have opened Yemen to the revolutionary ideas brought in by the Soviet Bloc and Egyptian experts. If Yemen had remained secluded and protected from foreign influences, the revolution might have been considerably postponed.

British policy may be considered an additional cause, for had Great Britain been willing to come to some sort of agreement concerning the future of the Protectorates, the Imāms, and particularly Aḥmad, would undoubtedly have devoted greater time and energy to coping with Yemen's internal problems. To do this, however, it would have been necessary for the Imāms to find a way of providing Yemen with gradual reform to replace violent revolution as a method of achieving progress—a vain hope, it would seem, for underdeveloped countries in the twentieth century.

39. This campaign was directed by 'Abd al-Raḥmān al-Bayḍānī, a Shāfi'ī who was born and raised in Cairo by a Yemeni father and served as Aḥmad's Ambassador to West Germany for a few years while obtaining his Ph.D. in economics, a position he undoubtedly received with al-Badr's assistance. He was, briefly, later closely associated with 'Abdullāh al-Sallāl in the 1962 revolution. The texts of the sixteen radio broadcasts which he made were printed immediately after Aḥmad's death (*Asrār al-Yaman* [Cairo: Kutub Qawmiyya, 1962]), complete with anti-Imām cartoons.

40. *New York Times*, February 6, 1962.

PART IV: THE CIVIL WAR

Chapter VIII

THE CIVIL WAR, 1962–1966

As had been the case with the revolutions of 1948 and 1955, accurate information concerning the revolution of 1962, its leaders, their motives, and their goals is extremely difficult to obtain. Although it is obvious that many of the circumstances and developments associated with this most recent attempt to overthrow the Imamate are similar to previous efforts, it is also immediately evident that the events taking place in Yemen are now of greater concern to other nations than previously.

On the morning of September 27, 1962, the newly formed Council of the Revolutionary Command, headed by ʿAbdullāh al-Sallāl, announced the establishment of the Yemen Arab Republic. In a determined effort to avoid having the Imām become the natural focus for all those opposed to the change in government, a concerted campaign was undertaken by the now revolutionary media of the state (as well as the media of the United Arab Republic, within only hours after the revolution) to convince the Yemeni population and the world at large that the Imām was dead.[1] Despite the seeming effectiveness of the *coup d'état*, its first few days were characterized by considerable confusion on the part of foreign observers—a fact which tended to give the claims and statements of the new government greater validity than they deserved. Conflicting stories appeared in the international press, and the residents of Yemen themselves, with the possible exception of those in Ṣanʿāʾ, knew very little about the new government, its leaders, programs, and objectives. Given their desire for some change in the government, as well as their sympathy for previous revolutionary attempts, it seems probable that the majority of the residents of the three major cities of

1. This remained true even after it had been reliably established that Muḥammad al-Badr had, in fact, escaped. Although the Western press first reported that the Imām was still alive in early October (*Christian Science Monitor*, October 3, 1962; *The Times* [London], October 4, 1962), it was not until about ten days later that Cairo admitted he was still alive (*The Times* [London], October 13, 1962).

Ṣan'ā', Ta'izz, and al-Ḥudayda greeted the new regime with some enthusiasm; but it may also be assumed that most politically aware Yemenis were somewhat skeptical of its ability to remain in power. Fully aware of the fate of their predecessors, the revolutionaries immediately attempted to obtain as much support as possible, domestically and internationally.

Although the first cabinet was composed largely of military officers, some prominent and respected members of the Free Yemeni Movement were carefully included; for example, Muḥammad Maḥmūd al-Zubayrī and Qāḍī 'Abd al-Raḥmān al-Iriānī. The new leadership could count on the support of the inhabitants of the major cities as well as some of the tribal confederations and individual tribes which for a variety of reasons had opposed Imām Aḥmad, such as the Hāshid tribes under Shaykh 'Abdullāh al-Aḥmar, who was released from prison by the new government. Nevertheless, the leaders were aware that these elements could not withstand alone a concerted attempt to overthrow them by the traditionally conservative and powerful tribes of the northern Zaydi highlands, led by an Imām. Two previous attempts at revolution had clearly demonstrated this. No matter how quickly the appurtenances of a modern state were created and additional support obtained from the urban centers, there would not be enough time to set up a genuinely popular government with its own citizen-soldiery which could withstand an attack from the north.

The leaders of the Republic had but one alternative: to seek international support. This was not a simple matter. Previous rebellions in Yemen had been crushed within a matter of weeks at most, and it was to be expected that most nations would be reluctant to grant recognition until they were certain of the regime's ability to remain in control. Nevertheless, recognition was not long in coming from some states: the United Arab Republic, the Soviet Union, and most nations of the Bloc granted it on September 29.[2] The major countries of the Western world waited for additional information on which to base their decisions. Saudi Arabia, Jordan, and Morocco, on the other hand, refused to recognize the basically antimonarchical coup. As a result, the political lines were drawn even before the end of September; the

2. *New York Herald Tribune*, September 30, 1962; *Neue Zürcher Zeitung*, October 1, 1962.

"progressive" and republican governments of the Middle East recognized and supported the new regime, while the conservative and monarchical governments did not. The political consequences of this were to prove to be immensely significant.

At the time, the revolutionaries had one obvious supporter in the Middle East: the United Arab Republic. The capital of the Egyptian republic had for years played host to the individuals and groups who wanted to bring reform to Yemen—the Free Yemeni Movement and the Yemeni Union. The government of Jamāl ʿAbd al-Nāṣir had for some time been publicly committed to the introduction of republican regimes in other Arab lands and actively promoted antimonarchical propaganda in favor of "progressive Arab nationalist" governments. In fact, Cairo's response to the new Republic's request for assistance was astoundingly swift—a fact which led to the belief in many quarters that the *coup d'état* had been engineered from Cairo by President ʿAbd al-Nāṣir.[3] By October 1, Egyptian paratroopers and matériel had already begun to arrive in Yemen;[4] by the seventh, Egyptian ships had landed in al-Ḥudayda;[5] and by November 10 a mutual defense treaty had been signed between the Yemen Arab Republic and the United Arab Republic.[6] This agreement was designed to replace the shaky legal basis on which the original support had been supplied—the Jidda Pact of 1956.

THE COUNTERREVOLUTION

It was soon obvious that this support was going to be necessary. The Imām, Muḥammad al-Badr, had been able to escape from the palace during the artillery barrage. In the early hours of the morning of September 27, he had been hidden and disguised by some of Ṣanʿā's residents and somewhat later had made his way into the northern mountains to seek refuge as well as support for a counterrevolution.[7] While it seems unlikely that the revo-

3. See, for example, Neil McLean, "The War in the Yemen," *Journal of the Royal United Service Institution*, CXI (February, 1966), 14–29; *The Times* (London), December 21, 1962 (article by Neil McLean).

4. *The Times* (London), October 2, 1962.

5. *New York Times*, October 7, 1962; *The Times* (London), October 8, 1962.

6. *The Observer* (London), November 11, 1962; *New York Times*, November 12, 1962.

7. The fullest report of the Imām's escape is to be found in his own account to newsmen at his mountain stronghold in early November, 1962. See: *New York*

lutionaries were not aware of al-Badr's escape (and therefore acted to obtain support from all quarters as soon as possible), this was not immediately known to the outside world. Al-Badr's uncle Ḥasan, still in New York as Yemen's representative to the United Nations, assumed the title of Imām upon hearing the original news reports. He proclaimed his intention of returning to Yemen in order to lead the forces which would restore the "legitimate government." Traveling via London, Beirut, and Jidda, he joined the other members of the Ḥamīd al-Dīn family who had been able to escape summary trial and execution or imprisonment.[8] Upon learning that al-Badr was still alive, Ḥasan renounced his claim to be Imām and recognized him. The campaign to restore the Ḥamīd al-Dīn clan to the throne of Yemen now began in earnest. Depending on traditional loyalties as well as the liberal use of funds, Ḥasan, al-Badr, and some of their cousins and other relatives set out to rally the Zaydi tribes of the northern regions and to begin the counterrevolution.

The forces of the Imām and his supporters, or Royalists as they soon came to be called, were also able to obtain outside assistance for their cause. Present in Yemen at the time of the coup was a small team of Jordanian military advisers, who, it was reported, assisted the Imām in organizing his irregulars into fighting units.[9] In addition, the government of Saudi Arabia proffered assistance, for it could not afford to remain idle while the United Arab Republic introduced men and matériel into the peninsula. The simple fact that in many of the Republic's first pronouncements 'Abdullāh al-Sallāl proclaimed his intention of eventually establishing a "Republic of the Arabian Peninsula" certainly did

Times, *New York Herald Tribune*, and *Washington Post*, November 11, 1962; *The Times* (London) and *Daily Telegraph* (London), November 12, 1962.

8. A number of members of the royal family who were in the city of Ṣan'ā' on the day of the revolution, as well as some members of Imām Aḥmad's and Imām al-Badr's governments, were executed during the first few days of the Republic; wholly accurate figures are not available, although it seems clear that at least fifteen had been executed by October 1. *Washington Post* and *Neue Zürcher Zeitung*, October 1, 1962.

9. The original nine-man mission sent to Yemen during the summer of 1962 was expelled in early October (*The Observer* [London], October 7, 1962). Jordan, however, offered assistance to the Royalists (*New York Times*, October 21, 1962), and in an interview in mid-November, King Ḥusayn admitted there were sixty Jordanian officers with the Imām's forces (*Neue Zürcher Zeitung*, November 16, 1962).

nothing to convince Saudi Arabia that the revolutionaries were concerned solely with bringing reform to Yemen.[10] In the desire to protect themselves from a possible extension of revolution into their own territory, the Saudis provided assistance to the Royalists immediately after the U.A.R. announced its intention of supporting the Republic; ironically, the legal basis for this support was the same as that originally invoked by the U.A.R.: the Jidda Pact of 1956.

By early October the Royalists were able to report the capture of Mā'rib; al-Shinnar, Jabal Ḥarāz, Ḥarīb, and Ṣirwaḥ, fell by the end of the month.[11] Members of the Ḥamīd al-Dīn family had taken charge of tribal units in various regions of the country; 'Abd al-Raḥmān ibn Yaḥyā, for example, was at first in command of the forces fighting in the regions northwest of Ṣan'ā'; 'Abdullāh ibn al-Ḥusayn headed forces operating in the Jawf regions; and Ḥasan ibn al-Ḥasan, as well as Ḥasan himself, operated in the southeastern desert regions.[12]

INTERNATIONAL INVOLVEMENT

Egypt and Saudi Arabia

It appears in retrospect that the leaders of both Saudi Arabia and the United Arab Republic understood from the outset the possible international significance of this latest attempt to bring revolutionary ideologies to the Arabian Peninsula.[13] It was pre-

10. On October 11, 1962, 'Abd al-Raḥmān al-Bayḍānī, the Vice-Premier, was quoted as saying that "Yemen considers itself at war with Saudi Arabia" (*Washington Post*, *New York Times*, and *New York Herald Tribune*, October 11, 1962.) On November 4, 1962, 'Abdullāh al-Sallāl was quoted as saying, "Our massed forces have orders from the Yemeni supreme command to march into Qizan [*sic*] and Najran and recover Yemen's stolen territory." (*New York Times*, November 5, 1962; *Neue Zürcher Zeitung*, November 16, 1962.) And on November 14, 1962, al-Sallāl announced the formation of the Republic of the Arabian Peninsula. (*Neue Zürcher Zeitung* and *Le Monde* [Paris], November 15, 1962.)

11. *The Times* (London), October 11, 1962; *New York Times* and *Washington Post*, October 22, 1962; *Neue Zürcher Zeitung*, October 30, 1962; *New York Times*, November 5, 1962.

12. *Neue Zürcher Zeitung*, October 26, 1962.

13. It should be noted that these two nations were not the only ones to see a wider significance to the revolution in Yemen. Jordan interpreted a victory for the Republic as a possible model for the export of revolution by the U.A.R., and Iran, which became involved somewhat later through its military support of the Royalists (*The Observer* [London], February 28, 1965), saw a victory for revolu-

cisely this internationalization of the Yemeni conflict which was to make a lasting settlement so difficult to achieve.

Nevertheless, there were forces that influenced the U.A.R. and Saudi Arabia to discuss a peaceful solution. In the case of the U.A.R., these were a complex combination of economic and domestic political factors; in the case of Saudi Arabia, it was a combination of foreign pressure and the unshakable conviction that a Royalist victory was inevitable.

On the economic side, it was obvious that the cost of the war in Yemen was anything but a minor item in the U.A.R.'s national budget. By mid-November, 1962, it was estimated that there were at least 10,000 Egyptian troops in Yemen, as well as an immense amount of war matériel in the form of infantry weapons, communications equipment, planes of various types, tanks, and armored and scout cars, not to mention artillery and other field weapons.[14] It was widely estimated that the cost of this operation was in the neighborhood of a million dollars a day; however, most observers later placed the cost at closer to $350,000 to $500,000 per day.[15] The U.A.R.'s foreign-exchange reserves were being rapidly depleted, and those still available were needed to pay for the imports necessary to keep domestic industrial enterprises operating. It was obviously in the best interests of the Egyptian economy that some limitation be placed on the rate of foreign expenditures.[16]

At the same time, there were indications from the U.A.R. before the end of 1962 that domestic opposition to the war in Yemen was rising. Reports had reached Egypt that Egyptian troops were being killed in large numbers and often mutilated by the barbarous tribesmen of Yemen. Furthermore, there was

---

tionary Arab nationalism in the peninsula as a potential threat to its own position on the Gulf, as well as its Arab minority in Khuzistan.

14. According to 'Abd al-Qādir Hatīm, the Minister of Culture and National Guidance, the U.A.R. had sent between 5,000 and 10,000 troops. (*New York Times*, November 9, 1962.)

15. Probably the highest estimate was made by the *Daily Telegraph* (London) on December 21, 1962: 400,000 pounds ($1,120,000) per day. The lowest estimate of the military costs to the U.A.R. was also made by a British writer, 30 million pounds ($84 million) for the period September, 1962, to July, 1963. See G. H. Jansen, "The Problems of South-west Arabia," *The World Today*, XIX (August, 1963), 341. The *New York Times*, December 25, 1962, reported $1 million per day (according to Western intelligence sources).

16. See the financial pages of the *Neue Zürcher Zeitung*, October–December, 1962, *passim*; *Die Welt* (Hamburg), November 29, 1962.

a marked unwillingness to fight in Yemen on the part of Egyptian soldiers. It is difficult to say whether or not this was because the army had now become somewhat familiarized with the nature of the terrain and the foe that it faced and had decided that a "total victory" was an unlikely if not impossible outcome. In any event, the U.A.R. government had indicated by November that it was willing to discuss a settlement of the conflict.[17]

The Saudi Arabian government, on the other hand, was not concerned with the financial aspects of assisting the Royalists. Its oil revenues could easily absorb the costs of providing such assistance without straining the national budget. Crown Prince Fayṣal (the brother of King Sa'ūd, and similarly a son of 'Abd al-'Azīz ibn Sa'ūd), who became Prime Minister of the country on October 17, 1962, and was the *de facto* ruler of Saudi Arabia, realized that a protracted war in the southwestern corner of the Arabian Peninsula could create a dangerous focus for opposition to the traditionalist Saudi government at a time when real reforms were being instituted for the first time.[18] With a readily accessible center of political opposition and a source of propaganda and weapons with which to carry out clandestine operations designed to overthrow that government, any existing opposition to Fayṣal and the Saudi royal family would not remain idle. The longer such a center existed, the greater the threat to the Saudi monarchy.

At the same time, the Saudis were convinced that the Republican government in Yemen could not possibly remain in power without the assistance and support provided by the Egyptians. It therefore followed, in the Saudi view, that the withdrawal of the Egyptian expeditionary forces would result in the resumption of power by the Royalists without further Saudi help.

Kennedy's Peace Proposal

On November 27, 1962, it was announced in Washington that President John F. Kennedy had sent messages to Fayṣal, King Ḥusayn of Jordan, President 'Abd al-Nāṣir, and 'Abdullāh al-Sallāl, in which he proposed steps toward the settlement of the Yemeni conflict. In essence, these proposals suggested the fol-

17. *Daily Telegraph* (London), November 14 and 19, 1962; *Washington Post*, November 27, 1962; *New York Times*, December 25, 1962.

18. *New York Times*, November 8, 1962; *The Observer* (London), March 24, 1963.

lowing solution: the U.A.R. would withdraw its troops, aircraft, and other military equipment from Yemen, while Saudi Arabia, Jordan, and the Shaykhs and Sultans of the South Arabian Federation would cease all assistance to the Royalist forces.[19]

Saudi Arabia answered on the following day, in effect rejecting President Kennedy's proposals. According to sources close to Fayṣal, the reasons for this rejection were (1) that Saudi Arabia considered the Imām and his government the legal rulers of Yemen; (2) that a majority of the Yemeni people still supported the Imām and his government; and (3) that it was likely, indeed probable, that the Imām and his supporters would be able to defeat the Republican forces before the end of the winter.[20]

Taken at face value, these beliefs were no deterrent to accepting Kennedy's proposals. It seems logical to conclude that Fayṣal was convinced that the real objective of the U.A.R. in sending the expeditionary force to Yemen was to gain a foothold on the peninsula from which to overthrow the Saudi monarchy and gain control of the vast oil resources which it possessed. The Saudis were convinced that their assessment of the situation was correct because the Egyptians had increased their military activities to such an extent that the Royalist counteroffensive had been arrested,[21] because Egyptian planes had bombed and strafed Saudi cities,[22] and because ʿAbdullāh al-Sallāl had publicly threatened to march his forces into Saudi Arabia as well as to "recover Yemen's stolen territory."[23]

The Egyptian response was also issued the following day, November 28, 1962, in *al-Ahrām*, the major government paper; this constituted the first authoritative statement of the U.A.R.'s outlook and policy with respect to Yemen and in effect also rejected President Kennedy's proposals. In the article the following points were made: (1) that it was Saudi Arabia which was the aggressor state because of the activities it had undertaken

19. *New York Times* and *The Times* (London), November 27, 1962.
20. *New York Times*, November 30, 1962.
21. *New York Times*, November 22, 1962.
22. *Sun* (Baltimore), November 4, 1962; *Daily Telegraph* (London), November 5, 1962; *New York Times*, November 7, 1962; *Daily Telegraph*, November 13 and 30, 1962.
23. *New York Times*, November 5, 1962; additional threats to bomb Saudi Arabia were reported by the *New York Times* on November 16, 1962, as well as by the *Christian Science Monitor* on December 6, 1962.

against the Yemeni Republic; (2) that the U.A.R. had sent forces to Yemen solely to "counteract the dangers of foreign invasion" (in fact, these troops had not been dispatched to fight, but only to prevent war and "convince the Saudi government that its aggression cannot continue without being punished"); (3) that neither the U.A.R. nor the Yemeni Republic wished to bring about the downfall of the Saudi (or Jordanian) monarchies. The U.A.R.'s only purpose in sending the troops was to consolidate the Yemeni revolution and insure its continued existence and stability.[24] Unlike Saudi Arabia, however, the U.A.R. offered to withdraw its troops from Yemen if it were assured that all threats to the continued existence of the Republic would cease.[25]

As far as the Yemenis were concerned, the Imām and his supporters were angered by the fact that they had not even been consulted. 'Abdullāh al-Sallāl, on the other hand, appeared to be the only party to the conflict to welcome President Kennedy's offer of mediation. In an interview with the Middle East News Agency on December 9, al-Sallāl said that the United States had offered to use its influence to prevent any "Saudi Arabian or Jordanian" aggression on the northern borders of Yemen.[26] Although the Yemeni leader did not speak of any *quid pro quo*, it was generally assumed that once all Saudi and Jordanian assistance to the Royalists ceased, this would enable the U.A.R. to withdraw its troops. In an effort to mollify the United States, which had already indicated its concern over continued Republican threats to go to war with Saudi Arabia, al-Sallāl also declared that "we have no aggressive intentions against the Arab people in Hijaz." [27]

United States Interest in the Conflict

The United States had become concerned not only with the threats of the Republicans vis-à-vis Saudi Arabia but also with increasing Soviet assistance to the Republican government. It was felt in Washington that if the United States did not soon recognize

24. *Washington Post*, November 29, 1962; *Oriente Moderno*, XLII (December, 1962), 957.
25. *Sun* (Baltimore), November 28, 1962.
26. *Daily Telegraph* (London), November 29, 1962; *Deadline Data*, "Yemen," December 9, 1962, p. 26.
27. *Deadline Data*, p. 26.

the Republican government, its opportunity to exercise a moderating influence on the policies and objectives of that government would be lost.[28] This fear was heightened by the Republican threat, made December 14, to close the embassies and diplomatic missions of all countries which had not as yet officially recognized the Republic.[29] Apparently, American officials were sufficiently alarmed to speed recognition, or they had already satisfied themselves that the major United States preconditions had been met; on December 19, 1962, the United States granted diplomatic recognition to the Republican government.[30]

American recognition was of immense importance to the United Arab Republic, as well as to the Republican leaders, and they had devoted considerable effort to obtain it. Although it could not guarantee the continued existence of the new government, American recognition had the effect of implying American sanction for the assistance the U.A.R. was supplying. Despite his awareness that the United States had a special interest in Saudi Arabia, President ʿAbd al-Nāṣir interpreted American recognition of the Republican government to mean that, short of outright war with the Saudis, the U.A.R. would be permitted to carry on the activities it had already undertaken. No doubt the fact that the United States agreed to loan the U.A.R. $12.9 million for "budgetary support" shortly thereafter served to assure the U.A.R. of the correctness of this assumption.[31] Monarchic regimes in the Middle East which had not recognized the Republican government quickly reached the same conclusion, and both Saudi Arabia and Jordan publicly expressed their disappointment over the United States action.[32]

American motives in recognizing the Republican government remain unclear. It has been suggested that the United States was determined to disassociate itself from "feudal" regimes in the area and for the first time directly associate itself with more

28. Phillips Talbot, Assistant Secretary of State, in a letter to Senator Bourke Hickenlooper, on July 26, 1963, expressed most clearly the thinking of the Department of State on United States involvement in the Yemeni civil war. Mr. Talbot's letter was printed in the *Congressional Record* of July 30, 1963, p. 12902, at the request of Senator Hickenlooper.

29. *Le Monde* (Paris) and *Daily Telegraph* (London), December 15, 1962.

30. *Department of State Bulletin*, XLVIII (7 January 1963), 11–12.

31. *Washington Post*, January 8, 1963.

32. *Ibid.*, January 5, 1963.

progressive Arab governments and leadership. At the same time, recognition was intended to "scare" the more conservative governments into reforming themselves and perhaps make them more receptive to the demands of their people for reform and greater economic and political freedom.

While it was perhaps hoped that the above goals would also be achieved, the most convincing explanation is that the United States action was intended to enable President ʿAbd al-Nāṣir to withdraw gracefully and thereby bring about an end to the war. It was recognized in Washington that it would be impossible to obtain Egyptian withdrawal without providing for an exit that could be both graceful and "face-saving." It was assumed that American recognition would be followed by that of most other countries, including Great Britain. The fact that the United States recognized the Republic would cause both the Saudis and the Jordanians to hesitate in their support of the Imām, if only because of their dependence on the United States for military assistance. The falling-off of aid to the Royalists from these two sources would permit ʿAbdullāh al-Sallāl and his government to become established. In this expected lull, President ʿAbd al-Nāṣir could withdraw his troops honorably, claiming that even the "imperialists" had conceded that the Republic was the rightful government of Yemen and firmly established.[33]

It became apparent somewhat later that American recognition of Yemen was part of an "agreement" which had been worked out between the United States and the United Arab Republic. It was undoubtedly the negotiations for this "agreement" to which al-Sallāl had referred earlier. According to contemporary accounts, the U.A.R. agreed to withdraw its forces in return for recognition of the Republic, conditional upon the cessation of Saudi and Jordanian aid to the Royalists.[34]

Reaction to United States Recognition

What in fact occurred after United States recognition was quite different. Although more than fifty countries followed the American lead, and the United Nations on the next day (December 20, 1962) seated the Republican delegation in place of the Imām's

33. Patrick Seale, "The War in Yemen," *New Republic*, CXCVIII (January 26, 1963), 10–11.
34. *Ibid.*, p. 11.

representatives, Great Britain was not one of them. The Imām and his supporters showed not the slightest inclination to retire from the field of battle. Saudi Arabia, fearing the expansion of Egyptian power and ideology in the peninsula, appeared very reluctant, despite American assurances of support, to end her assistance to the Imām.

As a result, President ʿAbd al-Nāṣir was placed in a serious dilemma: he could withdraw his troops ignominiously, or he could escalate his commitment to the Republican government in the hope of finally achieving victory through superior land and air power. Given the Egyptian theory that the failure of the first attempt at Arab unity—the United Arab Republic of Egypt and Syria from 1958 to 1961—was due not to any deficiencies on the part of the Egyptian government or its administration, but rather to a treacherous alliance between the "imperialists" and the "reactionaries," it was of course unthinkable to permit these same forces once again to stand in the way of progressive government and a new attempt at Arab unity. The U.A.R. chose to increase its commitment.

The Egyptian decision was soon clear: between December 30, 1962, and January 1, 1963, the Saudi cities of Jizān and Najrān were subjected to extensive bombardment by Egyptian high-altitude bombers.[35] Although the Egyptians had previously bombed Saudi cities,[36] the new bombings, coming immediately after United States recognition, marked an intensification of the conflict. The almost simultaneous announcement by Radio Ṣanʿāʾ that the Yemeni Republic possessed modern rockets which it intended to use against the royal palaces of Saudi Arabia and Jordan indicated that Egyptian assurances of continued support had buoyed the confidence of the al-Sallāl government.[37]

The air raids had an immediate effect in Washington. The next day a statement by the Department of State "deplor[ed] these incidents, which threaten to expand the Yemen conflict" and made it clear that the United States has an "interest in the preservation of [Saudi Arabia's] integrity, as well as that of other states of the area."[38] In order to underline its displeasure with

35. *Washington Post*, January 1, 1963.
36. See sources cited in footnote 22 (above).
37. *The Times* (London), December 28, 1962.
38. *Department of State Bulletin*, XLVIII (21 January 1963), 90–91.

the U.A.R. action, the United States also dispatched a number of jet fighters, a destroyer, and American paratroopers to Saudi Arabia.[39] In the words of *The Times* of London, " No one [in the Middle East] misses the point that American oil interests make Saudi Arabia a special American ward." [40]

Despite the warning, again in February, March, and May, Egyptian high-altitude jet bombers attacked and bombed Jīzān and Najrān, as well as smaller towns on the border, such as Khāmis Mishayt.[41] As a result, it was obviously no longer possible for the United States to effect an end to the war. By voluntarily supporting the Republican government and its U.A.R. allies in public, as well as providing both with agricultural (P.L. 480) and other economic assistance, the United States had lost its diplomatic power to obtain a *quid pro quo* from the U.A.R. government.[42] The circumscribed nature of American demonstrations in Saudi Arabia had not served their objective, although they had probably increased the confidence of the Saudis and perhaps contributed to the latter's willingness to continue their support of the Royalists. In accordance with the general guideline of " noninvolvement " in Middle Eastern disputes adopted by the United States as a policy in the late nineteen-fifties, there was a pronounced reluctance to intervene any further.

ATTEMPTS AT MEDIATION

Despite the mutual recriminations, by early 1963 both the Saudis and the Egyptians had expressed a desire to end the

39. *Washington Post*, January 7, 1963; *Neue Zürcher Zeitung*, January 8, 1963.

40. *The Times* (London), January 7, 1963.

41. *Neue Zürcher Zeitung*, February 16, 1963; *Le Monde* (Paris), March 3–4, 1963; *Washington Post*, March 3, 1963; *Neue Zürcher Zeitung* and *L'Orient* (Beirut), June 8, 1963; *The Times* (London), June 10, 1963; *L'Orient* (Beirut), June 16, 1963; *Neue Zürcher Zeitung*, June 17, 1963; *Newsweek*, June 24, 1963, p. 32; *L'Orient* (Beirut), June 26, 1963.

42. On October 8, 1962, a three-year agreement was signed with the United Arab Republic in which the United States agreed to provide $390 million in surplus agricultural commodities under the provisions of P.L. 480, the Agricultural Trade Development and Assistance Act. It was argued by the opponents of American policy that this agreement provided additional proof of United States support, not only for President 'Abd al-Nāṣir's foreign policy in general, but more specifically for his dispatch of more than 10,000 troops to Yemen, in view of the fact that the agreements had been signed after the civil war and Egyptian intervention had begun. The specific provisions of the agreement are in Department of State, *Treaties and other International Acts Series*, No. 5179; Washington, D.C., 1962.

hostilities; their opinions over the means to achieve this goal were at variance with each other, and it was decided that only a neutral mediator might be able to bring about any effective agreement.

The United States at first attempted to fill this role and, at the same time, bring in the United Nations for the same purpose. During early March, 1963, President Kennedy sent former ambassador Ellsworth T. Bunker to the Middle East to undertake the necessary negotiations leading up to a "disengagement agreement." Concurrently, the United Nations, at the prodding of the United States, sent its own emissary, Ralph Bunche, the U.N. Undersecretary for Special Political Affairs.[43]

It was soon evident, however, that neither the United States nor the United Nations was genuinely interested in making an impartial study of the situation in Yemen. Neither Bunche nor Bunker made any attempt to see representatives of the Royalist side of the conflict; indeed, Bunche, as a result, was not permitted to visit Saudi Arabia. Consequently, there was an understandable resistance on the part of the Imām and his supporters to the idea that either the United States or the United Nations could fulfill the role of the neutral mediator. The Republicans and their U.A.R. supporters, on the other hand, looked upon the visit of the two "mediators" as an opportunity for proving the justice of their cause.

Shortly after the United States and the United Nations discussed the possibility of sending fact-finding missions to the area with representatives of the U.A.R., the latter drastically increased the number of troops and equipment being delivered to Yemen. At the same time, a new Republican offensive was begun in the eastern regions against the two major towns of that area, Mā'rib and Ḥarīb, hitherto held by the Royalists.[44] Unable to defend them against the armored columns and air attacks of the Egyptians, the Royalists withdrew. As a result, the Republican government and its U.A.R. advisers were able to conduct Ralph Bunche to Mā'rib to demonstrate the extent of Republican control of the country.[45] Mr. Bunche, upon his return to Cairo, met with the reporters and informed them that he "was most impressed by

43. *Washington Post*, March 8, 1963; *New York Times*, February 27, 1963.
44. *Washington Post*, March 7 and 8, 1963.
45. *The Times* (London), March 2 and 4, 1963.

the earnestness, seriousness of purpose and strength of the President [al-Sallāl]" and that he felt Republican Yemen should be given all possible assistance in order to put an end to "infiltration."[46]

Ambassador Bunker, meanwhile, had gone about his meetings and discussions with Saudi and Egyptian leaders with considerably more secrecy and circumspection. As a result of his negotiations with the two nations, by mid-April he was able to obtain a commitment from both that they would act in concert to see that a "disengagement" was begun in Yemen.[47]

On April 30, 1963, Secretary-General U Thant informed the Security Council of the agreement, under the terms of which the Saudi government agreed to cease all aid to the Imām and his supporters, as well as to prohibit the use of Saudi territory as a sanctuary or staging post for the Royalists. The U.A.R. for its part agreed to begin the phased withdrawal of its estimated 25,000 troops in Yemen and not to undertake any punitive action against the Royalists nor against the territory of Saudi Arabia. In addition, the U.A.R., Saudi Arabia, and the Republican government of Yemen also agreed to permit United Nations observers access to all regions of the country necessary to insure compliance.[48]

The Secretary-General went on to explain the role of the United Nations in seeing that the terms of the agreement were carried out. Major General Carl Carlsson von Horn, chief of the Palestine Truce Supervisory Organization, would be sent to Yemen to determine the needs of the United Nations team, the cost of which, estimated at $807,500 for a four-month period, would be borne equally by Saudi Arabia and the U.A.R.[49] However, in his report to U Thant, prepared after a week of talks with government officials in Cairo, Jidda, Jīzān, Najrān, al-Ḥudayda, and Ṣan'ā', as well as a brief survey of the territory in which the United Nations would be operating, von Horn was anything but optimistic. Nevertheless he carefully listed the amount of equipment and supplies and the number of men and their duties which he felt were necessary to

46. *Washington Post*, March 6, 1963.
47. *New York Times*, April 14, 1963.
48. *The Times* (London), May 1, 1963.
49. *United Nations Review*, July, 1963, p. 17; *The Times* (London), June 5, 1963.

carry out properly the intended purpose of the United Nations presence.

In early June, the Security Council met to consider U Thant's request for approval of his proposals; on June 11 the United Nations Yemen Observation Mission (U.N.Y.O.M.), consisting of 200 men, was approved for a period of two months with a provision for extensions, if necessary.[50] Actual operations, however, did not officially begin until July 4, 1963. It was evident almost from the outset that the size of the mission, combined with the nature of the terrain to be policed, prevented it from fully carrying out the duties assigned to it, that is, to insure that no Saudi aid would cross the northern Yemeni frontier and that no new Egyptian troops would be brought into the country while those already present were being progressively evacuated.

Before U.N.Y.O.M. had completed its first two months of operation, on August 20, 1963, Major General von Horn announced his intention of resigning. In his letter to the Secretary-General, von Horn wrote:

> In spite of repeated assurances from yourself [and] Bunche, . . . that every possible effort would be made to meet my requirements, as stated in my report [of] 11 May 1963, I have been compelled repeatedly to draw Headquarters attention to the fact that the support so far provided is inadequate. . . . When my dutybound representations so often are boomeranged as "unwarranted remarks" I feel having [*sic*] lost your confidence and therefore I have no other choice but to herewith tender my resignation.

In public statements, as well as in additional private letters to the United Nations, von Horn complained that U.N.Y.O.M.'s work was being hampered by managerial incompetence on the part of the Secretariat, by its neglect and dismissal of his reports on the problems which he encountered, by its unwillingness to insure the safety of his men through the allotment of sufficient funds to provide for the necessary maintenance of equipment, by the unrealistic attitude of the Secretariat toward U.N.Y.O.M. and its capabilities, and perhaps, most important, by its prohibition

50. *New York Times*, June 12, 1963; *Department of State Bulletin*, XLIX (8 July 1963), 71–72.

of any contact with the Royalists (until, after many protests, three days before von Horn left Yemen, on August 24, 1963).[51]

With von Horn's resignation and the relative lack of success of U.N.Y.O.M. in achieving its objectives, it appeared that the United Nations presence would be terminated.[52] In a sharp about-face, however, U Thant announced in early November, 1963, that Saudi Arabia and the U.A.R. had agreed to pay the costs of continuing U.N.Y.O.M.'s existence.[53] The Mission was regularly extended every two months thereafter, under a succession of new commanders, throughout 1963 and into 1964. Finally, on September 2, 1964, U Thant announced that U.N.Y.O.M. would be withdrawn and its functions terminated on September 4, 1964.[54]

Although the Secretary-General praised the Mission and the men who had worked for it, it was evident to all that it had been unable to fulfill its objectives. According to some of the observers, as well as the interim reports of U.N.Y.O.M., Saudi Arabia had observed its obligations under the disengagement agreement for a sizable portion of its duty period.[55] By the time U.N.Y.O.M. was officially disbanded, however, the Saudis had resumed their support of the Royalists. Similarly, although the United Nations observers reported at first that some Egyptian troops had been withdrawn, it was observed shortly thereafter that these were

51. *The Observer* (London), September 8, 1963; *Daily Star* (Beirut), August 31, 1963; *The Times* (London), September 2, 1963.

52. *New York Times*, September 1 and 5, 1963, and *The Sunday Times* (London), September 1, 1963, indicate the doubt evident after only two months. For the real crisis which occurred after four months, see *Washington Post* and *New York Times*, October 30, 1963.

53. *Washington Post*, November 1, 1963; *New York Herald Tribune*, November 3, 1963; *Newsweek*, November 11, 1963, p. 41.

54. *New York Times* and *Washington Post*, September 3, 1964.

55. *The Observer* (London), July 14, 1963; *Newsweek*, August 5, 1963, p. 36; *Neue Zürcher Zeitung*, September 9, 1963. One month prior to the close of the Mission's operations, the United Nations officially reported the same result: *U.N. Monthly Chronicle*, I (August, 1964), 29. It should be added, however, that these results may have been the result of the United Nations' simple inability to patrol the whole northern Yemeni border; in its final report, the United Nations was at pains to point this out: *U.N. Monthly Chronicle*, I (October, 1964), 34–36. In conversations with members of the United Nations Mission, however, the author discovered the widespread conviction that Saudi Arabia had for some months made a concerted effort to fulfill its obligations in order to avoid being accused of responsibility for continued Royalist military operations. It was more than likely, however, that many individuals carried on a lucrative trade in weapons and supplies on their own during this period.

being replaced by fresh units, some of which were brought to Yemen in a manner calculated to avoid United Nations observation. By September of 1964, it was generally estimated that the total of Egyptian troops in Yemen was in the neighborhood of 40,000.[56] U Thant, in his closing summary, expressed the hope that "sincere efforts would be made by the Governments of Saudi Arabia and the United Arab Republic to settle their needless and now senseless dispute"; [57] in expressing himself in this manner, the Secretary-General was, in effect, arguing that only the two major foreign powers involved in the conflict would be able to effect a settlement. The day for neutral mediation was past.

REPUBLICAN PROBLEMS

On the military front during 1963, the Royalists once more seized the initiative. Following their loss of Mā'rib in March of 1963, some of the Royalist commanders held a military conference in Riyāḍ, at which the strategy for the succeeding months was presumably mapped out.[58] Beginning in the summer of 1963 and lasting into spring 1964, the Royalists regained most, if not all, of the ground lost to the Egyptians during the latter's spring 1963 offensive. Such important fortress towns as al-Ḥazm, cutting off the only overland link between Mā'rib and Ḥarīb, and al-Qafla, which commands an important road junction between Ṣan'ā' and Ṣa'da, fell in June. In addition, a number of important locations in the Jawf, as well as in the area northwest of Ṣan'ā', either fell immediately or, as in the case of Ḥajja and 'Amrān, were heavily besieged.[59]

Undoubtedly at least partially due to the Royalist successes, the position of the Republic, both domestically and internationally, underwent a serious deterioration. There were frequent reports

56. *New York Times*, September 1, October 15 and 24, 1964. Other sources had reported the figure 40,000 as early as May; see *Washington Post*, May 5, 1964; *The Times* (London), July 4, 1964; *Neue Zürcher Zeitung*, July 12, 1964.

57. *U.N. Monthly Chronicle*, I (October, 1964), 36.

58. Dana Adams Schmidt, in an interview in Beirut on April 24, 1963. This conference was attended by Crown Prince Fayṣal and some Saudi intelligence officers, as well as by Aḥmad Muḥammad al-Shāmī, the Royalist Foreign Minister, Prince 'Abdullāh ibn Ḥusayn, Qāḍī Aḥmad al-Siyāghī, the Royalist Deputy Premier and Minister of the Interior, among others.

59. *The Sunday Times* (London), June 16 and 20, 1963; *New York Times*, May 29, 1963.

of assassination attempts upon the lives of important officials of the Republic and the U.A.R. in Yemen; the attempt of August, 1963, upon ʿAbdullāh al-Sallāl was serious enough to require that he be taken to Egypt for proper treatment,[60] while in December, 1963, the U.A.R. commander-in-chief of the expeditionary force, General Anwār al-Qāḍī, was so badly wounded that he had to be replaced.[61]

Internal Dissensions

There were numerous other signs of weakness in the Republic: a number of important tribes and tribal leaders (including Shaykh ʿAbdullāh al-Aḥmar of the Ḥāshid) were discovered either to have defected to the Royalist side or to have had discussions with Royalist leaders;[62] a Shāfiʿī underground organization, al-Jīl al-Jadīd (The New Generation), which was formed to protest against the domination of the Republic by the Zaydis (specifically ʿAbdullāh al-Sallāl) and the Egyptians, was discovered;[63] some leaders of the Republic, including such highly respected figures as Muḥammad Maḥmūd al-Zubayrī, undertook unauthorized discussions with the intention of seeking to come to some sort of agreement with the Royalists and lessening the dependence of the Republic on the U.A.R.;[64] senior officers of the Yemeni Republic's army petitioned President ʿAbd al-Nāṣir to replace al-Sallāl, thus indicating their displeasure with his leadership;[65] and perhaps

60. *Daily Star* (Beirut), August 14, 1963; *Neue Zürcher Zeitung*, August 17 and 18, 1963; *L'Orient* (Beirut), August 25, 1963. According to the Egyptian authorities, however, al-Sallāl was suffering from a "duodenal ulcer," which had apparently first been diagnosed as anemia. (See also *Le Monde*, July 31, 1963, for an alleged earlier attempt.)

61. *The Times* (London), December 24, 1963.

62. *The Observer* (London), July 14, 1963; *Daily Star* (Beirut) and *L'Orient* (Beirut), August 15, 1963; *Daily Telegraph* (London), September 9, 1963; *Le Monde* (Paris) and *Neue Zürcher Zeitung*, September 28, 1963.

63. *Daily Star* (Beirut), August 20, 1963. It has not been possible to obtain any additional information on the origins or later activities of this organization. Another secret underground organization also made its appearance in mid-1963: the Popular Liberation Front. Unlike al-Jīl al-Jadīd, however, its membership was made up of both Shāfiʿīs and Zaydis, apparently united in their opposition to the Republican government. See the *Daily Star* (Beirut), September 3, 1963.

64. *Daily Star* (Beirut) and *L'Orient* (Beirut), August 15, 1963; *Daily Star* (Beirut), August 21, 1963; *The Times* (London), October 18, 1963; *Daily Star* (Beirut), October 31, 1963; *The Economist* (London), January 11, 1964; *Daily Telegraph* (London), November 19, 1963; *New York Times*, December 1, 1963.

65. *New York Times*, September 13, 1963.

most damaging of all, senior officers and field commanders of the U.A.R. forces in Yemen were signing truces with the Royalists in exchange for "safe conducts" from their beleaguered positions.[66] It was even reported that the U.A.R. Vice-President, 'Abd al-Ḥakīm 'Āmr, had met with Royalist commanders, while other officials had discussed with Royalist leaders the possibility of an Egyptian withdrawal.[67]

Egyptian–Republican Dissension

Although the U.A.R. forces continued to carry out their air attacks upon Saudi cities and the towns and villages of Royalist-held areas, there appears to have been a serious attempt on the part of President 'Abd al-Nāṣir to extricate himself from sole responsibility for sustaining the Republic in the latter part of 1963. While a variety of military officials in Yemen sought for some way of obtaining Royalist co-operation for a U.A.R. withdrawal, officials in Cairo attempted, without success, to replace the troops of the U.A.R. with an "all-Arab" force similar to that organized to defend Kuwait in 1961.[68]

The activities of the Egyptians in their search for a graceful exit from Yemen did not go unnoticed by 'Abdullāh al-Sallāl and his close supporters. Fearing that the U.A.R. was perhaps ready to abandon the Republic, the Yemeni President undertook to obtain other sources of support. In March of 1964, he left for the Soviet Union and was soon able to report the signing of a treaty under the terms of which the U.S.S.R. was to provide economic and technical assistance to the Yemeni Republic.[69]

The combination of almost uninterrupted Royalist victories and the successful trip of President al-Sallāl to Moscow in search of independent support for his failing government prompted the "surprise" visit of the U.A.R. President to Yemen in late April, 1964, in order to investigate the situation there at first hand.[70]

66. *Daily Telegraph* (London), September 9, 1963; *Neue Zürcher Zeitung*, November 30, 1963; *New York Times*, December 1, 1963.

67. These accounts were first published by the *Daily Star* (Beirut) on September 8, 1963, and were the result of an interview with Paul Bristol, M.P., who had just returned from Yemen.

68. *Daily Telegraph* (London), November 6, 1964.

69. *The Times* (London), March 16 and 23, 1964; *Neue Zürcher Zeitung*, March 27, 1964.

70. *The Times* (London), April 24, 1964; *Christian Science Monitor*, April 27, 1964.

The visit of 'Abd al-Nāṣir was followed by two important moves. The first of these was the promulgation of a new constitution for the Yemeni Republic (as well as a change in the cabinet).[71] The second, even more significant, step taken by the U.A.R. leader was an escalation in the number of troops and the amount of military matériel being committed to the Republic. Shortly after the visit, U.A.R. troops, together with their generally acknowledged weak and ineffectual Republican allies,[72] undertook a major offensive in the north which was designed to surround the Imām's major bastions, capture him, and destroy the Royalist armies. This was, in fact, "probably the biggest single military operation . . . in [the] nearly two years of campaigning" since the establishment of the Republic.[73] It was a two-pronged attack, using an estimated 5,000-plus troops directed against the northwestern mountain strongholds of Washha and Qāra, as well as the eastern armies under the leadership of Ḥasan. Although at one point the Republican and Egyptian forces came close to capturing these strongholds of the Royalists, the latter counterattacked, broke the Egyptian offensive, regained nearly all the territory they had lost, and captured large amounts of men and equipment.[74]

71. Antonio D'Emilia, "Intorno alle costituzioni provvisorie repubblicane del Yemen," *Oriente Moderno*, XLIV (May, 1964), 301–312.

72. According to the reports of the correspondents who visited Yemen, very few men were trained and armed in order to create a citizen-soldiery which could be termed a genuine "Army of the Yemen Republic." Those few Yemenis sent abroad, either to Egypt or the Soviet Union, for military training were not permitted to take part in military operations because of Egyptian doubts concerning their loyalty in combat. Apparently past experience had led to this conclusion. In fact, of course, the warriors in Yemen are the tribesmen; the urban Yemenis have never demonstrated any martial qualities, and for this reason they have generally been considered beneath contempt by the tribesmen of the mountains. Although the Egyptians at first were able to obtain the co-operation and assistance of many tribes, more and more of them deserted the cause of the Republic for the Royalist side as the conflict dragged on. Considerable sums were expended by both sides in subsidies to their tribal allies (a precedent which will undoubtedly cause considerable difficulty for whoever becomes the final "victor" and inevitably must eliminate or decrease these subsidies when peace is achieved); yet Egyptian campaigns in any particular region usually resulted in mass desertions from their ranks by those tribesmen whose homes and fields were immediately affected by the action. This is undoubtedly one of the major reasons for continued influxes of Egyptian troops—their loyalty to the U.A.R. cause and the Republic was at least assured; no doubt their regular pay and allowances often came to less than the subsidy which some tribes demanded for their co-operation.

73. *New York Times*, August 28, 1964.

74. *Ibid.* and *Christian Science Monitor*, September 2, 1964.

At the same time, President ʿAbd al-Nāṣīr also apparently decided on a new tack with respect to the stated purpose of the Egyptian presence in Yemen. Whereas in previous public statements the emphasis had been on the necessity of supporting the progressive regime of Republican Yemen (even though it was acknowledged that Yemen had become a "proving ground" for U.A.R. forces),[75] the U.A.R. leader now attempted to turn the war into an "anti-imperialist" campaign against Great Britain's position in southern Arabia. Presumably to draw attention away from the relative lack of success in Yemen, the U.A.R. supported, from all available evidence, tribal rebellions in the South Arabian Federation; specifically, training and military equipment were given to the tribes of the Radfān region of the former Western Aden Protectorate.[76]

PEACE NEGOTIATIONS

At this juncture, seemingly as a direct result of the defeat of the Republican campaign and the inability of the Radfān operations to achieve any notable success, direct negotiations between the Saudis and the Egyptians were taken up for the first time. In discussions held after the close of the Second Arab League Summit Conference in Alexandria in early September, 1964, Fayṣal and ʿAbd al-Nāṣir agreed to "fully cooperate in mediation with the concerned parties in order to reach a peaceful solution of all problems in Yemen" and to continue these efforts "until conditions stabilize there." [77]

In many respects, the Saudi–Egyptian agreement was similar to the earlier United Nations "disengagement" plan. In this instance, however, a joint Saudi-Egyptian force would play the peace-keeping role originally carried out by U.N.Y.O.M. The most interesting provision of the new agreement was the decision to "replace" the leaders of the opposing factions in Yemen itself and create a new government which would include some

75. *Le Monde* (Paris), December 26, 1963, reporting on President ʿAbd al-Nāṣir's annual Port Saʿīd speech.

76. *The Observer* (London), April 26, 1964; *Neue Zürcher Zeitung*, May 4, 1964; on the fighting in the Radfān mountains during May, 1964, and thereafter, see such British papers as *The Times* (London), *Daily Telegraph* (London), and *Guardian* (Manchester and London), *passim*.

77. *New York Times*, September 15, 1964.

Royalists, but no members of the Ḥamīd al-Dīn family. As a result of these talks, representatives of the two Yemeni factions met on the neutral ground of Erkwit, in the Sudan, between October 30 and November 4, 1964. They agreed that a cease-fire would go into effect on November 5, 1964, and that on November 23 a National Congress would be held somewhere in Yemen, to be attended by 169 tribal, religious, and military leaders in addition to those who originally participated in the meeting at Erkwit. However, the Congress never took place because the various factions could not agree on a formula for representation or even on a mutually satisfactory location.[78]

Appearance of a "Third Force"

The cease-fire which had accompanied the talks broke down almost immediately. After the renewal of the fighting, the Royalists expanded their operations and once again embarked on a major counteroffensive, including campaigns in the southern mountains for the first time in many months.[79] At the same time, the breakdown of the Conference and the Royalist victories brought into the open evidence of a major rift in Republican ranks. Although there had been serious disagreements among the revolutionaries in the past on the role and function of the Egyptians in the Republic, this was the first time that such differences had become widely evident. It seems reasonable to assume that the rift was attributable to the dissatisfaction that some Republican leaders felt concerning the intransigent attitude assumed by their official representatives to the Erkwit talks and to later discussions concerning representation at, and the purpose of, the National Congress which had never convened.

On December 11, 1964, the President of the Consultative Council, Aḥmad Muḥammad Nuʿmān, and the two Deputy Premiers, Muḥammad Maḥmūd al-Zubayrī and Qāḍī ʿAbd al-Raḥmān al-

78. *New York Times*, November 6, 1964; *The Times* (London), *New York Times*, *Neue Zürcher Zeitung*, November 9, 1964; *The Times* (London), November 20, 1964; *New York Times*, November 15 and 21, 1964; *Neue Zürcher Zeitung*, November 28, 1964; *New York Times*, December 8, 1964; *Washington Post*, December 13, 1964; *Neue Zürcher Zeitung*, December 15, 1964.

79. *The Times* (London), January 14, 1965; *Neue Zürcher Zeitung*, January 16 and 19, 1965; *Washington Post*, January 17, 1965; *New York Times*, January 23, 1965.

Iriānī, resigned.[80] According to reports at the time, their resignations were part of an increasing wave of sentiment in the capital and other Republican cities against the al-Sallāl government, as well as the provisions of the 1964 Constitution—an interpretation that was borne out in the next few weeks, when more than twenty additional members of the government resigned.[81] President al-Sallāl, who had been in Cairo on one of his many trips for a variety of diplomatic and health reasons, hurried back to Yemen and proclaimed a state of emergency. He replaced Premier Ḥamūd al-Jā'ifī with General Ḥasan al-'Amrī (often characterized as the " strongman " of the Republic) and issued instructions to bring some of the former ministers of the cabinet to trial for " crimes against the state." [82] It was obvious that the political grouping which had earlier been characterized as the " Third Force "—that is, those Republicans who were opposed to al-Sallāl and who felt that a settlement of the three-year-old war could be achieved only by an agreement worked out among the Yemenis themselves—had appeared on the Yemeni political scene to stay.

This " Third Force " was made up of a number of prominent Yemenis who had impeccable credentials insofar as their opposition to the regimes of previous Imāms were concerned. Among their number were prominent leaders of the old Free Yemeni Movement (al-Zubayrī and Nu'mān), as well as such respected members of the Republican government as Qāḍī al-Iriānī. Aware of the growing reaction to the Egyptian presence in Yemen, the " Third Force " sought to create an atmosphere conducive to some sort of compromise with the Royalists and thereby end the war.

Once again, secret talks were undertaken with Royalist leaders upon the initiative of this group.[83] There were, however, many officials of the Republic and the U.A.R. administration in Yemen who disapproved of these discussions; their argument was that they weakened the effectiveness of the Republic and contributed measurably toward a lessening of its prestige among those tribes

80. *New York Times*, December 13, 1964; *Neue Zürcher Zeitung*, December 16, 1964.

81. *New York Times*, December 27, 1964; *Washington Post*, December 28, 1964.

82. *New York Times* and *Washington Post*, January 6 and 7, 1965; *Neue Zürcher Zeitung*, January 8 and 13, 1965.

83. *The Economist*, CCXV (April 3, 1965), 34.

and other groups which tended to waver in their support. At the same time, of course, they enhanced the prestige of the Royalists. It was, perhaps, for these reasons that on April 1, 1965, the leader of the "Third Force," Muḥammad Maḥmūd al-Zubayrī, was assassinated. Although the Republican leaders immediately made him a martyr to the cause of the Republic, it was generally assumed that it was in fact Egyptian elements which had carried out the act.[84]

Fearing that the prestige of the Republic was now at an all-time low among the Yemenis themselves, and fully aware of the increasing opposition to the continued presence of large numbers of Egyptian troops, President al-Sallāl decided to attempt a reconciliation. On April 18, 1965, he replaced the "hard-lining" General Ḥasan al-ʿAmrī as Premier with Aḥmad Muḥammad Nuʿmān.[85] Immediately upon assuming office, the new government which Nuʿmān appointed undertook a National Peace Conference of Republican leaders with the chiefs of several powerful Yemeni tribes at Khāmir, in northern Yemen, from April 30 to May 5. Although the supporters of the Imām refused to attend, the Conference decided to form a special committee to make peace overtures to the Royalist leaders.[86]

This was a radical departure from the previous attitudes of Republican political leaders; indeed, it has been called "the second Yemeni revolution." It was soon obvious that these initiatives did not have the support of al-Sallāl, nor apparently of President ʿAbd al-Nāṣir; immediately after the Khāmir Conference closed, it was reported that the U.A.R. had once again dispatched more men and equipment to Yemen.[87] By June 28 Nuʿmān was forced to resign, and al-Sallāl appointed himself as Premier, together with a cabinet of unconciliatory military officers.[88]

Evidently this solution did not have the support of the U.A.R. either, and on July 11 al-Sallāl flew to Cairo for "consultations." The view of the Egyptian High Command was that a military government would not have sufficient popular support; accordingly, another new cabinet was named on July 20. Although

84. *New York Times*, April 2, 1965.
85. *New York Times* and *Washington Post*, April 22, 1965.
86. *The Times* (London), May 6, 1965; *Washington Post*, May 3, 4, and 5, 1965; *Neue Zürcher Zeitung*, May 7, 1965.
87. *New York Times*, May 30, 1965.
88. *New York Times*, June 29, July 2 and 12, 1965.

Ḥasan al-ʿAmrī remained Premier, the new government also included two members of the Nuʿmān cabinet, as well as a former Royalist who had been imprisoned by the Republicans for three years.[89] It was quite clearly an attempt to obtain greater popular support, but it either came too late or was considered insufficient, for on the next day 37 Republican leaders accompanied by over 200 of their supporters crossed the border into the Amirate of Bayḥān.[90]

This voluntary exile by so many leaders (all of whom took part in the Khāmir Conference) may well prove to have been one of the most significant events in the history of the Yemeni Republic. Among the individuals who left were Shaykh Nuʿmān ibn Qāʾid ibn Rajīh, a member of the Republican Council during the Nuʿmān government; Shaykh Sinān Abū Luhūm, the Minister of the Interior in the first al-ʿAmrī cabinet; and, most important of all, Shaykh ʿAbdullāh ibn Ḥusayn al-Aḥmar, Minister of the Interior in the Nuʿmān cabinet and a paramount leader of the Ḥāshid tribal confederation—one of the earliest supporters of the new Republic against the Imām.[91]

On the military front, the Royalist counteroffensive during this period was enjoying successes over large areas of the country. In early 1965 they had been able to take Jabal Rāzih, a strategic fortress controlling much of the land communications of the north;[92] in early March, the important city of Ḥarīb in the southeast returned to Royalist control;[93] somewhat later, another strategic fortress town, Sirwāh, returned to Royalist hands; and in the struggle for al-Jūba the U.A.R.'s most knowledgeable Yemen specialist, Brigadier Maḥmūd al-Qāsim, fell in battle.[94] By summer, Royalist forces (now receiving better training at the hands of a small number of European mercenaries)[95] also recaptured

89. *Arab World* (Beirut), July 21, 1965.
90. *Ibid.*, July 22, 1965.
91. *Ibid.*
92. *Neue Zürcher Zeitung*, January 16, 1965.
93. *Washington Post*, March 11, 1965; *New York Times*, March 25, 1965.
94. *Neue Zürcher Zeitung*, May 26, 1965; *New York Times*, May 30, 1965.
95. A number of correspondents reported that some French, Belgian, and British mercenaries were assisting the Royalists in the training of their tribal warriors. See, for example, *New York Times*, December 18, 1963; *New York Herald Tribune*, August 3, 1964; *New York Times*, May 22, 1965; *Christian Science Monitor*, July 13, 1965.

Mā'rib, al-Qafla, al-Mutamma, and a number of other towns; in the process, they succeeded in capturing large amounts of equipment, completely isolating or taking hundreds of Egyptian prisoners.[96] By early August, it was generally conceded that they had seized more than one-third of the area formerly held by Egyptian forces and that probably more than 50 per cent of the country was under their control.[97]

These successes, combined with the deep division in Republican ranks (once again, secret peace feelers had been undertaken, and assassination attempts upon the leaders of the various factions were increasingly frequent),[98] necessitated a new move toward "disengagement" or peace. Although al-'Amrī accused the dissident Republicans of being "traitors," President 'Abd al-Nāṣir of the U.A.R. announced that peace talks had been resumed.[99]

Meanwhile, more than 200 Royalist and Republican delegates held a two-week conference in Ṭā'if, Saudi Arabia, during early August. Representing the "dissident Republicans" (including the recently formed Ḥizb Allāh [Party of God])[100] and major leaders of the Royalist side, the Conference was able on the thirteenth to announce over Radio Makka a three-step plan to end the civil war.[101] Nevertheless, both Nu'mān (in Cairo) and al-Sallāl (in Ṣan'ā') rejected and disowned the proposals and the discussions which had been held.

'Abd al-Nāṣir–Fayṣal Peace Plan

Shortly thereafter, on August 22, 1965, President 'Abd al-Nāṣir arrived in Jidda to confer with King Fayṣal personally on a means

96. *Christian Science Monitor*, May 10, and 20, 1965; *New York Times*, May 22, 1965; *Neue Zürcher Zeitung*, June 29, 1965; *New York Times*, June 9, 1965.

97. *Washington Post*, August 7, 1965, and sources cited in footnote 96, above.

98. *New York Times*, July 14, 1965; *The Times* (London), July 13, 1965, p. 13; *Washington Post* and *Neue Zürcher Zeitung*, August 7, 1965; *The Times* (London), September 17, 1965.

99. *The Times* (London), August 2, 1965. (During early July, nearly fifty followers of Nu'mān had also been arrested for their alleged criticism of the Republic government and participation in an assassination attempt: *New York Times*, July 8 and July 24, 1965.)

100. Ḥizb Allāh was founded by Muḥammad Maḥmūd al-Zubayrī after his resignation from the Republican government in December, 1964. Its headquarters were in the Jawf region, at Jabal Baraṭ, near Ṣa'da, presumably to make unofficial contacts with the Royalists easier. See *Jeune Afrique*, No. 231 (May 9, 1965), pp. 19–21; *The Economist* (London), CCXV (April 3, 1965), 34.

101. *New York Times*, August 14, 1965.

toward settlement of the conflict.[102] By the twenty-fourth, the two leaders had reached an agreement for peace in Yemen. Their plan provided that: A national plebiscite be held in Yemen no later than November 23, 1966, to permit the Yemenis to determine which form of government they wanted. (2) A Transitional Council would be created, consisting of fifty members to represent all national interests in Yemen. This Transitional Council would decide on the system of government during the "transitional period" until the plebiscite and on the form and system of the plebiscite itself. It was to hold its first meeting in the Yemeni town of Ḥarāḍ on November 23, 1965. (3) The Saudi and U.A.R. governments pledged their support to the resolutions of the Transitional Council and agreed to establish a neutral committee made up of representatives from both countries to supervise the plebiscite if the Transitional Council so desired. (4) Saudi Arabia would begin to withhold immediately all military assistance to the Royalists and refrain from permitting the use of its territory as a base for operations against the Republican government of Yemen. (5) The U.A.R. would withdraw all its troops from Yemen over a ten-month period beginning on November 23, 1965. (6) A cease-fire would take effect immediately. (7) The U.A.R. and Saudi Arabia would establish a joint peace committee to supervise borders and ports in Yemen and to insure that no military assistance was furnished to either side. (8) The Peace Committee so established would have authority to operate anywhere in Yemen and would have at its disposal a joint force made up of Saudi and U.A.R. troops. (9) King Fayṣal and President ʿAbd al-Nāṣir would agree to maintain constant contact in order to overcome any possible difficulties in the implementation of the agreement.[103]

The reception accorded the agreement was generally favorable, although the al-Sallāl government displayed a noticeable lack of enthusiasm.[104] The facts that the two leaders had not listed any preconditions, that all eventualities appeared to be covered in great detail, and that the U.A.R. leader had come to Saudi Arabia in order to work out the compromise all augured well for its

102. *New York Times*, August 23, 1965.

103. *Arab World* (Beirut), *New York Times*, and *The Times* (London), August 24 and 25, 1965.

104. *The Times* (London), August 26, 1965.

success. By the end of the month, it was reliably reported that the cease-fire was in effect.

In an effort to close Republican ranks prior to the opening of the Ḥarāḍ Conference, President al-Sallāl announced the formation of a new Republican Council in early September; significantly, although it included al-ʿAmrī, it also included Nuʿmān and al-Iriānī.[105] At the same time, the government released the dissident Republicans who had been imprisoned after Nuʿmān's resignation in June.[106] In late October, al-Sallāl flew to Cairo following a conference of Republican leaders at Janad which unexpectedly had expressed support for the resolutions of the abortive Khāmir Conference.[107]

The Ḥarāḍ Conference

To the surprise of many, the Ḥarāḍ Conference actually convened on November 23, 1965; neither al-Sallāl nor the Imām was present, although the personal representatives of both Saudi Arabia and the U.A.R. were. It was soon apparent, however, that there was little ground for optimism. The head of the Republican delegation, Qāḍī al-Iriānī, protested that he had been unaware of the fact that the Jidda Agreement had seemingly abolished both the Republic and the Imamate and that the only function of the Conference was to choose a government neither Republican nor Imamic.

It was precisely this point which became the main stumbling block to any agreement at the Conference. The Jidda Agreement had left some points open to differing interpretations; the most important of these was the provision that the Conference should determine the method of government during the Transitional Period until the plebiscite. The Republican delegates argued that this implied that the Conference should decide once and for all that Yemen was a Republic in which the Ḥamīd al-Dīn family had no place. The Royalists, on the other hand, insisted that all the Conference was required to do was to set up a provisional

105. *Arab World* (Beirut), and *Washington Post*, September 5, 1965; *Neue Zürcher Zeitung*, September 9, 1965.

106. *The Times* (London), October 23, 1965.

107. *New York Times*, November 30, 1965; *The Observer* (London), December 19, 1965; *The Times* (London), December 22, 1965; *Arab World* (Beirut), December, 1965, *passim*.

administration for a "state of Yemen" and that the decision as to whether Yemen was a republic or any other kind of government was outside the competence of the Conference. As a result, further disagreements broke out on when the plebiscite should or could be held as well as on the timetable for Egyptian withdrawal. The Conference became deadlocked.[108]

Failure of Peace Efforts

It was, nevertheless, obvious that both Saudi Arabia and the U.A.R. desired to see a settlement. In his efforts to save the Conference, President 'Abd al-Nāṣir had al-Sallāl remain in Cairo throughout its deliberations in order to avoid any prejudicial activities on his part, and he also sent a personal representative, Ḥasan Ṣabrī al-Khūlī, to persuade the Republican delegation to come to some sort of agreement.[109] These attempts at bringing about a greater willingness to compromise on the part of the Republicans failed, and with the beginning of Ramaḍān, the Conference was adjourned until February 20, 1966.[110]

Almost immediately charges of bad faith, broken promises, obstructionism, and a threat to return to war were heard. On January 7, 1966, Premier Ḥasan al-'Amrī resigned, to be succeeded once again by Qāḍī al-Iriānī.[111] It was asserted at the time that this resignation was the result of "Egyptian disenchantment with the intransigence of Yemeni Republicans at, and after, the Ḥarāḍ Conference."[112] Indeed, the fact that al-'Amrī had paid a number of visits to the Conference in order to "harden" the Republican stand and had broadcast over Radio Ṣan'ā' that the Republic would "remain forever" and that the army would crush anyone opposed to Republican rule at the precise time when the Conference was in session certainly did little to convince the Saudis or the Royalists that the Republicans (and the Egyptians) were acting in good faith.[113]

108. See the references in note 107, above.
109. *The Observer* (London), December 5, 1965.
110. *The Observer* (London), December 19, 1965; *The Times* (London) and *Neue Zürcher Zeitung*, December 22, 1965; *Washington Post*, December 26 and 30, 1965.
111. *The Times* (London), January 8, 1966; *Neue Zürcher Zeitung*, January 9, 1966.
112. *The Times* (London), January 8, 1966.
113. *The Times* (London), January 8 and 14, 1966.

In mid-February, a high-level U.A.R. delegation (Vice-President 'Abd al-Ḥakīm 'Āmr, Ḥasan Ṣabrī al-Khūlī, and Anwār al-Sadāt) arrived in Ṣan'ā' to discuss the approaching resumption of the Ḥarāḍ Conference. It was assumed that 'Abd al-Nāṣir and the Egyptians were attempting to break the deadlock by exerting further pressure on the intransigent Republican leadership.[114] In fact, however, the Ḥarāḍ Conference failed to reconvene on February 20 as originally planned, and a noticeable hardening of positions on both sides took place shortly thereafter.

Observers of the Middle Eastern scene were quick to offer possible explanations. One prominent factor which was widely discussed was the single largest sale of modern jet aircraft and other sophisticated military equipment in the Middle East in many years to the Saudi Arabian government in late 1965 by the United States and Great Britain.[115] It was argued that this build-up of Saudi Arabia at a time when that country and the U.A.R. were in a bitter military (over Yemen) and psychological (over the "Islamic alliance") war for predominance in inter-Arab affairs was a calculated blow to the prestige of President 'Abd al-Nāṣir which he could not afford to ignore. Indeed, the latter interpreted it as part of an "Anglo-American conspiracy to destroy the Arab front"; it was, therefore, argued that it had contributed to Egypt's decision to remain in Yemen and to refuse to compromise.[116]

In other quarters it was suggested that promises of direct Soviet support for the Republican regime in the event of an Egyptian withdrawal gave certain of the Republican leaders new confidence and strengthened their resolve not to yield in any respect. It was true that significant amounts of new Soviet military aid were delivered to Yemen during January and February, 1966, perhaps as a result of a bilateral agreement between the Republicans and the Soviet Union.[117] If this were true, it meant that 'Abd al-Nāṣir had been placed in a difficult dilemma—one which ironically bore

114. *Washington Post*, February 19, 1966.

115. *The Times* (London), December 22, 1965.

116. *Arab Observer* (Cairo), January 10, 1966, p. 17; and *The Times* (London), January 4, 1966.

117. *The Times* (London), January 4 and 13, 1966. The Saudis, on the other hand, had a different explanation: the Soviet Union sees a continued conflict in Yemen as the best means for expanding its foothold on the peninsula. Saudi officials made reference to an article appearing in *Al-Ahrām*, written by Muḥammad Ḥasanayn Haykal, which said that although the war had been expensive for Egypt, the expenses had been more than covered by an agreement signed by President

certain similarities to his relationship with the old Yemen of Imām Aḥmad. Now, as in the nineteen-fifties, it appeared that the promise of Soviet support for the Republican regime, independent of U.A.R. support and control, made the U.A.R. leader extremely wary and perhaps convinced him that only by keeping the initiative in the defense of the Republic in his own hands could the threat of extensive Soviet penetration and intervention in Arab affairs be avoided.

Growing Polarization

For whatever reason, however, in early January new Egyptian troops, equipment, and other military matériel were landed.[118] By late February, in a speech on the anniversary of the abortive union of Egypt with Syria, President ʿAbd al-Nāṣir declared that the U.A.R. was prepared to stay in Yemen as long as necessary and that the withdrawal of Egyptian troops was contingent on the formation of a government that would conduct a plebiscite. He added that "unless this government is created, we shall not withdraw our troops until the Yemeni revolution is able to defend itself against the conspiracies of imperialism and reaction."[119] The implication seemed to be that if the two sides could agree on a transitional government, the U.A.R. was still willing to withdraw its troops.

By mid-1966, this hope had begun to fade.[120] Military operations by the Royalists had once more begun in earnest, and their forces drove deep into territories formerly held by the Republicans and the Egyptians. Reports indicated that many of the traditional supply routes of Egyptian forces were almost permanently in Royalist hands; certainly, all the cities and towns of the northwest, north, east, and much of the west were now under Royalist control.

Faced with an increasing number of defeats as well as a largely

ʿAbd al-Nāṣir in Moscow immediately after signing the August, 1965, agreement. This agreement "saved" Egypt $460 million, and the Saudis interpreted this to be the price which the Soviet Union was willing to pay to prevent implementation of the peace agreement. See *New York Times*, January 3, 1966.

118. *The Times* (London), January 13, 1966; *Washington Post*, January 14, 1966.

119. *New York Times*, February 23, 1966.

120. The proposed resumption of the Ḥaraḍ Conference, for example, never took place. *The Times* (London), February 21, 1966; *Arab World* (Beirut), February, 1966, *passim*.

demoralized army, the Egyptians decided on a new tactic: the "long breath." According to the military editors of such prominent Egyptian papers as *al-Akhbār*, *al-Ahrām*, and *al-Jumhūriyya*, this consisted of withdrawing Egyptian troops from the whole northern regions and regrouping them in the southern triangle formed by the three cities of Ṣan'ā', Ta'izz, and al-Ḥudayda.[121] In consolidating Republican troops and equipment in this area, it was obvious that the U.A.R. had abandoned the idea of a complete victory over all of Yemen. Whether the motivation was the defeat which the Royalists inflicted on the Egyptians east of Ṣan'ā' (which brought a request for Red Cross assistance from the U.A.R. leadership in Yemen),[122] or the recognition that an extensive area of inaccessible terrain without efficient communications and administrative network was next to impossible for a limited number of trained men (regardless how well equipped) to subdue when a determined group of "insurgents" had both the support of the populace and a protected supply route from outside the country, or the progressive breakdown of the largely agricultural Yemeni economy (leading to requests for sizable amounts of United States surplus foods),[123] the Egyptian retreat took most of March to May, 1966.[124]

121. *Al-Ahrām*, March 26, 1966; *Al-Jumhūriyyah*, March 30, 1966; *Al-Akhbār*, April 18, 1966. See also *Neue Zürcher Zeitung*, March 28, 1966; *The Observer* (London), March 20, 1966.

122. *Washington Post*, March 12, 1966; *New York Times*, March 11, 1966; *Neue Zürcher Zeitung*, March 24, 1966.

The International Committee of the Red Cross (I.C.R.C) began operations in Yemen early in the conflict. It sent an observer in 1962 to investigate the situation and, because of the reluctance of any national Red Cross to provide medical assistance to the combatants, undertook one of its rare unilateral missions. For further information on the operations, hospital, and personnel of the I.C.R.C. at al-Uqd (in Royalist territory), see *Neue Zürcher Zeitung*, January 31, June 19, September 28, 1963; *The Times* (London), September 25, 1963; *Neue Zürcher Zeitung*, October 23, 1963; *The Times* (London), October 31, 1963; *Neue Zürcher Zeitung*, Nevember 15 and 29, 1963, January 15, 1964, December 12, 1963, May 9, June 27, August 7, 1964; *New York Times*, May 30, 1965.

123. The question of American surplus food being delivered to Yemen, and specifically to the Royalist side, had originally been raised in mid-1965. (*New York Times*, March 9 and 10, 1965.) Once again, in mid-1966, at a time when there were many reports of starvation among the Yemenis as the result of a prolonged drought, the United States took up the issue. Although a number of objections were raised on political grounds, it was finally decided to send such supplies and have the neutral International Committee on the Red Cross act as the distributor. See *New York Times*, May 2, 25, and June 8, 1966; *Washington Post*, June 8, 1966.

124. *New York Times*, May 7, 1966.

Two Yemens?

The corollary of this action was immediately apparent to all concerned with developments in Yemen: a possible partition of the country into Republican and Royalist regions, the former being primarily Shāfiʿī, the latter primarily Zaydi. This was an alternative which, to all appearances, was relished by no one. Although it had been reported previously in the conflict that the idea had been broached,[125] neither the Republican nor Royalist leadership ever seriously proposed this alternative as a possible solution to the war. Indeed, although some of the opposition groups that had arisen in the Republican region had as their motivation an anti-Zaydi zeal, the Royalist leadership had gone to considerable lengths to point out to the population at large that it was fighting not for a restoration of the Imamate as it had been under Imām Aḥmad, but rather for a purely Yemeni regime in which the Imām would play the role of a " constitutional monarch " along Western lines.[126] In this it seemed to be quite successful, for by 1966 the formerly anti-Zaydi groups in the Shāfiʿī regions appeared to have lost any political significance, and correspondents were able to report that even the Shāfiʿī regions were sympathetic, to a certain degree, to the departure of the Egyptians and a return to Royalist rule.[127] The basic assumption underlying all attempts at peace had continued to be that Yemen was a single country undergoing the unfortunate and horrible experience of a civil war; in time, the war would end and the residents of the country—Shāfiʿī or Zaydi, Republican or Royalist—would once again work to create a viable and modernized whole.

125. *Daily Star* (Beirut), May 25, 1963; *New York Times*, September 13, 1963; *Neue Zürcher Zeitung*, February 16, 1966.

126. The idea of an Imām with very restricted powers in the field of religious affairs only had also been suggested earlier, even by ʿAbdullāh al-Sallāl himself. (*Washington Post* and *New York Times*, May 19, 1963.) Off and on during the conflict, the possibility of eliminating both al-Sallāl and the Imām from the political scene in an effort to bring about an agreement between the two sides was also discussed. (*Sunday Telegraph* [London], October 6, 1963; *Newsweek*, October 14, 1963, pp. 28 and 31.)

Various correspondents, after interviews with the Imām in his mountain strongholds, reported that he was not intractably opposed to the proposition, but by 1965–1966 the whole idea appeared to have been forgotten.

127. *Neue Zürcher Zeitung*, February 16, 1966.

THE SITUATION IN MID-1966

It is, of course, too early to make any certain statements concerning the eventual outcome of the Yemeni civil war. In mid-1966, however, the outlook for peace seemed dim, at best. On the international plane, the conflict contributed significantly to the acrimoniousness of inter-Arab disputes, despite the attempt by some nations (Kuwait and Sudan) to undertake neutral mediation once again as a possible means of ending the war. On the domestic level, a new spate of assassinations of prominent Republican figures, the enforced exile of many former strong supporters of the Republic, as well as mass arrests and summary executions of others, revealed the continued instability of the new government. On the other hand, it appeared that the U.A.R. was committed more strongly than in the past to remaining in Yemen (at least until 1968, the date of the independence of the South Arabia Federation); combined with the static military situation, this made the outlook for an eventual return to power of the Royalists extremely unlikely. Previous plans for another national conference at which the various factions might be able to work out a Yemeni solution which would allow the Egyptian troops to leave and also preserve the gains of the revolution seemed to have been abandoned. On the basis of the past four years, however, it would certainly appear that any workable solution will have to be extraordinarily astute in its assessment of the domestic and international factors involved.

It may, of course, be argued that each country is unique; rarely, however, has that adjective been applied more appropriately than to Yemen. Its social, religious, political, and geographical realities were unknown, perhaps even unfathomable, to many of the nations who became involved in the conflict. Because of the acuteness with which Saudi Arabia and Great Britain, who both took a "conservative" view of Yemeni affairs, assessed the political situation, the Royalists became associated with the idea of preventing all change in Yemen. In fact, there is considerable truth to the assertion on the part of many of the leaders of the Royalist cause that this was never their goal. Indeed, many of the Imām's advisers and assistants throughout the civil war were precisely those individuals who had been imprisoned by Imām Aḥmad for their opposition activities, such as Qāḍī Aḥmad al-Siyāghī, Aḥmad Muḥammad al-Shāmī, and members of the al-Wazīr clan, as well as numerous tribal leaders. A number of the correspondents who visited with the major Royalist leaders came away impressed; they were "sensible, open-minded and decent young men—the very best sort of American University of Beirut intellectual" is the way one correspondent described the sons of Ḥasan and Ḥusayn, who expressed the belief that "if we were fighting to preserve the throne alone, we would not deserve to win."

Inevitably, however, and deservedly at first, the Republican side received more sympathetic international treatment: it desired change, and it accomplished a great deal in updating the medieval social, political, and economic structure which had existed. Sizable portions of the population needed to be convinced that modernization was desirable and inevitable, even though most of the people were quick to realize and appreciate the benefits which were the result of more modern Egyptian (and other foreign) technologies. It was the fact of continued Egyptian occupation and administration which brought about the inevitable dislike—even hatred—which such foreign forces often engender.

In retrospect, it would appear that it was the almost perverse inability of most countries to recognize the unique nature of Yemeni culture and the consistent unwillingness of the extremists on both sides of the conflict to come to any rational compromise with their antagonists which contributed most to the length of the war, as well as all its cruelties, stupidities, and waste—both in human and economic terms. One may only hope that in the efforts at peace which must surely continue to be made, the participants will reflect upon the horrible consequences and costs of the past four years and expend even greater efforts at conciliation, compromise, and perhaps mediation than in the past, in order to avoid completely destroying a fascinating and beautiful country.

Chapter IX

CONCLUSIONS

The Imāms of Yemen in the twentieth century lived and ruled according to the tenets of the Zaydi faith, for whose adherents they were the living spiritual representative of God on earth. By and large, they succeeded to a degree matched by few other monarchs who ruled by divinely ordained power. I have tried to demonstrate that the Imāms were not primitive and irrationally motivated despots bent solely upon their own glorification and the amassing of immense wealth and power. It would be more accurate to characterize both Imāms Yaḥyā and Aḥmad as primarily religious leaders who, upon having secular power added to their responsibilities, attempted to carry out a series of specific temporal programs.

Despite their position as scion of God on earth and the divinely inspired descendant of the Prophet, they were not free to act as they pleased. Their policies were severely limited by the tenets of their own faith, by the community of Sayyids, the 'Ulamā', and other Zaydi notables, as well as by the powerful families who, like them, possessed the requisite qualifications for the Imamate. These traditional elites opposed the introduction of any meaningful changes in the political and religious institutions of Yemen—the former because such changes might diminish their own power, and the latter because it was not possible to alter in any way an edifice erected according to God's will.

The basic exclusiveness of Zaydi Islam and the Yemeni experience of Ottoman administration combined to make a policy of isolationism almost inevitable, once independence had been achieved. Nevertheless, both Imāms saw themselves forced to break with this policy in order to exercise their claim to historical jurisdiction over areas occupied by the British in south Arabia. In allying themselves with other nations and attempting to adopt some of the technology which they possessed for their own ends, the Imāms brought important portions of the population into contact with the ideas, ideals, and techniques of the twentieth century—with predictable results.

The domestic policies of the Imāms were designed to solve the most obvious problems of Yemen: a divided population, a lack of public security, and a dearth of uniformly administered laws. These policies were not designed to cope with the demands of the increasing number of Yemenis for programs of reform and modernization in step with the currents of nationalism and progress sweeping the rest of the Arab world.

In fine, the Imāms were not able to adjust to pressures and demands from reformers and traditional political forces at the same time. Indeed, there was neither the machinery nor inclination to do so. Both Imāms regarded all opposition as treason and heresy and met what they felt to be a personal threat to their position with ever more stringent controls on all phases of Yemeni life.

By 1962 Imām Aḥmad was faced with overwhelming opposition from all shades of political opinion—from the progressive, urban reformist to the ultraconservative religious and tribal traditionalist. The new and inexperienced Imām who replaced him could not possibly have solved the issues and problems which occasioned this opposition in the one week he ruled before the revolution.

Events since that time, however, have amply demonstrated that the establishment of a " modern " state in place of the traditional monarchy has not been the panacea for Yemen's problems its authors expected it to be. The revolutionary government has apparently been unable or unwilling to recognize the historical and religious role which the Imamate fulfilled in addition to its political one. Consequently, it seems unlikely that the almost insurmountable internal problems which characterize Yemen will be solved in the near future.

The revolution has nevertheless achieved at least two worthwhile ends. It has eliminated most of the influence and power of the Sayyid class, probably the largest stumbling block to reform in the past; and it has effectively convinced the traditional political circles that Yemen cannot exist in a vacuum or a superseded past—that reforms are both necessary and desirable. Perhaps now, when the Yemenis are once again permitted to solve their own problems, they will be able to do so.

Unfortunately, the introduction of thousands of foreign troops has created a situation similar to that which existed prior to Yemeni independence. It has become increasingly obvious that the Imamate has once again become the rallying point for the basically xenophobic Yemenis. As a result, it is possible that a new division has been created in the population: this time between those who will refuse any reduction in the Imām's power because he presents the best (and perhaps only) unifying symbol for a future united Yemeni state, and those who will refuse to accept anything less than a republic as the best assurance that Yemen will not return to the customs of the past.

The historical traditions of Yemen would indicate that the disparate groups existing there must co-operate if there is to be an independent and united Yemeni state. If the lessons of the past are heeded, perhaps by now establishing a "constitutional Imamate," it is quite possible that the Yemenis can demonstrate that complete population homogeneity is not a necessary prerequisite to the creation of a viable and stable state in the twentieth century.

APPENDIXES

APPENDIX A

The Sons of Imām Yaḥyā

In Chronological Order, Eldest First:

Name	*Date of Death*	*Comments*
Aḥmad	September, 1962	Natural death; his son, Muḥammad al-Badr, acceded to throne; reputation for courage, ability, and cruelty.
Muḥammad	March, 1934	Drowned in Red Sea attempting to save life of a servant; only one daughter as offspring; most popular son.
Ḥasan		Now fighting with Royalists; serves as Prime Minister for al-Badr; at least five sons, most educated at A.U.B. and also with Royalists; former xenophobia moderated by many years spent abroad.
Ḥusayn	February, 1948	Assassinated by revolutionaries in 1948; at least five sons, most now fighting with Royalists; most pious son.
'Alī	September, 1962	Death by firing squad by Republican government; some sons; reputation for high living.
Muṭahhar	Early 1952	Died of stomach disease in hospital in Eritrea; at least one son.
Qāsim	September, 1962	Death by firing squad by Republican government; some sons; usually filled post of Minister of Health under Aḥmad; apolitical.
'Abdullāh	April, 1955	Beheaded on Aḥmad's orders after attempted coup of March, 1955; died without any male or female heirs; probably Yaḥyā's favorite; scholarly, most internationalist; ambitious but not popular.
Ibrāhīm	April, 1948	Executed on Aḥmad's orders after participation in coup of February, 1948; only daughters as offspring.
Ismā'īl	September, 1962	Death by firing squad by Republican government; often imprisoned by Aḥmad, but reasons for their disagreements not known, perhaps high living.
'Abbās	April, 1955	Beheaded on Aḥmad's orders after attempted coup of March, 1955; usually filled post of Minister for Tribal Relations because of popularity with northern tribes.

Name	*Date of Death*	*Comments*
Yaḥyā	1950's	Natural death of diseases; probably the wisest and "best" of Yaḥyā's sons, but apolitical.
Muḥsin	February, 1948	Assassinated by revolutionaries in coup of 1948.
'Abd al-Raḥmān		Educated in Europe, now fighting with Royalists; in his late twenties.

APPENDIX B

IMĀMS OF YEMEN IN THE TWENTIETH CENTURY

I. Legitimate Imāms

1891–1904 Imām al-Mansūr Billāh Muḥammad ibn Yaḥyā Ḥamīd al-Dīn
Born: 1839
Became Imām: May, 1891
Died: June 4, 1904

1904–1948 Imām al-Mutawakkil 'alā Allāh Yaḥyā ibn Muḥammad Ḥamīd al-Dīn
Born: July, 1869
Became Imām: June 4, 1904
Died: February 17, 1948

1948–1962 Imām al-Nāṣir li-Dīn Allāh Aḥmad ibn Yaḥyā Ḥamīd al-Dīn
Born: 1891 (?)
Became Imām: March 15, 1948
Died: September 18, 1962

1962—— Imām al-Mansūr Billāh Muḥammad al-Badr ibn Aḥmad Ḥamīd al-Dīn
Born: 1926 (?)
Became Imām: September 19, 1962

II. Usurpers

1948 Imām al-Hādī 'Abdullāh ibn Aḥmad al-Wazīr
Born: 1888 (?)
Declared Imām: February 18, 1948
Deposed: March 15, 1948
Died: April 9, 1948

1955 Imām 'Abdullāh ibn Yaḥyā Ḥamīd al-Dīn
Born: 1912 (?)
Declared (Self) Imām: March 31, 1955
Deposed: April 5, 1955
Died: April 13, 1955

BIBLIOGRAPHY

Official Publications

Hoskins, Halford L. *Soviet Economic Penetration in the Middle East* (Special Study prepared for The Hon. Hubert H. Humphrey). U.S. Senate, Document No. 58, 86th Congress, 1st Session. Washington, D.C., 1959.

United Nations. *United Nations Bulletin.* 1947–1965.

U.S. Department of Commerce. Bureau of Foreign Commerce. *Basic Data on the Economy of Aden Colony.* No. 58–62, Part 1 (August, 1958). Washington, D.C.

———. *Basic Data on the Economy of Yemen.* No. 60–2, Part 1 (January, 1960). Washington, D.C.

U.S. Department of Commerce. Bureau of International Commerce. *Basic Data on the Economy of Aden and the Federation of South Arabia.* OBR 64–71 (June, 1964). Washington, D.C.

U.S. Department of State. Foreign Service Despatches. Aden: No. 52 (23 April 1945); 241 (13 January 1919). Taiz: 131 (18 November 1959); 18 (9 October 1961); A–197 (6 May 1964).

———. *Department of State Bulletin.* 1946–1965 *passim.*

———. *Papers Relating to the Foreign Relations of the United States 1927.* Vol. III of 3 vols. Washington, D.C., 1942.

———. *Treaties and Other International Acts Series.* Washington, D.C.

U.S. Joint Publications Research Service. Dr. Abdul-Rahman El-Bidani, *The Yemenite Economy.* JPRS: 12036 (18 January 1962). Washington, D.C.

U.S. Senate. Committee on Foreign Relations. *Hearings on the Foreign Assistance Act of 1963 (S. 1276).* 88th Congress, 1st Session. Washington, D.C., 1963.

Yemen. *The Kingdom of Yemen.* Washington, D.C.: The Legation of Yemen, n.d.

———. *The Kingdom of Yemen.* Revised ed. Washington, D.C.: The Legation of Yemen, n.d.

———. *The Yemen Arab Republic.* Washington, D.C.: Embassy of the Yemen Arab Republic, n.d.

———. Arab Yemeni Republic [sic]. *The revolution in 3 years.* N.p., n.d. [Printed in 1965 by the Government Printer, Cairo, United Arab Republic.]

Books

Books in Arabic

'Abd al-Hādī, Muḥammad Hinā'ī. *Intiṣār Thawrat al-Yaman.* Cairo: Ikhtirnā Lil-Jundī (No. 16), 1963 (?).

'Abd al-Raḥmān, Muḥammad Muḥammad. *Arḍ al-Baṭūlāt wa al-Amjād.* Cairo: Maṭba'at al-Taḥrīr, 1964.

'Abdullāh, Muḥammad Anwār. *'Ūdat al-Abṭāl min al-Yaman.* Cairo: Ikhtirnā Lil-Jundī (No. 36), 1963.

Aql, Muḥammad Ṣadīq, and 'Āfiyyah, Hiyām Abū. *Aḍwā' 'alā Thawrat al-Yaman.* Cairo: Kutub Qawmiyya, 1963.

al-'Arshī, Ḥusayn ibn Aḥmad. *Bulūgh al-Marām.* Edited and completed to 1939 by Père Anastase-Marie de St.-Elie. Cairo: Imprimerie C. E. Albertiri, 1939.

al-Aṣbaḥī, Muḥammad Sa'īd. *Sulālat Qaḥṭān.* Aden: Maṭba'at Fatāt al-Jazīra, 1941.

Ayūb, Muḥammad al-Sayyid. *Al-Yaman bayna al-Qāt wa Fasād al-Ḥukm qabl al-Thawra.* Cairo: Dār al-Ma'ārif, 1963. (Volume 246 in the " Iqrā' " Series.)
al-'Aẓm, Nazīh Mu'ayyad. *Riḥlat fī Bilād al-'Arabiyya al-Sa'īda min Miṣr ilā Ṣan'ā'.* 2 vols. Cairo: Maṭba'at 'Isā al-Bābī al-Ḥalabī wa Shurakāh, n.d.
al-Barrāwī, Rāshid. *Al-Yaman wa al-Inqilāb al-Akhīr.* Cairo: Maktabat al-Nahḍa al-Maṣriyya, 1948.
al-Bayḍānī, 'Abd al-Raḥmān. *Asrār al-Yaman.* Cairo: Kutub Qawmiyya, 1962.
al-Dabbāgh, Muṣṭafā Murād. *Jazīrat al-'Arab.* 2 vols. Beirut: Manshūrat Dār al-Talī'a, 1963.
Fakhrī, Aḥmad. *Al-Yaman.* " Ma'had al-Dirāsāt al-'Arabiyya al-'Āliyya." Cairo: Jāmi'at al-Duwal al-'Arabiyya, 1957.
Faraj, Muḥammad. *Yamaniyāt.* Cairo: Ikhtirnā Lil-Jundī, 1963.
al-Ḥajrī, Muḥammad ibn Aḥmad. *Khulāṣat Tārīkh al-Yaman.* N.p.: Maṭba'at Tajlīd al-Anwār, n.d.
Ḥasan, Ḥasan Ibrāhīm. *Al-Yaman.* " Ikhtirnā Lak, No. 52." Cairo: Dār al-Ma'ārif, n.d.
Ḥasan, Muḥammad. *Qalb al-Yaman.* Baghdad: Maṭba'at al-Ma'ārif, 1947.
al-Jarāfī, 'Abdullāh ibn 'Abd al-Karīm. *Al-Muqtaṭaf min Tārīkh al-Yaman.* Cairo: Dār Ihyā' al-Kutub al-'Arabiyya, 'Isā al-Bābī al-Ḥalabī wa Shurakāh, 1951.
Kaḥḥāla, 'Umar Riḍā. *Mu'jam Qabā'il al-'Arab.* 3 vols. Damascus: Al-Maktaba al-Hāshimiyya, 1949.
Kutub Qawmiyya. *Al-Yaman, Thawrat wa Salām.* Cairo: Kutub Qawmiyya (No. 317), 1965.
al-Mamlaka al-'Arabiyya al-Su'ūdiyya, Wazārat al-Khārijiyya. Bayān 'an al-'Ilāqāt bayn al-Mamlaka al-'Arabiyya al-Su'ūdiyya wa al-Imām Yaḥyā Ḥamīd al-Dīn. Makka: Maṭba'at Umm al-Qurā, 1934.
Manṣūr, Anīs. *Al-Yaman . . . dhālik al-Majhūl.* Cairo: Al-Dār al-Qawmiyya Lil-Ṭabā'a wa al-Nashr, 1963 (?).
al-Munajjid, Ṣalāh al-Dīn. *Al-Yaman wa al-Muttaḥida.* Beirut: Dār al-Kitāb al-Jadīd, 1962.
al-Ramādī, Jamāl al-Dīn. *Al-Yaman.* Cairo: Kutub Qawmiyya, 1963.
al-Rayḥānī, Amīn. *Mulūk al-'Arab.* 2 vols., 4th ed. Beirut: Dār al-Rayḥānī, 1960.
Rifā'ī Bey, Aḥmad Farīd. *Riḥlatī ilā al-Yaman.* Cairo: Maṭba'at Muḥammad 'Alī Ṣabīḥ wa Awlāduh, 1951.
Sa'īd, Amīn. *Al-Yaman.* Cairo: Dār Ihyā' al-Kutub al-'Arabiyya, 'Isā al-Bābī al-Ḥalabī wa Shurakāh, 1959.
Sālim, al-Sayyid Muṣṭafā. *Takwīn al-Yaman al-Ḥadīth.* Cairo: Al-Maṭba'a al-'Ālimiyya, 1963.
al-Sallāl, 'Abdullāh, *et al. Min Warā' al-Aswār.* Beirut: Dār al-Kātib al-'Arabī, 1964. (Contains speeches and statements by: 'Abdullāh al-Sallāl, Aḥmad Muḥammad Nu'mān, Aḥmad al-Marūnī, Aḥmad al-Mu'allimī, Aḥmad 'Abdullāh al-Fasīl, Muḥammad Aḥmad Ṣabra, 'Abd al-Raḥmān al-Iriānī, 'Abd al-Salām Ṣabra, 'Alī Nāṣir al-'Ansī, Muḥammad Aḥmad al-Siyāghī, and Muḥammad Aḥmad Nu'mān.)
al-Saqqāf, Aḥmad Muḥammad Zayn. *Anā 'Ā'id min al-Yaman.* Revised ed. Cairo: Dār al-Kātib al-'Arabī, 1962.
al-Sha'bī, Qaḥṭān Muḥammad. *Al-Isti'mār al-Baritānī fī Janūb al-Yaman.* Cairo: Dār al-Nāṣir, 1962.
Sharaf al-Dīn, Aḥmad Ḥusayn. *Al-Yaman 'ibr al-Tārīkh.* Cairo: Maṭba'at al-Sinna al-Muḥammadiyya, 1963.

al-Shawkānī, Muḥammad ibn 'Alī. *Al-Badr al-Ṭāli'.* 2 vols. Cairo: Maṭba'at al-Sa'āda, 1929.

Tarsīsī, 'Adnān. *Al-Yaman wa Ḥaḍārat al-'Arab.* Beirut: Dār Maktabat al-Ḥayāt, 1963.

al-Wāsi'ī, 'Abd al-Wāsi' ibn Yaḥyā. *Tārīkh al-Yaman.* Cairo: Al-Maṭba'a al-Salfiyya, 1927.

al-Waysī, Ḥusayn ibn 'Alī. *Al-Yaman al-Kubrā.* Cairo: Maṭba'at al-Nahḍa al-'Arabiyya, 1962.

al-Wazīr, Ibrāhīm 'Alī. *Bayn Yaday al-Ma'sāt.* Beirut: Dār al-Andalus, 1962.

———. *Li-Kay La Namdī fī al-Zalām?* Beirut: Dār al-Andalus, 1963.

Al-Yaman. "Kutub Siyāsiyya, No. 49." Cairo: Dār al-Qāhira li al-Ṭibā'a, 1957.

Al-Yaman al-Manhūba al-Mankūba. N.p., n.d.

Al-Yaman Ẓāhiruhā wa Bāṭinuhā. N.p. n.d.

Zabāra, Muḥammad ibn Muḥammad. *Nayl al-Watr.* 2 vols. Cairo: Al-Maṭba'a al-Salfiyya, 1929–1931.

———. *Nubalā' al-Yaman bi al-Qarn al-Thānī 'Ashr li al-Ḥijra—Nashr al-'Araf li al-Nubalā' al-Yaman bi 'Abd al-Ālif ilā 1375 Ḥijriyya.* Cairo: Al-Maṭba'a al-Salfiyya, 1957.

Books in European Languages

Ansaldi, Cesare. *Il Yemen nella storia e nella leggenda.* "Collezione di Opere e di Monografie a cura del Ministero delle Colonie, No. 17." Rome: Sindicato Italiano Arti Grafiche Editore, 1933.

Antonius, George. *The Arab Awakening.* London: Hamish Hamilton, 1938.

Aponte, Salvatore. *La Vita segreta dell'Arabia Felice.* Milano: A. Mondadori, 1936.

Arendonk, C. van. *Les Débuts de l'Imamat Zaidite au Yemen.* "Publications de la fondation de Goeje, No. 18." Leiden: E. J. Brill, 1960.

Balsan, François. *Arabie du Sud.* Paris: Fernand Nathan, 1957.

———. *Inquiétant Yemen.* Paris and Geneva: La Palatine, 1961.

Bent, James T. and Mabel. *Southern Arabia.* London: Smith, Elder, 1900.

Berreby, Jean-Jacques. *La Péninsule Arabique.* Paris: Payot, 1958.

Bethmann, Erich W. *Yemen on the Threshold.* Washington. D.C.: American Friends of the Middle East, 1960.

Bisch [*sic*], Jørgen. *Behind the Veil of Arabia.* London: George Allen & Unwin, 1962.

Bowen, Richard LeBaron, and Albright, Frank P. *Archeological Discoveries in South Arabia.* Baltimore: Johns Hopkins Press, 1958.

Brémond, Edouard. *Yémen et Saoudia.* Paris: Charles-Lavauzelle, 1937.

Bullard, Sir Reader, ed. *The Middle East.* 3rd ed. London: Oxford University Press, 1958.

Bury, G. Wyman. *Arabia Infelix.* London: Macmillan, 1915.

Cooke, Hedley V. *Challenge and Response in the Middle East.* New York: Harper, 1952.

Coon, Carleton S. *Measuring Ethiopia and Flight into Arabia.* Boston: Little, Brown, 1935.

———. *The Races of Europe.* New York: Macmillan, 1939.

Cortada, James N. *The Yemen Crisis.* Los Angeles: University of California Press, 1965.

Craufurd, C. E. V. *Treasure of Ophir.* London: Skeffington [1929].

El-Attar, Mohamed Said. *Le sous-développement économique et social du Yemen: perspectives de la révolution Yemenite.* Algiers: Edition Tiers-Monde,

1964. [Also available in Arabic, published by al-Matba'āt al-Waṭaniyya al-Jazā'iriyya in 1965.]
EL-KHATIB, M. FATHALLA, and BABAA, KHALID I. *British Penetration and Imperialism in Yemen.* "Information Papers Number 6-A." New York: Arab Information Center, 1958.
EL-SHOUREKI, IBRAHIM. *The Bloody Strife in Yemen.* Tehran: Ettala'at Press, 1965.
Encyclopedia of Islam. 4 vols. and Supplement. Leiden: E. J. Brill, 1913–1938.
FARAGO, LADISLAS. *Arabian Antic.* New York: Sheridan House, 1938.
———. *The Riddle of Arabia.* London: Robert Hale, 1939.
FAROUGHY, ABBAS. *Introducing Yemen.* New York: Orientalia, 1947.
FAYEIN, CLAUDIE. *Une française médecin au Yemen.* Paris: René Julliard, 1955.
FISHER, W. B. *The Middle East: A Physical, Social and Regional Geography.* London: Methuen, 1950.
FORBES, ROSITA. *Women Called Wild.* London: Grayson & Grayson, 1935.
FREEMAN-GRENVILLE, G. S. P. *The Muslim and Christian Calendars.* London: Oxford University Press, 1963.
GAURY, GERALD DE. *Rulers of Mecca.* London: G. G. Harrap, 1951.
GERLACH, EVA. *Aus dem Harem in die Welt.* Leipzig: VEB F. A. Brockhaus, 1962.
GERLACH, RICHARD. *Sonne über Arabien.* Leipzig: VEB F. A. Brockhaus, 1960.
GIROLAMI, MARIO. *Viaggio alle Terre della Regina di Saba.* Firenze: Coi tipi dell'Instituto geografico militare, 1953.
Great Britain. Naval Intelligence Division, Admiralty. *A Handbook of Arabia.* London: His Majesty's Stationery Office, 1920.
———. Reference Division, Central Office of Information. *The Yemen.* London: Her Majesty's Stationery Office, 1958.
GRIESSBAUER, LUDWIG. *Die internationalen Verkehrs- und Machtfragen an den Küsten Arabiens.* Berlin: H. Paetel, 1907.
GROHMANN, ADOLF. *Arabien.* "Kulturgeschichte des Alten Orients: 3er Abschnitt, 4er Unterabschnitt." Munich: C. H. Beck'sche Verlagsbuchhandlung, 1963.
———. *Südarabien als Wirtschaftsgebiet.* 2 vols. Vol. 1, Vienna: Forschungsinstitut für Osten und Orient, 1922. Vol. II. "Schriften der philosophischen Fakultät der deutschen Universität in Prag." Brno, Czechoslovakia: Rudolf Rohrer Verlag, 1933.
GRUNEBAUM, G. E. VON. *Muhammadan Festivals.* New York: Henry Schuman, 1951.
HAMILTON, A. (The Master of Belhaven). *The Kingdom of Melchior.* London: John Murray, 1949.
———. *The Uneven Road.* London: John Murray, 1955.
HARRIS, WALTER B. *A Journey through the Yemen.* Edinburgh: William Blackwood, 1893.
HAZARD, HARRY W. (ed.). *Southern Arabia.* New Haven: Human Relations Area Files, 1956.
HELFRITZ, HANS. *Glückliches Arabien.* Zürich and Stuttgart: Fretz und Wasmuth, 1956.
———. *Im Lande der Königin von Saba.* Wiesbaden: E. Brockhaus, 1952.
———. *Land ohne Schatten.* Leipzig: Bibliographisches Institut, 1934. English edition: *Land without Shade* (New York: National Travel Club, 1936).
HEYWORTH-DUNNE, GAMAL-EDDINE [JAMES]. *Al-Yemen.* Cairo: Renaissance Bookshop, 1952.
HICKINBOTHAM, TOM. *Aden.* London: Constable, 1958.

HOECK, EVA. *Als Ärztin unter Beduinen.* Einsiedeln, Switzerland: Benziger Verlag, 1958.

HOGARTH, DAVID G. *The Penetration of Arabia.* New York: Frederick A. Stokes, 1904.

HUREWITZ, J. C. *Diplomacy in the Near and Middle East.* 2 vols. Princeton: D. van Nostrand, 1956.

INGRAMS, DOREEN. *A Survey of Social and Economic Conditions in the Aden Protectorate.* Eritrea: The Government Printer for the British Administration, 1949.

INGRAMS, HAROLD. *Arabia and the Isles.* 2nd ed. London: John Murray, 1952.

———. *A Report on the Social, Economic, and Political Condition of the Hadhramaut.* London: Colonial Office, 1937.

———. *The Yemen.* London: John Murray, 1963.

JACOB, HAROLD F. *The Kings of Arabia.* London: Mills and Boon, 1923.

———. *Perfumes of Araby.* London: Martin & Secker, 1915.

JAMME, A. *Sabaean Inscriptions from Maḥram Bilqîs (Mârib).* Baltimore: Johns Hopkins Press, 1962.

KAMMERER, A. *L'Abyssinie, la Mer Rouge et l'Arabie.* London: Royal Geographical Society of Egypt, 1935.

KHALIL, MUHAMMAD. *The Arab States and the Arab League.* 2 vols. Beirut: Khayat's, 1962.

KIERNAN, R. H. *The Unveiling of Arabia.* London: G. G. Harrap, 1937.

KING, GILLIAN. *Imperial Outpost: Aden.* London: Oxford University Press, 1964.

KIRK, GEORGE. *Survey of International Affairs 1939–1946. The Middle East in the War.* London: Oxford University Press, 1952.

LAWRENCE, T. E. *The Seven Pillars of Wisdom.* New York: Doubleday, 1935.

LENCZOWSKI, GEORGE. *The Middle East in World Affairs.* 3rd ed. Ithaca: Cornell University Press, 1962.

LEONE, ENRICO DE. *Le prime ricerche di una colonia e la esplorazione politica, geografica ed economica.* Rome: Poligrafico dello Stato, 1955.

———. *Le relazioni Italo-Yemenite negli ultimi ottanti anni.* Padua: Sadam Editore, 1956.

LEVY, REUBEN. *The Social Structure of Islam.* Cambridge: Cambridge University Press, 1957.

LIPPENS, PHILLIPE. *Expédition en Arabie Centrale.* Paris: Adrien Maisonneuve, 1956.

LONGRIGG, STEPHEN H. *Oil in the Middle East.* 2nd ed. London: Oxford University Press, 1961.

MACRO, ERIC. *Bibliography on Yemen and Notes on Mocha.* Coral Gables, Fla.: University of Miami Press, 1960.

MANSUR, ABDULLAH [G. WYMAN BURY]. *The Land of Uz.* London: Macmillan, 1911.

MANZONI, RENZO. *El Yemen, tre anni nell'Arabia Felice.* Rome: Tipografia Eredi Botta, 1884.

MARSTON, THOMAS E. *Britain's Imperial Role in the Red Sea Area 1800–1878.* Hamden, Conn.: The Shoe String Press, 1961.

MASSIGNON, LOUIS. *Annuaire du Monde Musulmane.* 4th ed. Paris: Presses Universitaires de France, 1955.

MEULEN, DANIEL VAN DER. *Aden to the Hadhramaut.* London: John Murray, 1947.

———. *Faces in Shem.* London: John Murray, 1961.

———, and WISSMANN, H. VON. *Hadhramaut—Some of Its Mysteries Unveiled.* Leiden: E. J. Brill, 1932.

The Middle East. London: Europa Publications, 1948–1963.

Middle East Record, 1960. Tel Aviv: The Israel Oriental Society, n.d.

MONFRIED, HENRI DE. *Les derniers jours de l'Arabie heureuse.* Paris: Gallimard, 1935.

———. *Secrets de la Mer Rouge.* Paris: Livre de Poche, 1959.

MOUSSA, FARAG. *Le Service Diplomatique des Etats Arabes.* Geneva: L'Institut Universitaire de Hautes Etudes Internationales, 1960.

PAWELKE, GÜNTHER. *Der Jemen—Das verbotene Land.* Düsseldorf: Econ Verlag, 1959.

PEARN, NORMAN S., and BARLOW, VERNON. *Quest for Sheba.* London: Ivor Nicholson & Watson, 1937.

PHILBY, H. ST. JOHN B. *Arabia.* New York: Charles Scribner's Sons, 1930.

———. *Arabian Highlands.* Ithaca: Cornell University Press, 1962.

———. *Arabian Jubilee.* New York: John Day, 1953.

———. *The Empty Quarter.* London: Constable, 1933.

———. *Sa'udi Arabia.* London: Ernest Benn, 1955.

———. *Sheba's Daughters.* London: Methuen, 1939.

PHILLIPS, WENDELL. *Qataban and Sheba.* New York: Harcourt, Brace, 1955.

RABIN, CHAIM. *Ancient West-Arabian.* London: Taylor's Foreign Press, 1951.

REILLY, SIR BERNARD. *Aden and the Yemen.* London: Her Majesty's Stationery Office, 1960.

RIHANI, AMEEN. *Arabian Peak and Desert.* London: Constable, 1930.

———. *Around the Coasts of Arabia.* London: Constable, 1930.

ROSSI, ETTORE. *L'Arabo parlato a San'a'.* Rome: Istituto per l'Oriente, 1939.

ROSSI, VINCENZO. *Le quistioni del Medio Oriente.* Rome: Casa Editrice Italiana, 1906.

SANGER, RICHARD H. *The Arabian Peninsula.* Ithaca: Cornell University Press, 1954.

SCHMIDT, WALTHER. *Das südwestliche Arabien.* Frankfurt on the Main: Heinrich Keller Verlag, 1913.

SCOTT, HUGH. *In the High Yemen.* London: John Murray, 1942.

SETON-WILLIAMS, M. V. *Britain and the Arab States.* London: Luzac, 1948.

SHARAFADDIN, A. H. *Yemen.* Rome: Daily American Press, 1961.

SIMMONS, JAMES STEVENS, *et. al. Global Epidemiology.* 3 vols. Vol. III: *The Near and Middle East.* Philadelphia: J. B. Lippincott, 1954.

STARK, FREYA. *The Coast of Incense.* London: John Murray, 1950.

———. *Dust in the Lion's Paw.* London: John Murray, 1961.

———. *East Is West.* London: John Murray, 1945.

The Statesman's Yearbook. London: Macmillan, 1918–1962.

STORM, W. HAROLD. *Whither Arabia?* London: World Dominion Press, 1938.

STUHLMANN, FRANZ. *Der Kampf um Arabien zwischen der Türkei und England.* Hamburg: George Westermann Verlag, 1916.

TARCICI, ADNAN. *Yemen.* N.p., 1947.

THESIGER, WILFRED. *Arabian Sands.* London: Longmans, Green, 1959.

THOMAS, BERTRAM. *Arabia Felix.* New York: Charles Scribner's Sons, 1932.

TOPF, ERICH. *Die Staatenbildungen in den arabischen Teilen der Türkei seit dem Weltkriege, nach Entstehung, Bedeutung und Lebensfähigkeit.* Hamburg: Friederichsen, De Gruyter, 1929.

TOYNBEE, ARNOLD J. *Survey of International Affairs, 1925.* Vol. I, *The Islamic World since the Peace Settlement.* London: Oxford University Press, 1927.

———. *Survey of International Affairs, 1928.* London: Oxford University Press, 1929.

TRITTON, ARTHUR S. *Rise of the Imams of Sanaa.* London: Oxford University Press, 1925.

TWITCHELL, KARL S. *Saudi Arabia.* 3rd ed. Princeton: Princeton University Press, 1958.

VERG, ERIK. *Halbmond um den Davidstern.* Berlin: Ullstein Verlag, 1964 (pp. 163–178).

VOCKE, HARALD. *Das Schwert und die Sterne: ein Ritt durch den Jemen.* Stuttgart: Deutsche Verlags-Anstalt, 1965.

VOLTA, SANDRO. *La Corte di Re Yahia.* Milan: Garzanti, 1941.

WAVELL, A. J. B. *A Modern Pilgrim in Mecca and a Siege in Sanaa.* London: Constable, 1912.

WEISL, WOLFGANG VON. *Zwischen dem Teufel und dem Roten Meer.* Leipzig: F. A. Brockhaus, 1927.

WEISS-SONNENBURG, HEDWIG. *Zur verbotenen Stadt Sana'a.* Berlin: Eigenbroedler Verlag, 1928.

WILLIAMS, JOHN ALDEN. *Islam.* "Great Religions of Modern Man." New York: George Braziller, 1961.

WISSMANN, HERMANN VON, and HÖFNER, MARIA. *Beiträge zur historischen Geographie des vorislamischen Südarabien.* Wiesbaden: Franz Steiner Verlag, 1952.

———, and RATHJENS, CARL. *Südarabien Reise.* 3 vols. Vol. III: *Landeskundliche Ergebnisse.* Hamburg: Friederichsen, De Gruyter, 1931–1934.

ZWEMER, SAMUEL M. *Arabia: The Cradle of Islam.* New York: Fleming H. Revell, 1900.

Unpublished Manuscript

LUQMAN, HAMED MUHAMMED. *The Yemenite Revolution of 1948.* Typescript Study prepared by the author as B.A. project at the American University of Cairo, April, 1949.

ARTICLES

Articles in Arabic

Aḥmad ibn Yaḥyā, Imām. "Naṣīḥat tuhda ilā Kull al-'Arab," *Al-Ayyām* (Aden), December 9, 1961.

"Muḥāwalāt li-Qalb al-Imām Aḥmad," *Al-Ḥayāt* (Beirut), December 25, 1960.

al-Muwāhilī, Muḥsin Ḥasan. "Hadhihi hiya al-Yaman," *Al-Ḥayāt* (Beirut), October, 1962.

Riḍa, Mamduḥ. "'Ashr Ayyām fī al-Yaman," *Rūz al-Yūsuf* (Cairo), Nos. 1498–1500 (1957).

"Al-Yaman," *Al-Usbū' al-'Arabī* (Ma'maltayn/Beirut), IV, No. 24 (July 15, 1963), 48; No. 173 (October 1, 1962), 18–21; No. 174 (October 8, 1962), 38–59.

Zabāl, Salīm. "Al-Ḥudayda," *Al-'Arabī* (Kuwait), No. 60 (November, 1963), 68–97.

———. "Ṣan'ā'," *Al-'Arabī* (Kuwait), No. 58 (September, 1963), 68–107.

Ẓāhir, Ṣa'd, and Tabarik, Muḥammad. "Wuzarā' . . . min al-Yaman," *Rūz al-Yūsuf* (Cairo), No. 1578 (1958).

Articles in European Languages

ABERCROMBIE, THOMAS J. "Behind the Veil of Troubled Yemen," *National Geographic Magazine*, CXXV (March, 1964), 403–445.

ALBRIGHT, WILLIAM F. "In Defense of the American Foundation for the Study of Man," *The Middle East Journal*, VI (Winter, 1952), 111–112.

ANDERSON, W. A. "Aden of Araby," *Harper's*, CXXXV (September, 1917), 449–462.

BALSAN, FRANÇOIS. "La conjoncture yéménite," *Revue Militaire Générale*, March, 1963, 279–297.

BARTKE, WOLFGANG. "Die Beziehungen der VR China zum Nahen und Mittleren Osten," *Der Ostblock und die Entwicklungsländer*, No. 16 (July, 1964), 143–144.

BENEYTON, A. J. "Mission d'études au Yemen," *La Géographie*, XXVIII (October, 1913), 201–219.

———. "Trois années en Arabie Heureuse," *Bulletin de la Société de Géographie*, XXVII (June, 1913), 493–497.

BERREBY, JEAN-JACQUES. "Le Yemen," *Documentation française*, No. 2141 (February 18, 1956), 1 ff.

BOXHALL, P. G. "The Yemen—Background to Recent Events," *The Army Quarterly and Defence Journal*, LXXXVIII (July, 1964), 201–209.

BRITTON, EVERARD B. "The Use of 'Qat,'" *Geographical Journal*, XCIII (February, 1939), 121–122.

BROWN, WILLIAM R. "The Yemeni Dilemma," *The Middle East Journal*, XVII (Autumn, 1963), 349–367.

BUXTON, LELAND. "Arabia Felix," *Contemporary Review*, CXVI (December, 1919), 681–684.

CARVALHO, GEORGE DE. "A Weird Arabian Nights War with 100,000 Dead: Yemen's Desert Fox," *Life*, LVIII (February 19, 1965), 97–109.

CATTAN, SELIM. "Itinerario della Missione Janelli nel Yemen," *Levante*, I (October–December, 1953), 5–12.

CHAMIER, JOHN A. "Air Control of Frontiers," *Journal of the Royal Central Asian Society*, XXI, Pt. 3 (July, 1934), 403–419.

Christian Science Monitor (Boston), April 8, 1961, August 11, 1962, and August 21, 1962.

CLARK, HARLAN B. "Yemen—South Arabia's Mountain Wonderland," *The National Geographic Magazine*, XCII, No. 5 (November, 1947), 631–672.

COLOMBE, MARCEL. "La reconnaissance du gouvernment de la République Arabe du Yémen par les Etats-Unis," *Orient* (Paris), VI (4e trimestre, 1962), 161–164.

———. "Coup d'état au Yémen," *Orient* (Paris), VI (3e trimestre, 1962), 7–10.

CONDÉ, BRUCE. "Seven Weeks of Yemen in the Sixth Year of Ahmad," *Al-Kulliyah*, XXIX (February, 1954), 4–9, 24, 27.

COON, CARLETON S. "Southern Arabia, A Problem for the Future," *Papers of the Peabody Museum of American Archaeology and Ethnology of the Harvard University*, XX (*The Dickson Memorial Volume*) (1943), 385–402.

CRANE, CHARLES R. "Museum of Islam," *Near East and India*, XXXII (December 8, 1927), 713–714.

———. "A Visit to the Red Sea Littoral and the Yemen," *Journal of the Royal Central Asian Society*, XV (January, 1928), 48–67.

CRAUFURD, CHARLES E. "Hodeida Before and After the War," *Geographical Journal*, LVIII (December, 1921), 464–465.

———. "Yemen and Asir," *Journal of the Royal Central Asian Society*, XX (October, 1933), 568–576.

CUCINOTTA, ERNESTO. "L'opera degli Italiani per la conoscenza del Yemen," *Rivista Coloniale*, XXI (January–February, 1926), 414–416.

Daily Telegraph (London), September 20, 21, 25, and 26, 1962.

DE GRAMONT, SANCHE. "Inside the Yemen Republic, Once Called Happy Arabia," *New York Herald Tribune* (4 parts), August 2–5, 1964.

D'EMILIA, ANTONIO. "Intorno alle costituzioni provvisorie repubblicane del Yemen," *Oriente Moderno*, XLIV (May, 1964), 301–312.

ESS, JOHN VAN. "Arabian Aspects of the War," *Asia*, XVIII (October, 1918), 843–850.

FAGO, VINCENZO. "Italia e Yemen: gli Zaidite nel conflitto turco-yemenita," *Rivista Coloniale*, V (April, 1910), 45–49.

FERRARA, ROBERTO. "Le relazioni economiche fra Italia e Yemen," *Levante*, I (October–December, 1953), 23–31.

FORBES, ROSITA. "A Visit to the Idrisi Territory in Asir and Yemen," *Geographical Journal*, LXII, No. 4 (October, 1923), 271–278.

"Forbidden Yemen Yields to a Yankee's Offer," *Life*, XXXIX (December 5, 1955), 51–52.

GIANNINI, AMADEO. "La Questione del porto di Shaikh Sa'id nel Yemen," *Oriente Moderno*, XV (November, 1935), 549–554.

———. "Il Trattato di et-Ta'if e l'equilibrio dell'Arabia," *Oriente Moderno*, XV (October, 1935), 489–498.

GIROLAMI, MARIO. "Visita alle rovine della città di Saba," *Levante*, I (October–December, 1953), 32–41.

GLASER, EDUARD. "Die Kastengliederung im Jemen," *Das Ausland*, LVIII (March 16, 1885), 201–205.

"Gli Studi Italiani sul Yemen," *Levante*, I (October–December, 1953), 18–22.

HAHN, EDWARD. "Die Weltstellung Jemens," *Geographische Zeitschrift*, IX (December, 1903), 657–666.

HAINES, C. GROVE. "The Problem of the Italian Colonies," *The Middle East Journal*, I (October, 1947), 417–431.

HAMILTON, R. A. B. "Six Weeks in Shabwa," *Geographical Journal*, C (1942), 107–123.

HART, JANE SMILEY. "Basic Chronology for a History of the Yemen," *The Middle East Journal*, XVII (Winter–Spring, 1963), 144–153.

HAY, R. "Great Britain's Relations with Yemen and Oman," *Middle Eastern Affairs*, XI (1960), 142–149.

HELFRITZ, HANS. "The First Crossing of Southwestern Arabia," *Geographical Review*, XXV (July, 1935), 395–407.

———. "Land without Shade," *Journal of the Royal Central Asian Society*, XXIV (April, 1937), 201–216.

HEYWORTH-DUNNE, GAMAL ED-DINE [JAMES]. "The Yemen," *Middle Eastern Affairs*, IX (1958), 50–58.

HEYWORTH-DUNNE, J. "Témoignage sur le Yémen," *Orient* (Paris), VIII (3e trimestre, 1964), 21–73.

HOFE, KLOPP VON. "Der arabische Krieg," *Preussische Jahrbücher*, CCXXXVII (July, 1934), 21–31.

HOGARTH, D. G. "Some Recent Arabian Explorations," *Geographical Review*, XI (July, 1921), 321–337.

HOLDEN, DAVID. "At Cross-Purposes in the Sands of Yemen," *The Reporter*, XXVIII (February 14, 1963), 37–41.

HOOGSTRAAL, HARRY, and KUNTZ, ROBERT E. "Yemen Opens the Door to Progress," *The National Geographic Magazine*, CI (February, 1952), 213–244.

HORTON, PHILIP. "Our Yemen Policy: Pursuit of a Mirage," *The Reporter*, XXIX (October 24, 1963), 28–35.

HOSKINS, HALFORD L. "Background of the British Position in Arabia," *Middle East Journal*, I, No. 2 (April, 1947), 137–147.

HOTTINGER, ARNOLD. "Der Bürgerkrieg im Jemen: Wegbereiter des Kommunismus auf der Arabischen Halbinsel," *Europa-Archiv*, XXI (April 25, 1966), 297–306.

———. " A Journey through Royalist Yemen," *Swiss Review of World Affairs*, XII (April, 1963), 14–16.

———. " The Mechanism of Middle East Revolutions—Yemen and Iraq, Parallels and Discrepancies," *Swiss Review of World Affairs*, XII (February, 1963), 7–9.

———. " A Visit to Republican Yemen," *Swiss Review of World Affairs*, XIII (May, 1963), 11–12.

———. " The War in Yemen," *Swiss Review of World Affairs*, XV (September, 1965), 17–22.

———. " Yemen," *Swiss Review of World Affairs*, VI (March, 1957), 11–14.

" Imam Yahya and His Enemies," *Near East and India*, XXXI (April 21, 1927), 464–465.

" An Incident in the Yemen in 1934," *Journal of the Royal Central Asian Society*, XXIV (January, 1937), 125–127.

INGRAMS, HAROLD. " A Journey in the Yemen," *Journal of the Royal Central Asian Society*, XXXII (January, 1946), 58–69.

———. " The Outlook in Southwest Arabia," *Journal of the Royal Central Asian Society*, XLIII (July–October, 1956), 176–186.

———. " Southwest Arabia: Today and Tomorrow," *Journal of the Royal Central Asian Society*, XXXI (April, 1945), 135–155.

———. " What Next in al-Yemen? " *New Commonweal*, XL (March, 1962), 148–150.

INNES, HAMMON. " Ancient Desert Skyscrapers," *Holiday*, XVIII (November, 1955), 58–59, 149–156.

INSABATO, ENRICO. " Italia e Yemen," *Levante*, I (October–December, 1953), 13–17.

———. " Yemen: the Islamic World Turns Left? " *Mediterranean Meeting Point*, IV (January–February, 1963), 41–44.

JACOB, HAROLD F. " The Kingdom of the Yemen: Its Place in the Comity of Nations," *Transactions of the Grotius Society*, Vol. XVII, *Problems of Peace and War* (1933), 131–153.

———. " Resources and Commercial Possibilities of the Yemen," *Near East and India*, XXVII (March 5, 1925), 256–257.

———. " The Yemen," *Journal of the Royal Central Asian Society*, XII (January, 1925), 26–42.

———. " The Yemen," *Near East and India*, XXVI (October 30, 1924), 455–456.

JANNELLI, PASQUALE. " Auspicio di prosperità per il Yemen," *Levante*, I (October–December, 1953), 3–4.

JANSEN, G. H. " The Problems of South-west Arabia," *The World Today*, XIX (August, 1963), 337–343.

KAPELIUK, AMNON. " Stalemate in Yemen," *New Outlook* (Tel Aviv), VI (October, 1963), 551–563.

KHADDURI, MAJID. " Coup and Counter-coup in the Yaman, 1948," *International Affairs*, XXVIII, No. 1 (January, 1952), 59–68.

" Khat " [*sic*], *Geographical Journal*, CXXVI (March, 1960), 52 ff.

KOHN, HANS. " Arabien 1924–1928," *Zeitschrift für Politik*, XVIII, No. 3 (1928–1929), 171–183.

LAMARE, PIERRE. " A propos d'une exploration au Yemen," *Journal Asiatique*, CCXVII (1930), 307–313.

———. " L'Arabie heureuse—Le Yemen," *La Géographie*, XLII (June, 1924), 1–23.

———. " Une exploration française au Yemen," *La Nature*, LVIII, Pt. 2, No. 2844 (November 1, 1930), 394–399.

LAMBARDI, NELLO. "Divisioni amministrative del Yemen; con notizie econòmiche e demografiche," *Oriente Moderno*, XXVII, Nos. 7–9 (July–September, 1947), 143–162.

LAMBEL, ROBERT. "Les tribulations de l'Arabie heureuse," *L'Illustration*, CLXXXVIII (June 2, 1934), 170 ff.

"Land of Yemen," *Life*, November 18, 1946, 59 ff.

LAW, JOHN. "'Forgotten' War in the Desert: A First-hand Report," *United States News and World Report*, LVIII (May 24, 1965), 67–69.

———. "A Pawn in Nasser's Dream of Empire," *United States News and World Report*, LIV (December 31, 1962), 44–49.

LEONE, ENRICO DE. "L'assedio e la resa di San'a' del 1905 attraverso il carteggio inedito di Giuseppe Caprotti," *Oriente Moderno*, XXXVI (February, 1956), 61–81.

LIEBESNY, HERBERT J. "Administrative and Legal Development in Arabia: Aden Colony and Protectorate," *The Middle East Journal*, IX, No. 4 (Autumn, 1955), 385–396.

———. "International Relations of Arabia: The Dependent Areas," *The Middle East Journal*, I (April, 1947), 148–168.

MACLAURIN, E. C. B. "The Yemen," *Australia Outlook*, XII (September, 1958), 33–45.

MCLEAN, NEIL. "The War in Yemen," *Journal of the Royal Central Asian Society*, LI (April, 1964), 102–111.

———. "The War in the Yemen," *Royal United Service Institution Journal*, CXI (February, 1966), 5–29.

MACRO, ERIC. "Leland Buxton in the Yemen, 1905," *Journal of the Royal Central Asian Society*, XLVIII (April, 1961), 168–172.

———. "Yemen, a Brief Survey," *Journal of the Royal Central Asian Society*, XXXVI (January, 1949), 42–53.

———. "The Yemen, Some Recent Literature," *Journal of the Royal Central Asian Society*, XLV (January, 1958), 43–51.

MALVEZZI, ALDOBRANDINI. "L'insurezzione nello Yemen," *Nuova Antologia*, Series 5, CLII (March 16, 1911), 307–321.

MARCHAND, H. "Les questions d'Arabie: Le Yemen," *Questions Diplomatiques et Coloniales*, XXXI, No. 339 (April 1, 1911), 397–407.

MARTELLI, GEORGE. "A Journey through the Yemen," *The Geographical Magazine*, XXXV (April, 1963), 675–681.

MEULEN, D. VAN DER. "Hadhramaut Today," *Moslem World*, XXXIII (1943), 29–32.

———. "A Journey in the Hadhramaut," *Moslem World*, XXII (1932), 378–392.

MEYER, GEORGES. "Le conflit d'Arabie," *Europe Nouvelle*, XVII, No. 851 (June 2, 1934), 567–570.

———. "Le Paix en Arabie," *Europe Nouvelle*, XVII, No. 857 (July 14, 1934), 717–719.

———. "Regards sur la Mer Rouge," *Europe Nouvelle*, XX, No. 923 (November 6, 1937), 1079–1080.

MONTAGNE, ROBERT. "Au cœur de l'Arabie heureuse," *L'Illustration*, CLXXV (June, 1930), 254–260.

———. "Le Yemen," *L'Afrique et l'Asie*, XXXII (1955), 63–77.

MOSER, CHARLES. "The Flower of Paradise," *The National Geographic Magazine*, XXXII (August, 1917), 173–186.

"The New Frontier of the Aden Protectorate," *Geographical Journal*, XXVIII (December, 1906), 632 ff.

NUNE, E. "L'Inghilterra nella Penisola Arabica," *Oriente Moderno*, XXI (May, 1941), 209–232.

O'BALLANCE, EDGAR. "The Yemen," *Brassey's Annual*, LXXV (1964), 96–104.

Oil and Gas Journal (Tulsa, Oklahoma), March, 1961—September, 1962, *passim.*

PETRIE, PATRICK W. R. "Some Experiences in South Arabia," *Journal of Tropical Medicine and Hygiene*, XLII (December, 1939), 357–360.

PHILBY, H. A. R. "From the Yemen," *Middle East Forum*, XXXVIII (December, 1962), 10–11.

PHILBY, H. ST. JOHN B. "Arabia Today," *International Affairs*, XIV (1935), 619–634.

———. "The Land of Sheba," *Geographical Journal*, XCII (July and August, 1938), 1–21, 107–132.

PHILLIPS, WENDELL. "Exploring Queen of Sheba Land," *Collier's*, "Flavor of Romance and Spice of Danger" (April 7, 1951), "World under the Sand" (April 14, 1951).

PIETRAVALLE, PAOLO. "L'economia ed i lavori pubblici nel Yemen d'oggi," *Oriente Moderno*, XXXII (July–August, 1952), 165–189.

PIKE, R. W. "Land and Peoples of the Hadhramaut, Aden Protectorate," *Geographical Journal*, XXX (1940), 627–648.

Platt's Oilgram (New York), March, 1961—September, 1962, *passim.*

PRESENTI, GUSTAVO. "La situazione politico-militare nell'Arabia e gli'interessi dell'Italia," *Rivista Coloniale*, XII (January–February and April, 1917), 106–116, 165–171.

RATHJENS, CARL. "Exploration au Yemen," *Journal Asiatique*, CCXV (June–September, 1929), 141–155.

———. "Tâghût gegen scherî'a," *Jahrbuch des Linden-Museums* (Stuttgart), Neue Folge I (1951), 172–187.

———. and, WISSMANN, H. VON. "Sanaa," *Zeitschrift der Gesellschaft für Erdkunde zu Berlin*, No. 9/10 (1929), 329–353.

REILLY, BERNARD. "The Aden Protectorates," *Journal of the Royal Central Asian Society*, XXVIII (1941), 132–145.

RHODOKANAKIS, N. "San'a—City of Fanaticism," *Travel*, LV (August, 1930), 20–24.

RIHANI, AMEEN. "Ibn Saud und Imam Jahia," *Europäische Gespräche*, VII, No. 7 (July, 1929), 333–347.

———. "Image of Perfection in Sana'a," *Asia*, XXIX (October, 1929), 795 ff.

———. "In the Land of Wallah—We'll Slay Him," *Asia*, XXIX (September, 1929), 717 ff.

———. "Under the Roofs of Sana'a," *Asia*, XXIX (November, 1929), 878 ff.

ROBERTSON, WILLIAM [P. W. R. PETRIE]. "San'a, Past and Present," *Moslem World*, XXXIII, No. 1 (January, 1943), 52–57.

———. "San'a and the Qat-eaters," *Scottish Geographical Magazine*, CVIII (September, 1942), 49–53.

———. "Yemen Journey," *Scottish Geographical Magazine*, CIX (October, 1943), 63–70; CXI (September, 1945), 46–51.

RONDOT, PIERRE. "Une crise arabe 'étranglée': l'affaire du Yemen," *Revue de Défense Nationale*, XIX (February, 1963), 283–295.

———. "La crise du Yemen et ses nouveaux developpements," *Revue de Defénse Nationale*, XX (June, 1964), 1022–1038.

ROSSI, ETTORE. "Il diritto consuetudinario delle tribù arabe del Yemen," *Revista degli Studi Orientali*, XXIII (1948), 1–36.

———. "Un Libro di Nazih el-Muayyad el-Azm," *Oriente Moderno*, XX (September, 1940), 452–458.

———. "Note sull'irrigazione, l'agricoltura e le stagioni nel Yemen," *Oriente Moderno*, XXXIII (August–September, 1953), 349–361.

———. "La Stampa nel Yemen," *Oriente Moderno*, XVIII (October, 1938), 568–580.

ROSSI, GIOVANNI BATTISTA. "Nell'Jemen: impressioni di viaggio," *Rivista Coloniale*, II (September–October, 1906), 66 ff.

———. "Gli Yemen," *La Lettura*, XXVII (June, 1927), 417–422.

ROUCEK, JOSEPH S. "Yemen in Geopolitics," *Contemporary Review*, CCII (December, 1962), 310–317.

ROUET, GASTON. "La Question du Yemen," *Questions Diplomatiques et Coloniales*, XXIX, No. 316 (April 16, 1910), 475–491.

RYCKMANS, G. "Through Sheba's Kingdom," *The Geographical Magazine*, XXVII (July, 1954), 129–137.

"A Sad Little Sideshow of Desert War," *The Times* (London), July 19, 1965.

SAGE, C. E. "Catha Edulis," *Pharmaceutical Journal*, CLIII (1944), 128 ff.

San Francisco Examiner, January 12, 1961.

SASSON, PHILIP. "Air Power in the Middle East," *Journal of the Royal Central Asian Society*, XX (October, 1933), 394–405.

SCHIARINI, P. "Il Jemen in rivolta," *Rivista di Cavalleria*, XXVIII (August, 1911), 129–158.

SCHLOSS, ROLF W. "Al Baidani, the Real Ruler," *Atlas*, V (March, 1963), 161–165.

SCHMIDT, WALTHER. "Der Kampf um Arabien zwischen der Türkei und England," *Geographische Zeitschrift*, XXIII (May, 1917), 197–215.

———. "Der südarabische Kriegsschauplatz," *Geographische Zeitschrift*, XXII (August, 1916), 458–470.

EL-SCIAMI, ABDUL WAHAB. "Aspetti della moderna letteratura Yemenita," *Levante*, I, No. 2 (October–December, 1953), 42–45.

SCOTT, HUGH. "A Journey to the Yemen," *Geographical Journal*, XCIII (February, 1939), 97–121.

———. "The Peoples of Southwest Arabia," *Journal of the Royal Central Asian Society*, XXVIII (April, 1941), 146–151.

———. "The Yemen in 1937–1938," *Journal of the Royal Central Asian Society*, XXVII (January, 1940), 21–44.

SEAGER, BASIL W. "The Yemen," *Journal of the Royal Central Asian Society*, XLII, Pts. 3–4 (July–October, 1955), 214–230.

———. "The Yemen and the Arab Protectorates," *Contemporary Review*, CXCI (May, 1957), 296–299.

SEAGER, HEATHER. "Guests of the Imam," *Blackwood's Magazine*, CCLXXI (June, 1955), 481–491.

SEALE, PATRICK. "The War in Yemen: Did Nasser Lure the U.S. Out on a Limb?" *New Republic*, CXCVIII (January 26, 1963), 9–11.

SERJEANT, R. B. "The Mountain Tribes of the Yemen," *The Geographical Magazine*, XV, No. 2 (June, 1942), 66–72.

SMILEY, D. DE C. "The War in the Yemen," *Royal United Service Institution Journal*, CVIII (November, 1963), 328–335.

Der Spiegel (Hamburg), April 30, 1958, and September 26, 1962.

STACK, SIR LEE. "The Slave Trade between the Sudan and Arabia," *Journal of the Royal Central Asian Society*, VIII (July, 1921), 163–164.

STAHMER, A. M. "Erdölpartner Jemen," *Zeitschrift für Geopolitik*, XXIV, No. 1 (November 1, 1953), 615–616.

"Stark Desert War in Arabia," *Life*, LVII (September 8, 1964), 34–43.

STARK, FREYA. "In Southwestern Arabia in Wartime," *Geographical Review*, XXXIV (July, 1944), 349–364.

———. "Yemen Chose to Be Poor," *Asia and the Americas*, XLVI (February, 1946), 78–80.

STREIFF, ERIC. "Problematic U.N. Mission in Yemen," *Swiss Review of World Affairs*, XIII (October, 1963), 5–6.

———. "Red Cross Mission to Yemen," *Swiss Review of World Affairs*, XIII (December, 1963), 7–8.

STROTHMANN, R. "Zaidiya," *Encyclopedia of Islam*, IV (1936), 1196–1198.

SURIEU, ROBERT. "Problèmes yéménites," *Orient* (Paris), No. 7 (3e trimestre, 1958), 43–53.

TAILLER, F. "L'Arabie du Sud, Hadhramout et Yemen," *L'Asie Française*, XXXVII (July, August, 1937), 210–214, 237–244.

THESIGER, W. P. "The Badu of Southwest Arabia," *Journal of the Royal Central Asian Society*, XXXVII (January, 1950).

———. "A Journey through the Tihama, the Asir, and the Hijaz Mountains," *Geographical Journal*, CX (1947), 188–200.

TWITCHELL, KARL S. "In the Queen of Sheba's Kingdom," *Asia*, XXXIII (January, 1933), 4 ff.

———. "More Experiences in Arabia Felix," *Asia*, XXXIII (February, 1933), 106 ff.

———. "Operations in the Yemen," *Journal of the Royal Central Asian Society*, XXI (July, 1934), 445–449.

VECCIA-VAGLIERI, L. "Notizie aneddotiche su Ibn Sa'ud, l'Imam Yahya ed il Yemen," *Oriente Moderno*, XIV (September, 1934), 417–433.

VOCKE, HARALD. "Inside Yemen," *Atlas*, VIII (October, 1964), 161–166.

WALKER, BERNARD C. "Medical Work at San'a', Yemen," *Moslem World*, XXXI (September, 1934), 417–433.

"War in the Desert: Big Fight over a Small Country," *United States News and World Report*, LV (July 15, 1963), 62–63.

"The War with the Yemen," *Near East and India*, XLIII, No. 1204 (June 14, 1934), 457.

WAUGH, TELFORD. "The German Counter to Revolt in the Desert," *Journal of the Royal Central Asian Society*, XXIV (April, 1937), 313–317.

Die Welt (Hamburg), September 11 and 21, 1962.

WENNER, M. W. "Mocha and Coffee," *Middle East Forum*, XL (Late Autumn, 1964), 11–14.

WIESL, W. VON. "Fascism on the Red Sea," *Living Age*, CCCXXXII (May 15, 1927), 885–895.

———. "New Light on Arabia," *Living Age*, CCCXXXII (May 1, 1927), 795–801.

———. "Theocracy in the Yemen," *Near East and India*, XXXI (March 31, 1927), 367–368.

WOOLBERT, ROBERT G. "The Purchase of Assab by Italy," in MCKAY, DONALD C., *Essays in the History of Modern Europe*. New York: Harper, 1936.

WRIGHT, QUINCY. "Arbitration of the Aaroo Mountain," *American Journal of International Law*, XXXIII (1939), 356–359.

WYNN, WILTON. "Yemen under Imam Ahmad," *Middle East Institute Newsletter*, IV (October 1, and November 1, 1951), 4–6.

"The Yemen in Modern Treaty Pattern," *American Perspective*, I (April, 1947), 41–48.

"Yemen Observation Mission," *United Nations Review*, X (July, 1963), 16–20.

ZWEMER, S. M. "Ingrams' Peace in Hadhramaut," *Moslem World*, XXXIII (1943), 79–85.

Periodicals Consulted

The Arab World (Beirut), 1955–1966.
The Economist (London), 1950–1966.
Frankfurter Allgemeine Zeitung (Frankfurt on Main), 1958–1962.
Middle East Forum (Beirut), 1954–1965.
Middle East Journal (Washington, D.C.), 1947–1966.
The Mizan Newsletter (London), 1958–1966.
Le Monde (Paris), 1955–1966.
Near East and India (London), 1920–1940.
Neue Zürcher Zeitung (Zürich), 1957–1966.
New York Herald-Tribune, 1958–1966.
New York Times, 1940–1966.
The Observer (London), 1955–1966.
Oriente Moderno (Rome), 1920–1966.
The Sunday Times (London), 1955–1966.
The Times (London), 1920–1966.
Washington Post (Washington, D.C.), 1958–1966.

INDEX

Note: With the exception of members of royal families, and the names of the Ottoman Wālīs of Yemen, all Arabic names are indexed according to the last name without regard for the article " al- ".

A